D0392405

WITHDRAWN

AUG 11 2022

DAVID O. McKAY LIBRARY
RICKS COLLEGE
DAVID O. McKAY LIBRARY
BYU-IDAHO
REXBURG, IDAHO 83460-0405

# Puzzle Palaces and Foggy Bottom

# Puzzle Palaces and Foggy Bottom
*U.S. Foreign and Defense
Policy-Making in the 1990s*

## Donald M. Snow
University of Alabama

## Eugene Brown
Lebanon Valley College

St. Martin's Press
New York

*Executive editor*: Don Reisman
*Managing editor*: Patricia Mansfield-Phelan
*Project editor*: Diana Puglisi
*Production supervisor*: Alan Fischer
*Art director*: Sheree Goodman
*Cover design*: Marek Antoniak

Library of Congress Catalog Card Number: 92-62750

Copyright © 1994 by St. Martin's Press, Inc.
All rights reserved. No part of this book may be reproduced, stored in a retrieval system, or transmitted by any form or by any means, electronic, mechanical, photocopying, recording, or otherwise, except as may be expressly permitted by the applicable copyright statutes or in writing by the Publisher.
Manufactured in the United States of America.
8  7  6  5  4
f  e  d  c  b  a

For information, write:
St. Martin's Press, Inc.
175 Fifth Avenue
New York, NY 10010

ISBN:  0-312-08654-7 (paperback)
       0-312-10268-2 (cloth)

# Preface

The beginnings of *Puzzle Palaces and Foggy Bottom* date back to the traumatic period between 1989 and 1991, when the world as we had known it was rapidly changing. We observed and commented on those changes from our shared office as visiting professors at the United States Army War College in Carlisle Barracks, Pennsylvania. As the Cold War evaporated before our eyes, it was obvious that U.S. foreign and defense policy would inevitably change, but what was not quite so certain was how that change would occur.

If policy was going to have to adapt to a changing environment, so too would the mechanisms and processes by which policy is made. The structural foundation of foreign and defense policy-making before 1989 was rooted deeply in the national security requirements that were associated with the Cold War military and political confrontation between the United States and the Soviet Union. These structures had served us well, but we began to question their continuing relevance in a post–Cold War environment.

This question of structural change to adapt to a changing world energized our conversations and eventually our research. We agreed that world change was occurring in two basic areas—the international economic system and requirements for national security. Those areas form the recurring themes of the present volume.

In the midst of writing this book, another event occurred that reinforced our need to take a fresh look at the foreign and defense policy-making process. That event, of course, was the 1992 presidential election campaign which resulted in the first post–Cold War president, Bill Clinton. Throughout the campaign, Clinton emphasized economic problems. His first structural alteration of government, the formation of an Economic Security Council, had significant international economic implications. The Council would have an importance parallel to the National Security Council, a body born of the Cold War. This proposal illustrates the very process of change that we want to capture for the reader in the present work.

A word about the title is appropriate, for two reasons. First, it is purposely a bit more colorful than the titles ordinarily given for texts on the political process. In addition to trying to distinguish this effort as the first text to examine the policy process from the perspective of the post–Cold War era and the beginnings of the Clinton administration, we have consciously attempted to set a tone that is a bit less formal and even less somber than typical books on this subject. We hope the title conveys the notion that the book seeks to take a livelier, more interesting approach to the subject.

Second, those readers who are not already familiar with the subject will want to know what the title means. The term *puzzle palace* is a Washington nickname associated with two bureaucratic agencies. To most insiders, it is the name given to the super-secret National Security Agency, an intelligence agency in the arcane area of encrypting U.S. messages going abroad and intercepting messages coming into the United States. The other usage, and the one we have adopted, is Ronald Reagan's extension of the term to encompass the U.S. Department of Defense located in the Pentagon. Foggy Bottom, on the other hand, is the area near the Potomac River where the State Department is located. Frequently, the area is physically enshrouded in fog; some consider the thought process of the State Department to be equally opaque and soupy. Thus, the nickname of the area extends to the department.

From these nicknames emerges the symbolism of the title. The two major executive agencies historically engaged in foreign and defense policy are, of course, the Department of Defense (one of the Puzzle Palaces) and the Department of State (the one and only Foggy Bottom).

## The Plan and Organization of the Book

In this book, our analysis will proceed within the process of change, where the policy community tries gamely but not always successfully to mount and control events currently beyond their control. Because they represent the most important structural problems the system will confront, we will make extensive use of two examples as we describe and assess the policy process.

For those parts of the system whose orientation is primarily national security, our example will be the ongoing debate about U.S. strategy in the post–Cold War world. What threats does the United States face? What interests are in jeopardy? How do we fit into the "new world order" (assuming there is one)? What military preparations must the United States make to protect its interests? For the more traditionally foreign policy elements, the example will center on the problems of economic internationalization, with particular but not exclusive emphasis on the U.S.-Japan relationship. What is the process of internationalization and privatization of global economics? How well does the policy process understand this phenomenon? How can we maximize the United States' position in the economic order? These elements of policy come together in the changing debate; where change produces confluence, it will be emphasized.

Chapter 1 will survey the changing context for foreign and defense policy-making, outlining the international system along with the dynamics of the Cold War world and today's post–Cold War world. The remaining chapters will examine the major parts of the policy process in sequential order. Because the executive branch of government has historically been preeminent in this area, it will be the focus of Chapter 2, with some emphasis on the adequacy of current executive branch organization to deal with changing reality. Chapter 3 will highlight that change, focusing on the major executive branch agencies in foreign policy and how they are adapting. The discussion will then move in Chapter 4 to Congress, the second of the three branches of the federal government with major foreign and defense responsibility. A major theme will be the surge of congressional activism during the past decade, aimed principally at reform.

Chapter 5 will then look at how the government works with itself: how the myriad agencies within the executive branch coordinate their actions through the so-called interagency process; and the major mechanisms for interaction between the executive and legislative branches. The context for the discussion will be the real politics of interaction and places where change may dictate reform. Because it is rarely intrusive in defense and foreign policy-making, the judicial branch of government is not treated in a separate chapter.

With the institutional framework established, the discussion will move outside the formal processes of government. Chapters 6 and 7 will examine the multiple groups that seek to influence what the government does. In addition to traditional subjects such as interest groups and the general public, we will study the growing role of professional research organizations that are mostly centered around Washington, the media, and a new phenomenon that is a product of both, the "expert analyst" who was so evident during Desert Storm.

In Chapter 8, we will attempt to integrate the previous discussions through two case studies that also reflect our ongoing themes. To illustrate the rising importance of economics, we will look at the FSX fighter dispute between the United States and Japan; it is a story with multiple international and domestic economic and defense ramifications. To illustrate the national security side, we will discuss the politics of Desert Storm, first with regard to the process leading to congressional authorization of the use of force, and then also in terms of the policy spinoffs of actions taken during and subsequent to Desert Storm itself. In the final chapter, we will review our findings and make some suggestions toward the future.

## Acknowledgments

Any work of this nature is the product of the labors of more people than just the authors, and we would like to acknowledge those who also played a role. First, we would like to thank the Department of National Security and Strategy of the Army War College for bringing us together for a two-year period during which the collaboration was hatched. Our chairs, Colonel David Hansen and Colonel David Hazen, occasionally rued our irreverence of things Army and wondered if putting us alone in an office without proper Army "supervision" was a good idea; we are grateful.

Thanks are also clearly due to our St. Martin's editor, Don Reisman, who commissioned and encouraged the manuscript, and to the always excellent production staff who saw the project through to conclusion. A number of people read the first draft and made useful comments for which we are grateful. They are: Deborah J. Gerner, University of Kansas; Donald L. Hafner, Boston College; Richard A. Melanson, National Defense University; Michael A. Preda, Midwestern State University; Brian Ripley, University of Pittsburgh; and David W. Tarr, University of Wisconsin–Madison. Finally, we would both like to thank our families for putting up with us during the preparation of the book: Donna and Eric Snow, and Diane, Karen, and Jennifer Brown.

Donald M. Snow
Tuscaloosa, Alabama

Eugene Brown
Annville, Pennsylvania

# Contents

# Puzzle Palaces and Foggy Bottom

# CHAPTER 1

# Policy-Making in a Changing Environment

The past several years have witnessed dramatic and far-reaching changes in the international environment that provides the context for making foreign and national security policy. At the most obvious level, the events that began in the latter half of 1989 in Eastern and Central Europe—the fall of communist governments belonging to the old Warsaw Pact countries in 1989 and 1990, the disintegration of the Warsaw Treaty Organization (WTO) itself in 1991, and the voluntary dismemberment of the Soviet Union at the end of 1991—have transformed the geopolitical map of the world and hence the international problems which the United States must confront. The 1992 election capped that process: it was the first presidential election since the end of the Cold War, and it produced the first president who is arguably not a career "cold warrior."

The end of the Cold War was the most dramatic embodiment of change but by no means was it the only one. Indeed, several other forces altered the context of foreign policy. During the 1980s a truly global economy began to emerge, and policy-makers are only now beginning to come to grips with the policy implications of this phenomenon. Certainly, as the new Clinton administration has readily grasped, it has rendered conceptions of foreign policy that lack a significant international economic component less and less relevant.

Another force that is only vaguely understood is the telecommunications revolution, especially global television organizations such as Cable News Network (CNN). All world leaders watch CNN closely and occasionally communicate indirectly with one another via interviews with reporters on the network. As a result, we are witnessing a unique phenomenon: CNN influences the way people worldwide understand the issues of our times.

The primary purpose of this volume is not to examine in detail the substantive changes that have occurred and that are continuing in the foreign and defense policy-making arena, although we prominently feature such changes in the book. Rather, the major task we have set for ourselves is to examine the policy process itself: the focus is on *how* foreign and defense policy-making is accomplished, and not on *what* policy is ultimately formulated.

These two concerns can only partially be separated. Changing circumstances not only alter the international environment, but they also affect how the policy process itself operates. For instance, at the height of the Cold War in the 1950s and 1960s, when many of the political structures within which foreign and defense decisions are made were created, very little interest was shown in economic activity as a foreign policy concern. The reason, simply enough, was that the United States dominated the international economy: American goods and services were universally desired, and the U.S. dollar was the standard for international trade (the world's major so-called hard currency — a currency acceptable in international exchange).

Clearly, that scenario has changed. The United States remains one of the three economic "superpowers," along with Japan and the European Community (EC), but we no longer dominate the international economy the way we once did. Much of our relationship with Japan, and to a lesser extent the EC, is economic in content, and yet, as we will discuss in some detail later in this book, we made little institutional adaptation to the new importance of international economics until the Clinton administration, with its wave of economic changes, took office. Within the executive branch, for instance, the Departments of State and Defense dominated the foreign and defense policy-making process; economic issues such as trade were relegated to subdivisions within other government agencies (e.g., the international division of the Department of Agriculture for food sales or the U.S. trade representative with the status of an ambassador). We may have reached the point where the Clinton Economic Council may have influence equal to that of the State Department and Defense Department.

Because the substance of policy does affect the policy-making process, this chapter examines changes in the international system that are also causing adaptations in how policy is made. We will begin by looking at the nature of the international system and how foreign policy acts as a bridge between domestic politics and the broader world. We will then briefly describe the Cold War period, because East-West, Soviet-U.S. concerns dominated the 45-year period after the end of World War II. Many of the institutions and informal patterns that are still in place today were products of and responses to that period. We will then study some of the most important changes in the past decade and how they have altered both the context and structure of the policy process. The chapter will conclude by outlining some adaptations that have occurred or are occurring.

## The International System

Foreign policy is about how the United States, or any other nation-state, deals with the world outside its boundaries: the international system. The international system as we know it today is basically the product of the series of agreements that ended the Thirty Years' War, which had engulfed most of Europe between 1618 and 1648. Those agreements are known collectively as the Treaty of Westphalia, and the system it created is often called the Westphalian system. The building blocks of the Westphalian system are a series of *sovereign nation-states* that are designated as the principal political entities in the world. This term introduces two separate concepts, each of which is critical to understanding international politics and thus foreign policy.

The first concept is *sovereignty*, which we define as supreme authority. The entity that possesses sovereignty, whether it be government or individual, has no higher authority that can order or control its political fate. In the early days of the modern international system, sovereignty was thought to reside in the monarch, because the states of the international systems were uniformly ruled by monarchies (hence the interchangeable use of the terms *monarch* and *sovereign*). As the basis of governance broadened through seminal events such as the American and French revolutions, sovereignty came to be regarded as residing in individuals or the population of countries as a whole, which delegated part of their sovereignty to their governments. This concept has recently been challenged in places such as Somalia, where some assert that sovereign authority may be forfeited when a government overtly abuses all or some of its citizens.

The result was that sovereignty came to be considered an attribute of nation-states and, more precisely, the governments of nation-states. Once again, we have introduced a new term, *nation-state*. It is purposely hyphenated because it represents two different and sometimes inconsistent ideas. The first half of the word, *nation*, is an anthropological term, and it refers to group loyalties. The characteristics that usually define nationality include ethnicity, common language and historical experience, religion, or simply the feeling of belonging. My nationality, in other words, derives from my loyalty to some nationally defined group. Thus, some people think of themselves as Americans, some as Frenchmen, some as Russians. The other half, *state*, is a legal and political term that refers to exclusive jurisdiction over a piece of territory. The boundaries of a political map are state boundaries, and exclusive jurisdiction is the operational definition of sovereignty: states legally possess sovereignty.

The basis of this possession, and the principle that has stood at the base of international politics, is the right of each state to maintain total and absolute jurisdiction over its sovereign territory and those who live within that territory. Because this power has occasionally been abused and, recently, very publicly so in places such as Iraq, Yugoslavia, and Somalia, the principle has come under some criticism by people such as United Nations Secretary-General Boutros Boutros-Ghali.

The principle of sovereignty has quite opposite consequences within and between states. Internally, sovereignty creates authority (the power to make and enforce decisions about how relations between people and between people and the government will be regulated). Authority and jurisdiction are closely related, and the result is some semblance of physical order. In most Western systems, that authority is not imposed but is the result of the system's legitimacy, the right to govern which the people give freely to the government. In other, usually non-Western systems, authority is reinforced because of tradition (as in monarchies) or through coercion.

The consequences for the international system are quite the opposite. The same sovereignty that permits a government to govern within its territory prevents it from imposing its rules on other governments, since they possess sovereignty over their own territory. The result is the absence of authority in the relations between nation-states, or international politics. The international system is marked formally by a state of anarchy, the lack of government.

In this situation, international politics must operate very differently from domestic politics. The absence of government means the absence of enforceable rules to regulate how the state actors operate. As a result, international politics are inherently *power politics*, where states attempt to influence the behavior of other states but where they lack the authority to impose solutions reflecting their own positions.

U.S. foreign policy deals with how the United States, as only one (if a very important one) of the approximately 188 nation-states that are currently members of the United Nations, pursues its interests in a world over which the U.S. government lacks authority. The need for foreign policy arises because all nation-states have *interests* (conditions that are important to their well-being or even, in the extreme, their survival) that sometimes come into conflict with the interests of others. When conflicts of interest arise (situations where the United States and some other nation-state cannot simultaneously pursue their interests), then foreign policy attempts to resolve those disagreements.

At the top of the hierarchy of interests are *vital interests* — conditions and situations that are so important to national well-being or even survival that states will not voluntarily forfeit their desired interests. In the case of the United States, for instance, President Jimmy Carter in his 1980 State of the Union address deemed the free flow of oil from the Persian Gulf to be a vital American interest. This principle became known as the Carter Doctrine.

A vital interest is normally so important that in order to protect and maintain it the state will go to war. For example, when Iraq annexed Kuwait in August 1990, the United States felt it had to employ armed force to reverse the situation. (The alternative basis for using force was to punish Saddam Hussein for violating the rights of states, which he had done by infringing on Kuwait's sovereign territory.)

When vital interests and possible military action are involved, then foreign policy merges with something that is called *national security policy*, because the national security is defined in military terms. As we will see, during the Cold War foreign and national security policy were used synonymously. Technically, national security policy is a subset of foreign policy, which refers to all contacts with the outside world.

The Westphalian system is under at least some mild attack in the post–Cold War period. Two examples stand out. The first is the emergence of problems that transcend national boundaries and for which national solutions are inadequate or inappropriate. These transnational issues are illustrated by the Earth Summit of 1992. The second is the assertion that, at least in some cases, the rights of individuals and groups may transcend the rights of states. This has been a result of televised atrocities by governments. Saddam Hussein's attacks against the Kurdish minority in Iraq in 1991 as well as the desperate attempts by what was left of Yugoslavia to hold the country together by attacking separatist republics such as Bosnia and Herzegovina are examples. Operation Restore Hope in Somalia continues this assault, giving rise to concepts such as humanitarian vital interests (conditions vital to humanity for which the international use of force is justified despite state sovereignty).

## The Cold War World

In the present context, the Cold War seems like ancient history, but in fact, only five years ago it was still the dominant reality of international relations and foreign policy. The military competition between the West, led by the United States, and the East, led by the Soviet Union, was the single most important fact of life, and the government's mechanisms for foreign and defense policy-making were focused primarily, often exclusively, on managing that competition.

The encompassing Cold War competition was the result of the restructuring of the international system that occurred at the end of World War II. Prior to that war, a number of European states (especially Great

Britain, France, Germany, Italy, and the Soviet Union) had dominated international politics. The United States, a potential power of equal or greater magnitude, stood in "splendid isolation" from this system, which most Americans believed to be corrupt and irrelevant to their day-to-day concerns.

The war shattered the system and the United States' view of it. At the structural level, most of the traditional powers were prostrate or so greatly weakened that they no longer had the resources or energy to manage the system: Germany and Italy in Europe and Japan in the Far East were defeated and physically occupied, and Britain and France were exhausted physically and economically.

In this circumstance, the only nation-states to come out of the war with major power were the United States and the Soviet Union. Their power was not equal, however. The United States was the colossus: the U.S. economy, which had entered the war at something like 30 percent capacity, became the "arsenal for democracy" and was greatly strengthened by the war. U.S. casualties were comparatively light (about 300,000 killed), and the physical United States had been subjected to no physical damage. Moreover, the United States was the only country in the world that possessed nuclear weapons.

The situation was considerably bleaker for the Soviet Union. The bulk of the physical fighting in the war had been on the Eastern front, and the Soviets had suffered greatly. Estimates of Soviet losses stand at about 20 million and, especially if Stalin's purges during the 1930s are included, approach 30 million killed; two-thirds or more of the country's industry was destroyed; and thousands of towns and villages were leveled. The Soviets' major claim to power was the retention of a huge Red Army of occupation in those areas of Eastern Europe that it liberated from the Nazis. As time went by, that army looked increasingly ominous to the West.

Life had changed domestically in the United States as well. The chief victim of the war internally was the policy of isolationism. Many people had come to believe that, had the United States played an active role in restraining Germany during the early 1930s, war would not have come. Whether or not they liked the idea, most Americans recognized that the country would have to take a leading role in the postwar recovery.

As the smoke of the battlefield cleared, the central question about the new system was whether or not the wartime collaboration between the remaining powers would continue once the cause of collaboration was over. From the U.S. viewpoint, would "Uncle Joe" Stalin (as the Soviet leader was known during the war) remain the kindly uncle of the war, or would he revert to being the hideous, "godless communist" that he had been depicted to be before the war?

The answer, which was not immediately evident, would define the postwar system. During the war, a group of academics from the Western allies had drafted the United Nations Charter, which they hoped would provide the framework for organizing the postwar peace. Fearing confrontation but hoping cooperation would be the prevailing outcome, they drafted a document that could encompass either. If cooperation were possible, provision was made in Chapter VII for collective security measures to enforce the peace under U.N. auspices; if not, Article 51 provided authorization to form military alliances.

By 1947 it was apparent that the two powers would not be able to cooperate in organizing the peace. Possessing two very different political value systems and visions about how the world should be organized, the Americans and the Soviets could not agree on a peace to be enforced. Thus, the provisions of the U.N. Charter calling for collective actions against those who breached the peace remained dormant until 1990, when they were finally invoked against Iraq for its invasion and conquest of Kuwait.

The Soviet-U.S. confrontation had both ideological and military roots, and in combination, the competition dominated the policy of both nations for over 40 years. Ideologically, the barometer for U.S. policy was communism-anticommunism, and it affected both domestic and foreign policy. In the latter 1940s and 1950s, strong opposition arose in the United States to anyone who espoused what were viewed to be communist or Marxist ideas, culminating in the excesses of Wisconsin Senator Joseph ("Tail Gunner Joe") McCarthy's hearings to identify communists in the U.S. Army in 1954. Internationally, the competition was over allegiance to the communist or anticommunist movements, figuratively coloring the map red or blue.

At its height, this competition was viewed as encompassing and pervasive. The Yugoslav dissident Milovan Djilas described it as the "protracted conflict," indicating its enduring character. In the 1950s people debated whether "better red than dead" or "better dead than red" was the more desirable state of affairs.

The most obvious manifestation of the competition was in the military realm. The United States and the Soviet Union evolved rival military alliances in Europe: the North Atlantic Treaty Organization (NATO), which tied the United States to Canada and 14 Western nations in 1949, and the Warsaw Treaty Organization (WTO), which bound the Soviet Union and the Eastern European communist countries together in 1956.

The term *superpower* was fashioned to describe the military superiority of the world's two most powerful nations. At the pinnacle of this relationship was the possession of large thermonuclear arsenals on both sides aimed at the other. The United States became the first nuclear power, successfully testing an atomic (fission) bomb on July 16, 1945, three weeks before the only instances of such a device being employed in anger — against the Japanese cities of Hiroshima and Nagasaki. The Soviets first exploded a nuclear device in 1949, and in 1952 and 1953, respectively, the United States and the Soviets added thermonuclear (fission-fusion or hydrogen) weapons to their arsenals.

This military competition dominated foreign policy. Both sides maintained large active armed forces along the Iron Curtain in Europe to deter one another from attacking — at horrendous expense to both. At the end of the Korean War, for instance, the United States devoted 50 percent of the federal budget to defense, and it was not uncommon for 6 to 8 percent of gross national product (GNP) to be devoted to defense spending. Although exact figures are notoriously inaccurate, the Soviets were estimated to spend between 15 and 25 percent of their GNP on defense spending. As nuclear arsenals grew and became more sophisticated, both sides acquired the capability to destroy the other as functioning societies, a condition known as *mutual societal vulnerability* or *mutual assured destruction*.

It is impossible to overstate the fervor with which this competition was waged, especially in the formative years after World War II when the foreign policy structures and approaches that currently define the policy process were devised. Before World War II, foreign policy was a relatively minor concern handled by the State Department and the embassy system that it operated. When foreign policy became a life-and-death struggle in which the United States was a central character, the nature of the process was altered to meet the new demands.

The most visible, symbolic manifestation of that change was the National Security Council (NSC) system. This system was the product of the National Security Act of 1947, one of the landmark documents defining how Americans view both foreign and national security policy problems and processes.

Conceptually, the series of perceptions that underlay the National Security Act represented a sharp departure from how Americans had previously viewed foreign affairs. Prior to World War II, foreign affairs were a relatively minor part of the policy process. Most Americans found foreign policy, which they associated with the tainted power politics of Europe drawing us into World War I (the "Great War"), as distasteful, unpleasant, and essentially irrelevant to Americans. This was especially the case when our attentions were riveted on recuperating from the Great

Depression, which most Americans did not view as part of an international process. Moreover, the existence of two great oceans protected the United States from foreign military threats; thus, isolationism was both desirable and possible.

With foreign affairs relegated to the periphery of the political process, the United States' foreign interchange could be carried out quietly outside the spotlight. Institutionally, foreign policy and the State Department were more or less synonymous, and foreign policy essentially equaled diplomatic policy. The State Department was overwhelmingly the preserve of the Eastern liberal establishment, which had more interest in foreign affairs than the public at large. For most purposes, oversight by committees such as the Foreign Relations committees of the two Houses of Congress was mostly to ensure that the United States did not become too involved in the world.

The United States' active involvement in a competitive postwar system changed all that, a fact that came to be accepted during the war. As the only militarily significant states after the war, the United States and the Soviet Union viewed each other with increasing suspicion and hostility, fueling the possibility of armed conflict between them. As a result, for the first time a military dimension was added to the definition of U.S. foreign policy. The war and its aftermath indeed broadened this definition.

The evolving new system added a new ingredient to the old set of conceptions: a permanent Soviet military threat as the primary problem with which U.S. foreign policy would have to contend. U.S. foreign policy no longer equaled diplomacy. Instead, a new term came into being — *national security policy*—which was the sum of traditional diplomatic policy and defense policy. This transformation had at least three important consequences.

First, it gave foreign policy greater importance. Rather than being a peripheral matter, foreign policy became the concern of everyone, especially during the late 1940s and early 1950s, when the "red scare" made internal subversion by communists a part of the domestic agenda. In the process, the foreign policy establishment became larger and more visible. Many of the new participants were more liberal and internationalist in orientation than the public at large, and they became subject to scrutiny on patriotic grounds, for a number of them had flirted early in life with Marxism. Others, such as George F. Kennan, simply felt that the great majority of citizens was too ignorant of foreign affairs to offer intelligent opinions. Thus, he publicly groused that the public should leave the professionals alone to do their jobs, as they had in the past.

Second, adding a military threat to the foreign policy equation also added a patriotic dimension. Foreign policy was not only too important to be left to a narrow elite, but also it required the active and unified support of the American public and its servants. Politically, the idea of bipartisanship in foreign affairs became the watchword. Typified by the catch phrase that "politics ends at the water's edge," the idea was that, although the principal parties could disagree on domestic issues, they must refrain from partisan bickering on foreign affairs. In this way they would present a single voice and posture to the outside world. The viability of this distinction was sustainable at least in part because most domestic and foreign issues were distinct from one another.

One figure of the early postwar period who symbolized bipartisanship more than any other was Arthur Vandenburg, the Republican senior senator from Michigan who was chairman of the Senate Foreign Relations Committee and one of the Senate's most imposing members. Prior to World War II, Vandenburg had been one of the nation's foremost isolationists, tenaciously fighting President Franklin Delano Roosevelt's attempts to tie the United States to the allied cause. Converted to the necessity of U.S. involvement in the world by Pearl Harbor, Vandenburg became the leading symbol of the new bipartisan approach to world involvement after the war, joining old political enemy President Harry S Truman in the fight for the National Security Act.

Third, broadening the definition required bringing a broader range of expertise into the decision-making process. More specifically, the need to think about the military meant that the professional military officer corps of the United States had to be brought into the foreign policy-making process.

The resulting crash can still be heard today. The professional military officers who emerged from the war could hardly have been more unlike the Eastern establishment experts who dominated foreign policy processes. A relatively small, almost dynastic group tied to the service academies (the United States Military Academy at West Point, New York, and the United States Naval Academy at Annapolis, Maryland), the military was (and still is) an intensely conservative, patriotic, Spartan group. During the period between the two world wars, the military had been reduced in size, consigned to the periphery of American society. Thus, it had developed a sense of isolation from society that left it somewhat bitter and alienated from the political process.

This professional military and the urbane, sophisticated elite centered in the State Department took one look at one another, and a not always good-natured rivalry emerged that continues to the present. The competition has been characterized as a struggle between the "pointy heads" from State (the military's caricature of Foreign Service Officers or FSOs) and the "knuckle-draggers" from the military (State's equally pejorative caricature of the officers' supposed apelike intellectual qualities). This rivalry is, in some ways, only natural and healthy, for both groups bring different perspectives to problems that must be considered if wise policy is to result.

The result of these dynamics was the National Security Act of 1947, legislation that we now take for granted but had monumental institutional consequences. The act (1) created the Department of Defense (DOD) from the old Departments of War, the Army, and the Navy; (2) made the United States Air Force an independent branch (formerly, it was the Army Air Corps) and placed it, together with the Army and Navy, under the authority of the newly created secretary of defense; and (3) established the Central Intelligence Agency (CIA), the first civilian peacetime intelligence-gathering agency. The CIA's chief officer, the director of central intelligence (DCI), was designated as the coordinating officer for all governmental intelligence activities (see Chapter 2 for more details).

Of the greatest symbolic importance was the act's creation of the National Security Council as the coordinating body for national security policy deliberations. By statute, the NSC has four permanent members: the president, the vice president, and the secretaries of state and defense. The DCI and the chairman of the Joint Chiefs of Staff (JCS) are statutory advisers to the Council. The president may also include other governmental officials as he sees fit. John F. Kennedy, for instance, routinely included his brother, Robert F. Kennedy, the attorney general, in NSC deliberations. By design, the NSC is a deliberative body whose chief purpose is to give advice to the president. The NSC has no voting powers; rather, it only airs and discusses opinions from the various agencies.

The symbolism of the NSC lies in its apparent elevation of defense to coequal status with diplomacy by making the respective secretaries of the two major agencies the only other required members except the president and vice president. Thus, foreign policy was institutionally broadened beyond diplomacy to include military policy, and foreign policy became national security policy. Because most of the chief players today are products of this system, both institutionally and practically it has transcended the ending of the Cold War into the post–Cold War period.

## The Post–Cold War World

With the advantage of retrospect, we can now see that the long-standing Cold War confrontation was becoming increasingly tenuous in the years before Mikhail Gorbachev instigated—or at least did not oppose—the cascade of events that ended the competition. In turn, the cessation of that competition has changed the context and content of that policy in ways that we are only beginning to realize. Adapting to new conditions has been made all the more difficult because of the trauma of shedding the long-entrenched foreign policy process of the Cold War period.

## Motors of Change

The need to end the Cold War was most pressing to the Soviets, which is probably why they initiated the process, but the desire was not altogether absent in the United States. The impetus had both economic and military roots, each of which requires brief examination if we are to understand the changes that have occurred.

The economic dimension involved the widening gap between the economies of the First World (the most highly industrialized and prosperous nations of the West and Japan) and those of the Second (or socialist) World. This gap increased to a chasm during the 1970s and 1980s when the economies of the Western world experienced an unprecedented and mutually reinforcing prosperity and expansion, at the same time that the economies of most Second World countries, notably the former Soviet Union, not only failed to experience a similar expansion but even contracted. The availability of Western European television in the communist countries of Eastern Europe made the widening divergence in standards of living and productivity increasingly visible to all.

Economic expansion in the West had several motors. First, it was largely the result of applying the high-technology revolution to the productive system. High technological development is based on three fundamental pillars: great increases in knowledge generation and application as a result mainly of advanced computing capability; equally great expansions in knowledge dissemination within the pure and applied scientific communities as a result of the telecommunications revolution; and advances in a whole series of derivative technologies such as fiber optics, new materials science, robotics, and biotechnology. Each of these three pillars tended to be mutually reinforcing: computing advances sped up discoveries in derivative technologies like fiber optics, which in turn greatly increased telecommunications efficiency and hence the ability of scientists to interact and generate more new knowledge. As we will see in Chapter 3, President Clinton seems to fully appreciate the importance of this phenomenon.

Second, this revolution occurred within the context of a wave of privatization of economic activity throughout the First World. Freed of many of the shackles of governmental regulations, private investors and entrepreneurs came forward in high-risk but high-profit enterprises.

Third, the expansion not only was nurtured by the increasing internationalization of economic activity among the most developed countries but also contributed to it. With the capacity for instant communication of great bodies of data across national borders via computer modems and facsimile (fax) machines, international scientific collaboration accelerated enormously. Global telecommunications allowed the development of a truly global monetary and economic system. The age of economic interdependence, initially advertised in the 1960s, came to fruition in the 1980s, if not necessarily in the way it was predicted.

The policy and intellectual communities have not yet come to grips with these economic changes and their consequences for domestic and foreign policy. At best, their understanding of these dynamics is imperfect and currently is almost beyond the control of the policy process, which is trying to adapt to a changed environment it does not fully comprehend.

Instead of enjoying a prosperity comparable to that of the West, the Soviet economy in particular began to experience decreasing growth during the 1970s that flattened out to no growth. When Gorbachev came to power in 1984, his supporters identified the 1970s as the "period of stagnation." By standing still, the East was falling progressively further behind the West, especially in the crucial areas of high technology. To become economically vibrant and hopefully competitive, Gorbachev and his followers instituted a series of structural economic and political reforms intended to invigorate the economy. Put forward under the banners of *perestroika* (restructuring) and *glasnost* (openness or criticism), these reforms failed in their primary mission and eventually contributed to the process of national disintegration.

Parallel dynamics were occurring in the military competition between the superpowers. By the latter 1970s or early 1980s the military, and especially the thermonuclear, capabilities on both sides had grown to such proportions that a war between them employing nuclear weapons would ultimately destroy both as functioning societies. Nuclear war could not be won and thus had to be avoided at all costs. The result was a nuclear stalemate or necessary peace between the superpowers. With the consequences of nuclear exchange unacceptable to both sides, deterrence became their overt goal.

The avoidance of nuclear war had been an implicit part of the dynamic between East and West at least as far back as the Cuban missile crisis of 1962, when the two sides looked seriously at what a nuclear war would mean and recoiled from the realization. By the early 1980s, a difference had become evident: the two antagonists gradually recognized that the military stalemate now extended to the conventional balance as well. Two huge and enormously expensive conventional armed forces had faced one another off since the latter 1940s, but they could not be allowed to clash because any East-West war could escalate to the unacceptable nuclear exchange. Thus, the conventional confrontation became increasingly hollow and ritualistic: both armies practiced and perfected battle plans that neither had any intention of carrying out. Deterrence had become the only acceptable goal at the conventional level as well.

These two factors came together under Gorbachev and militated for an end to the Cold War competition. The Soviets had come to the conclusion that they could never share in the general prosperity until they adopted the very international economic and scientific system that they had emphatically rejected for years. Entrance into that system required joining the scientific and technological system that underlay the competition. As long as the Cold War persisted, however, the Soviets would be excluded inasmuch as the new technology was *dual-use*, that is, with both civilian and military applications. One does not sell the most advanced capability to the enemy; thus, a precondition of entrance was to cease being viewed as the enemy.

It was at this juncture that the military dimension entered the picture. The military competition was not only hollow, but it had also become an albatross around the Soviets' neck. At one level, the great expense of military preparedness contributed to the stagnation of the economy; reducing that expenditure might provide a "peace dividend" by allowing the Soviets to divert resources heretofore dedicated to the military to other priorities. At another level, the military confrontation between NATO and the WTO, along with the continued "enslavement" of Eastern Europe under unpopular communist rule, was the most obvious symbol of the antagonism that caused Soviet exclusion from the economic and technological cornucopia.

Under these circumstances, from the Soviet perspective ending the Cold War confrontation was not only attractive, but probably also necessary. In the process, the intellectual underpinnings of the United States' national security policy based in that confrontation were rendered largely irrelevant. As the Soviets knocked away the old symbols of competition, the director of the Soviets' USA and Canada Institute, Georgi Arbatov, noted wryly in 1989, "We have done a terrible thing to you. We have deprived you of the threat." Sifting through both the substantive and institutional consequences of the end of the Cold War continues to be a difficult task for U.S. policy-makers.

Although the entire kaleidoscope of change has not resolved itself into a clear and coherent pattern, certain results of change relevant to the war policy are becoming evident.

## Effects of Change

The post–Cold War world will provide a very different environment for foreign and national security decision-making than did the Cold War. As events in the Balkans and the former Soviet Union have already clearly demonstrated, it will not necessarily be a more peaceful or a more orderly place. The world may in fact become more disorderly and fractious than it was before.

This situation is already creating consternation among the world's policy-makers. In retrospect, the Cold War had a virtue in providing a certain orderliness and predictability. We all knew what the problems were, and we had devised both policies and policy processes to deal with the problems. The agenda was clear. In contrast, the new system lacks that clarity. Instead of the intellectually tidy framework of the Cold War that had organized our foreign policy, the new order is likely to be more fractious and even dangerous than was the Cold War. Events in the Balkans, especially Yugoslavia, in the former Soviet Union, and elsewhere serve as alarming examples of the new disorder.

Certain aspects of the new pattern are emerging and identifiable. For current purposes, we will identify six that appear to have particular policy and institutional significance.

**Collapse of the East-West Confrontation**   The East-West confrontation is no longer the centerpiece of U.S. and Soviet foreign policy. This change does not mean that the United States has no interest in the evolution of successor states to the former Soviet Union. Quite the contrary, events in these states are of great importance to how the new system evolves. It is the context of foreign policy that is different.

The military aspect of the relationship, as argued earlier, has virtually collapsed. As long as the successor states maintain large nuclear forces, they retain the capability, if not the likely intention, to cause great damage to the United States. The conventional military decline of the former Soviet Union, however, means that much of U.S. defense policy, strategy, and force mission and structure are rendered questionably relevant. As the process of reducing the size of the U.S. armed forces is debated and implemented, a major question that needs to be addressed is, For what purposes and needs should the armed forces be prepared in the future?

The real debate about relations with the former Soviet Union now centers on the role of the United States, along with the rest of the First World, in the process of political and economic development there that may help implement political democracy and encourage vibrant market economies. To date, the effort has centered on Russia, the largest and most consequential of the successor states, but it will doubtless spread to others as well.

This debate raises another interesting question: Who will set the agenda for the future of U.S. relations with the former Soviet Union? During the Cold War, the military confrontation dictated a heavily military orientation and thus the conservative defense community had primary influence. At the height of the Cold War, many Americans believed it unpatriotic to think in any other terms.

It is not so clear who will dominate the current debate. The end of military confrontation removes the strictures on the agenda and on those who can influence it. The Soviet threat no longer dominates the agenda; the successor states must now compete with other foreign and domestic pretenders to public attention. Thus, in the wake of the tragic rioting and destruction of Los Angeles in May 1992, members of Congress could question why the United States could afford to send aid to Russia but not to American cities. Thus, that summer members of Congress with a primarily domestic agenda were able to block assistance to Russia on domestic grounds. Such a consideration could hardly have been raised before.

***Reduced Emphasis on National Security Concerns***   The change in the East-West relationship has signaled a reduced emphasis on the national security content of U.S. foreign policy. While defense concerns will not disappear from the calculation of national security concerns, they will likely have less urgency and less predominance in the United States' view of the world.

This effect is, once again, largely the result of the end of the Cold War. In the Cold War period, U.S. interests and the threats to them largely coincided and thus guided policy. Now a kind of interest-threat mismatch has developed in which our most important interests (as in Europe) are not threatened militarily and most military threats are occurring in areas (e.g., the Third World) where we have marginal interests.

Part of the overall national debate on United States' policy toward the "new world order" has turned on how the United States will redefine the circumstances under which it will use military force to implement policy. Most of these situations will arise in Third World areas that have traditionally not been considered important enough to warrant use of force. Moreover, the situations that will likely arise will be unpredictable and often difficult and ambiguous. What will U.S. policy be?

A good example of this problem surrounds the tragedies of Yugoslavia and Somalia. As national self-determination turned to secessionism which brought violent reprisals from the largely Serbian remnants of the Yugoslavian armed forces, the international system had no effective mechanisms to contain the bloodshed. The European Community grappled with the difficulty, but because Yugoslavia is not a member, it decided it lacked jurisdiction. NATO used the same rationale. These decisions masked the determination that any involvement would be long, bloody, and probably inconclusive. By contrast, this same community that avoided Bosnian intervention thought ending Somali starvation seemed "doable."

In the spring of 1992, the United Nations responded by sending peacekeeping forces to Bosnia and Herzegovina, where the fighting was fiercest and the slaughter of innocent civilians most upsetting. The forces failed because they were inappropriate to the situation: peacekeeping forces presume that a ceasefire is in place and that both sides want someone to monitor and guarantee that peace. In the Yugoslav situation, it was not clear that either of those assumptions held. The controversy continued well into 1993.

The real problem in Bosnia and Herzegovina centered on the U.S. military's view of peace enforcement—the physical separation of warring parties and the imposition and enforcement of a peace on them when one or both parties (in this case the Serbians) may prefer to continue fighting. Filling this role is difficult, requiring robust and large armed forces such as the United States possesses.

But is that the direction U.S. foreign policy will take? Certainly it is one possibility and one the United States' intervention in Somalia seems to reinforce. In that case, defense concerns will remain a prominent part of the foreign policy agenda, for the Third World presents no shortage of potential situations like the one in Yugoslavia. The question is whether Americans want to so redefine their interests that Third World problems will become important foreign and defense priorities. If so, then national security concerns will retain some of their former urgency; if not, some of that urgency recedes.

*Nontraditional Elements of Policy*    The third pattern is the redefinition of national security and foreign policy to include nontraditional elements. The need to enlarge the agenda encompasses at least two different subsets of concern. The first and most conspicuous subset has been the emergence of a series of transnational issues: problems that transcend national borders and whose solutions can be attained only through international actions.

The transnational issue that has received the greatest attention and publicity is environmental degradation, which was the subject of the so-called Earth Summit, an international conference in Rio de Janeiro, Brazil, in June 1992. The environmental issue clearly exemplifies a transnational concern. It currently centers on ozone depletion, and is truly international in scope. For example, most of the carbon dioxide ($CO_2$) emissions that cause the depletion of ozone occur in the First World (automobile exhaust emissions being a primary culprit), whereas the destruction of the equatorial rainforests in places such as the Amazon Basin removes many of the trees that break down $CO_2$ into harmless elements. Moreover, atmospheric pollution is on the increase in the Third World, which now produces about 45 percent of all pollutants.

Environmental concerns, like other transnational issues, are also quasi-national security concerns that fall somewhere between traditional national security issues defined in military terms and foreign policy issues framed in diplomatic terms. They are national security concerns inasmuch as our sense of security and well-being will be affected negatively if ozone depletion is not arrested and reversed. On the other hand, they are not traditional national security issues inasmuch as military solutions do not apply. Similarly, they go beyond classic diplomatic concerns in their intractability and multinational character, and the need to take actions beyond simple negotiation. These difficulties were apparent at the Rio de Janeiro summit.

Several other issues fall within this general category, including the overwhelming indebtedness of Third World countries to the developed First World, and the problems of overpopulation and food supplies. Another issue is that of migration across national boundaries. Until recently, migration has largely involved the movement of peoples from the poor countries to the richer countries for economic reasons. Today many are forced to migrate because of war or political repression; these migrations have far greater explosive potentials. At the beginning of 1992, for instance, an estimated 15 million people fell into this category. If the precedents of the former Soviet Union and Yugoslavia apply more widely, this problem could grow in magnitude.

The second subset of concerns encompasses broadened conceptions of defense-applicable concerns. As the Cold War has faded and the traditional role of the armed forces has been arguably constricted, the Defense Department has embraced roles and missions that go beyond its traditional mandate and even interest. These roles involve interaction between the United States and the Third World, where national security interests have historically been marginal, as noted. Moreover they involve issues whose military solution is unclear or marginal.

This subset involves three different issues, all of which are on the DOD agenda. The most well-known issue is counternarcotics — participation by U.S. forces in the so-called war on drugs announced by President Bush to stem the flow of cocaine and other drugs from the Andean states of Peru, Bolivia, and Colombia to the United States. The armed forces are principally involved in so-called supply-side efforts: Army Special Operations Forces (SOFs) providing training for native forces to improve their abilities to destroy the coca crops from which cocaine is refined (source eradication); the Navy and Coast Guard (which is administratively housed in the Treasury Department and thus is technically not an armed force) in seizing sea-based smuggling; and the Air Force in aerial reconnaissance of airborne drug shipments (interdiction).

The military's participation in the war on drugs is both uncomfortable and controversial. It is uncomfortable because the actions being undertaken more closely resemble policing than military roles and because the military establishment, having known considerable success in the past few years, fears being tainted by what could easily be a losing effort. It is controversial because, to date, supply-side efforts have had only modest success (some would argue failure), despite the fact that 70 percent of American resources dedicated to these efforts has been for supply-side activities. President Clinton has announced a reorientation away from supply-side efforts. Many, including the president, feel that reducing the demand for drugs is the only approach that has any real chance of success.

Counternarcotics efforts are definitely North-South problems, since drugs are produced in the Third World for consumption in the First World. The other two issues involved in the subset — counterterrorism and peacekeeping — are similar to counternarcotics. Counterterrorism, which is essentially designed to shield U.S. citizens from terrorist actions, takes the forms of antiterrorist actions that seek to make society less vulnerable to terrorists (e.g., through use of metal detectors at airports, training business executives how to evade kidnappers) and counterterrorist actions that seek to punish terrorists (e.g., through capture of terrorists and disruption of terrorist organizations).

Since most terrorism is initiated in the Third World, especially the Middle East, this problem, too, has a North-South flavor. It is an untraditional role for the military; in fact, only very specialized military units, such as the Army's Delta Force, have the skills and training for this kind of activity.

Peacekeeping, the third mission, has been a U.N. role since the U.N. Emergency Force (UNEF) was interposed between Israel and Egypt at the end of the Suez War of 1956. It is a relatively new mission for the United

States, however. The United States' only real experience in this area was its supervision of the truce line between Israel and Egypt in the Sinai as a result of the Camp David Accords of 1978.

This mission has also become controversial. One important consideration concerns whether the international system will be more involved in peacekeeping or peace enforcement efforts in the future. If the emphasis goes to peacekeeping, then U.S. involvement will be only minor, if at all. If, on the other hand, peace enforcement becomes the more prominent of the two, countries with large, capable armed forces such as the United States will almost certainly be heavily involved. If Bosnia and Herzegovina are any indicators, the future may witness more peace enforcement than peacekeeping opportunities. The question that arises is how many times and in what places will the United States be willing to involve itself. Moreover, will the criterion for intervention be the prospect of quick and relatively easy solution as in Somalia, or some other standard?

Another consideration is that peacekeeping is not an area of traditional military expertise or emphasis. Within the Army, which would bear the brunt of peacekeeping efforts, only the Military Police (MP) receives relevant training. Finally, most of the peacekeeping–peace enforcement opportunities will occur in Third World areas where the United States' vital interests as traditionally defined have not been engaged. Humanitarian instincts notwithstanding, is a desire for world order sufficient motivation for going to war? In other words, will the United States embrace concepts like "humanitarian vital interests"?

*The Internationalization of Economic Activity*   The other three emerging patterns are more closely related to changes in the international environment. The fourth and by far most important of all six patterns is the internationalization of economic activity. Boosted by the telecommunications and technological revolutions and the adoption of policies that promote privatization of economic activity, the world's economy has changed in dramatic though poorly understood ways. At least within the First World, a truly global economy has emerged in which the economic systems of the three economic superpowers are tied together in ways that would be difficult to disaggregate. Thanks to the telecommunications revolution, for instance, stock markets are open 24 hours a day, because it is always the workday somewhere. Multinational buying and selling occurs in New York, London, and Tokyo, to mention the most obvious cases. If Wall Street is closed for the day, transactions can be made somewhere else. At the same time, businesses can communicate instantly with essentially any other entity on the globe. Thus, companies with far-flung affiliates can efficiently coordinate activity; through teleconferencing they can hold Board of Directors meetings with board members on several different continents. The cutting edge of this phenomenon is the so-called stateless corporation—the corporation that has become so internationalized in ownership, management, labor force, and product mix that it cannot be definitively identified with any single nation. Many traditional nationally defined companies—International Business Machines and Honda, to cite but two examples—are moving toward this status.

These processes have occurred and continue to evolve so rapidly that traditional means of understanding them are not adequate to explain their behavior and its effects. What does it mean, for instance, when Japanese automobiles are made in the United States and are even produced on the same production line as identical cars carrying "American" brand names? (The Eagle Talon, Plymouth Laser, and Mitsubishi Eclipse, all made in Bloomington, Illinois, are examples.) Is Honda, whose president is an American and which has recently moved its corporate headquarters to California, still a Japanese corporation? If so, what does that mean?

Of all the global interconnections, none is closer than that between the United States and Japan. This relationship is also the most controversial and most prominent in the policy process. Because Japanese-American relations affect jobs all over the country, they are by no means the sole preserve of the executive branch; all those members of Congress whose constituents have gained or lost jobs in their district owing to Japanese investment have a vital say in the defense of Japan or in "Japan-bashing."

The debate over what constitutes an American automobile, alluded to earlier, exemplifies this controversy. The lines of ownership have been blurred for three reasons: (1) American corporations have invested heavily in foreign automobile manufacturers (Jaguar is owned completely by General Motors, and Mitsubishi is a quarter owned by Chrysler); (2) joint ventures between automobile makers have taken place (Ford and Mazda, General Motors and Toyota); and (3) overseas manufacture of cars is common (Ford Crown Victorias in Mexico, Nissans in the United States). According to the current definition, an automobile is American if 75 percent of its parts are made in this country. The result can be anomalous: by this definition, Ford Crown Victorias are foreign cars, whereas Mazda 626s made in Japan are American.

*Global Television*   The impact of the telecommunications revolution is not limited to economic internationalization. An additional effect is global television that is also an agent transforming our understanding of the world. The bellwether has been Ted Turner's Atlanta-based Cable News

Network (CNN). Born in 1980, CNN was derided as a lunatic scheme with little chance for journalistic or financial success. By the time it began providing the standard-setting coverage of Operations Desert Shield and Storm, CNN was available in over 50 million American households and could be seen in over 100 foreign countries. Some estimates are that upward of 1 billion people worldwide watched some part of CNN coverage of the war in the Persian Gulf.

Global television impacts the foreign policy process primarily because political leaders watch the network. Former President Bush, for example, was known to be an avid watcher, as are many foreign leaders. In fact, it has become something of a status symbol within the government to have a television set tuned to CNN in one's office. CNN often provides these viewers the first information they receive on international affairs, and through the network's news coverage foreign leaders communicate indirectly with one another.

More and more individual citizens also watch CNN, especially during times of crisis, thereby increasing their knowledge of what is going on in the world around them. Extensive television coverage led by CNN no doubt influenced public awareness and condemnation of the People's Republic of China's violent repression of the democracy movement in Tiananmen Square in 1989.

Global television has yet another effect: because people are generally made more aware of foreign affairs, their elected representatives, notably in Congress, feel the increased need to show some knowledge and interest. In earlier times, most members of Congress could rely on the opinions of their colleagues — especially those known for great expertise — to form their opinions. Now, those who have no formed opinions can quickly be exposed to the voters back home.

The impact of global television is only beginning to be felt or understood. CNN is not, after all, a global television system; rather, it is a U.S. broadcast system that collects news and broadcasts in a number of countries. A European-based consortium that is the parallel of the stateless corporation is scheduled to begin broadcasting in 1994, and when it does, the process will be advanced another step.

*Rising Importance of the Third World*   A sixth phenomenon is the growing relative importance of the Third World to U.S. policy. In some ways, this is a natural outgrowth of the end of the Cold War: with East-West tensions no longer at the center of concern, the spotlight had to move somewhere else. Increasingly, the burdens and difficulties of the Third World, which have great violent potential, are forming the problem for systemic stability.

Economically, the countries of much of Africa, Asia, and parts of Latin America that comprise the Third World share economic underdevelopment and misery. By some measures, the conditions in many of these countries have deteriorated absolutely in the last decade; certainly the gap between the rich and poor nations has widened substantially. Historically, this situation has been regrettable but not of sufficient importance to warrant the concerted effort of First World nations, including the United States. In an increasingly global economic system, a major question is whether self-interest will lead to the nurturing of the Third World's labor and market potential as a means of stimulating global economic growth.

Politically, the Third World continues to be the least stable and most violent part of the world. Regional conflicts between historical enemies — India and Pakistan, for instance — are one form that instability takes. Another form is internal conflicts — wars between groups within Third World states for control of government.

Internal instability in the Third World may be a particular problem in the upcoming years. Most Third World governments today are plagued by illegitimacy: they do not have the willing consent of the population to govern. As democratization, one of the main outcomes of the revolutions of 1989, spreads from the Second World to the Third World, the results could be similar to those we are seeing in the former states of Yugoslavia and the Soviet Union: secessions often accompanied by violence.

The breakup of Yugoslavia offers a particularly chilling problem for U.S. and world policy. Many states in the Third World are like Yugoslavia: artificial aggregates of minority groups with much more loyalty to their groups than to the nation-state of which they are a part. As Yugoslav disintegration turned bloody in places like Croatia and Bosnia and Herzegovina, policy-makers in the United States and elsewhere looked on at the consequences in impotent horror. Organizing to prevent similar futures will be a major challenge in the 1990s and beyond.

## Adjusting to Change

The changes that are cascading through the international system will require substantive changes in policy that respond to new realities; and adaptations in the policy process itself, in terms both of institutional patterns and attitudes and the setting of the foreign and defense agenda. These are the major foreign policy challenges that face the Clinton administration.

Our major concern here, as we have said, is not to present a detailed examination of the content of future policy but rather to show how its content dictates change and adaptation within the process. Since the two forms of change are related, of course, we cannot look at one aspect and totally ignore the other.

Signs of some change have already begun to appear, although the final impacts are by no means clear. For purposes of illustration, we can identify three areas of change: a reorientation away from the idea of the national security state to some broader conceptual and institutional basis for the policy process; a growing awareness of the need to get a better institutional hold on the impact of economic internationalization and its effects on citizens and foreign policy; and the increased pace and intensity of foreign affairs fanned by global telecommunications.

As noted earlier in the chapter, much of the intellectual and institutional apparatus for making policy is a product of the Cold War obsession with containing Soviet communism. Institutionally, as we have said, this organization was largely created in the executive branch of government through the National Security Act of 1947, which produced a more militarized U.S. policy than had heretofore been the case. This pattern was also reflected in the kind of congressional committees that were formed to oversee the activities of the constituent parts of the NSC system. Intellectually, the fixation on the "communist menace" effectively created the definition of foreign policy as national security policy.

With the disintegration of the Soviet Union and the collapse of worldwide communism except in isolated pockets, the *raison d'être* for that system vanished and so it is that the conceptual and institutional relevance of the ongoing system is being questioned. With no visible, permanent military menace to counteract, is national security defined mostly in terms of military balances a relevant overriding organizational concept? If it is not, then we face the options of redefining national security to include a host of nontraditional concerns or of loosening or breaking the equation of foreign and national security policy.

In the evolving system, transnational problems and economic issues will increasingly fill the foreign policy agenda. If that is true, are those with the appropriate expertise in an institutional position to influence policy? The statutory members and advisers to the NSC reflect the old loading of the decision process toward the military dimensions of problems. Does a new order where the traditional concerns are less pressing require adjusting the personnel and institutions that form the core of the system to reflect the new realities?

The growing concern with international economic reality exemplifies the problem. Currently, governmental assets are scattered throughout the executive branch, largely through international divisions in different executive agencies (e.g., the Department of Commerce and Agriculture).

Until the Clinton administration created the coequal Economic Council, no single bureaucratic, cabinet-level focal point within the government was devoted solely to dealing with international economic issues on a plane, say, of the National Security Council and its interagency process. If economic issues become more important in the future, will the creation of an economic adviser and council create the level and intensity necessary to raise their status in the overall policy process? Clearly, President Clinton, who has a particular interest in economic matters, believes so.

Some institutional adjustment is already evident. Using the Goldwater-Nichols Defense Reorganization Act of 1986 as their guideline, the chair of the Senate and the former chair of the House Select Committees on Intelligence, Senator David Boren and Representative David McCurdy, both Democrats from Oklahoma, introduced what has become known as the Intelligence Reorganization Act (or Boren-McCurdy Act) in early 1992. The overall purpose of the bill is to streamline an intelligence complex of institutions developed and designed for the Cold War and in the process to reduce the size and redundancy of the system.

Events rapidly unfolding in 1992 and focusing on the violent disintegration of Yugoslavia suggested another externally imposed area of change: peacemaking. In documents that began to come available in that year the DOD, sensitive to the need to adapt to changing reality, apparently embraced a broader peacekeeping/peace enforcement role. This represents a fundamental change in the DOD's outlook. First, it has strong implications for force missions and structure. As noted, peacekeeping — as opposed to peace enforcement — skills are not widely taught in the U.S. military system except to the Military Police. Clearly, a new career track, complete with new patterns of training and equipping, will be necessary. Second, the idea that U.S. forces might come under the command of other than American commanders represents a fundamental departure, the ramifications of which have yet to be fully appreciated or felt. Once (or if) those forces are established, video images of suffering and atrocity will greatly enhance the temptation to employ them, as was the case during the attacks on the Bosnian capital of Sarajevo.

Adjustment to the new and evolving global economy may require more policy and institutional adaptation than any other emerging trend. The most important reason is that the United States' approach to this new system, including the degree of its competitiveness, will have a great deal to do with the prosperity of the average American in the future. This has become a major theme of the Clinton administration.

The situation is complex, dynamic, and poorly understood. Most Americans today know that something must be done about the nation's double deficits: the federal budget deficit and the trade deficit with the world, especially Japan. The two deficits are interrelated and weigh heavily on economic expansion. Were the trade balance more positive, it would mean either that we were importing less (thus buying more American goods) or exporting more (thus producing more goods to be sold overseas). With either outcome, more Americans would be working and paying more taxes that presumably could be used to reduce the budget deficit. At the same time, large budget deficits are increasingly underwritten by loans from foreign investors, giving them a leverage in the United States that makes many Americans apprehensive.

The new system challenges the United States' historical economic dominance. Although joint ownership of firms internationally conditions the extent to which it could occur, the situation is competitive in a variety of ways that are becoming commonplace. Education, for instance, is thought to be the motor that drives the high technology that increasingly underlays economic advantage in the global economy. Comparisons — often invidious — between the U.S. educational system and other First World countries are regularly made. The same is true for a variety of other measures, such as worker productivity or labor costs. The point is that all these comparisons used to be made on a strictly domestic basis: for example, performance on standardized tests by regions of the country or productivity by industry. Now, the comparisons are almost always international.

The problem we have to be concerned with in this international economic problem area is that no one seems to understand either its parameters or how to deal with it in a policy sense. The government has appointed a number of commissions, such as the Young Commission on Competitiveness in the mid-1980s, to study aspects of it, but the studies scarcely ever agree on definitions of problems or solutions. The result is that the public agenda on the subject is fuzzy, although President Clinton is going to great lengths to clarify that agenda. In addition, thanks to the penchant for noninterference in economic affairs by government that is a legacy of the Reagan-Bush years, the executive branch does not provide the kind of leadership that would clearly designate it as the prime agenda setter.

The result has been political chaos. The president normally sets the tone and agenda in foreign policy areas, but under President Bush, this was not the case in the economic area. A major reason was that the economic problem is neither an exclusively domestic nor an exclusively foreign/national security problem. Rather, almost any domestic economic decision will have foreign policy ramifications, and vice versa, a condition for which the term *intermestic* policy was devised in the 1970s. Because a foreign economic policy decision can have a direct impact on individual states and congressional districts within states, senators and representatives demand part of the agenda-setting role. In economic matters, politics decidedly no longer ends at the water's edge. Moreover, as long as the executive branch was controlled by one political party and the Congress by the other, there was little danger of a bipartisan approach.

If the economic question dominates over the rest of the century, it is not clear who will handle it or how. With regard to leadership or agenda setting, will the leadership in framing the questions and their answers come from the executive branch or Congress? Currently, neither branch has a focal point that obviously provides that emphasis. In that case, will the situation be handled primarily as a domestic problem, with emphasis on issues like education and job training? Or will it be treated as a foreign policy problem, with emphasis on items such as trade negotiations? Both strands can be found in President Clinton's economic and budget initiatives.

Because economic internationalization is both a domestic and a foreign policy phenomenon that currently has no compelling institutional home, it is likely a prime candidate for institutional innovation. The Economic Council will most probably form the institutional setting for this adjustment as this new structure and concept matures.

The rapidly evolving role of global mediation is also changing the context and structures of foreign and national security policy. This is especially true of global television, which has given a transparency to events worldwide that would have seemed inconceivable only a few years ago. Global television both informs us of and dramatizes world events with a speed and comprehensiveness that profoundly affects the work of government.

As already stated, CNN and similar organizations such as Independent Television Network (ITN) are responsible for much of this transformation, and television's reach is growing. CNN has been consistently first on the scene: with the Kurds in southern Turkey, providing coverage without which Operation Provide Comfort probably would not have occurred. ITN has been on the front lines in Bosnia when Serbian irregulars attacked civilians with a deadly mortar attack that aroused international calls for action. And all the television news-gathering organizations provided copious coverage of the suffering in Somalia. As that coverage moves to other tragedies like the Sudan, will policy be far behind?

By providing dramatic, instantaneous coverage of global events, global television has become part of the agenda-setting mechanism in ways that are not yet clearly understood. Policy-makers get their first information on many foreign events via television, and the fact that average citizens see and are affected by that same coverage means government is constrained to act in ways it might not if events were less public. Would most Americans have known or even cared about Bosnia and Herzegovina without global television?

It is, of course, a two-way street. Governments routinely use television to announce developments such as negotiating positions through televised news conferences piped worldwide. The commencement of the air campaign that began Operation Desert Storm was clearly timed to coincide with network news broadcasts: the first attacks on Baghdad occurred at 6:55 P.M. Eastern Standard Time on January 16, 1991. Moreover, congressional leaders, aware of the impact of televised events, use reportage as a means of communicating with their own constituents. This approach will almost certainly increase in a Clinton administration where the president seems especially attuned to the use of television to influence opinion.

Once again, the impact of global television, wrapped as it is in the high technology and telecommunications revolutions, is such a new phenomenon that we lack a detailed understanding of what it does and how it affects the structures of government. As a result, there is less agreement about what, if any, institutional adaptations will be required to deal with it.

## Conclusions

One of the most obvious shared characteristics of the new influences on foreign and defense policy-making is the way in which events and trends are being accelerated and condensed. Events simply happen faster than they used to, and the pace will not likely slow.

This tempo collides directly with a governmental process that is known for neither its speed nor its efficiency. In some important ways, this slowness was part of the Founding Fathers' purposeful design: the separation of powers would assure that no branch of government or any individual could accumulate too much power. Of course, the Founding Fathers did not anticipate the future extent of government, the nature and pace of events that would have to be governed, or, more relevantly for present concerns, the importance of foreign and defense matters.

The rapid changes, which are most evident in restructuring the geopolitical map of the world but also clearly reflected in the economic and political impacts of economic internationalization and high technology, are changing the context within which the policy process operates. As even the most casual observer will have noted, the policy process has not responded well to these changes.

The elements of change have come to a head in the Clinton administration. Both the president and vice president have more activist views on the role of government than did Presidents Reagan and Bush. The two Republicans shared the belief that government normally made worse decisions than the private sector, and thus the role of government should be to stay out of the way of private industry as much as possible.

Clinton and Gore believe that government can and must play a more activist role, and the policy and institutional consequences of their beliefs were clearly evident in their first year in office. Although the new president professed a primary concern with the domestic economy, he realized the role of global economic competitiveness and incorporated educational and tax incentives and research and development funds into his program. His explicit purpose was to make American industry more competitive with the advanced world. Secretary of Labor Robert Reich, long an academic advocate of global competitiveness, led the charge to the same end with organized labor.

Much of this activism centers on environmental issues and initiatives. The interest of Vice President Gore was well documented in the campaign and was translated quickly into intermestic policy. The new administration announced early on that a prime focus of its industrial policy would be on nurturing the environmental cleanup industry, a growing global economic area in which the United States lagged. The vehicle for this emphasis is the sharing of research commissioned by governmental agencies—principally the Department of Energy—with private firms to enhance their abilities to produce world-leading technologies for dealing with environmental degradation.

The activism extends to traditional areas such as the military. Clinton initially shocked the military establishment by announcing his intention to rescind the ban on gays and lesbians in the military, and he followed that with the announcement that he proposed to cut $60 billion more from the defense budget by fiscal year 1995 than had been proposed by the Bush administration.

Institutional change has been part of this process. As already noted, the Economic Security Council was rapidly put in place to coordinate the United States' economic competition with the world. Shortly after taking their offices, Secretary of State Warren Christopher and Secretary of Defense Les Aspin announced their intentions to put in place departmental reorganizations that would align their departments more closely with emerging trends. These proposed changes are discussed in Chapter 3.

In foreign and defense policy-making areas, we may come to view the 1992 election as a watershed event. Over 100 seats in the Congress changed hands—almost 20 percent new faces in a Congress where the turnover rate has normally been more like 3 or 4 percent. The "freshman class" is already proving to be vigorous and assertive. At the same time, the Clinton administration brings a new, more activist, and clearly more post–Cold War orientation than has been the case before.

As we move toward the middle of the 1990s, the trends born in the 1980s and culminating with the end of the Cold War collide with the first post–Cold War presidency. The results may prove volatile, not unlike a warm and moist low-pressure front meeting a cold high-pressure front. While the results can be volatile and unpredictable, they will almost certainly be interesting.

## SUGGESTED READINGS

Crabb, Cecil Van Meter. *The American Approach to Foreign Policy: A Pragmatic Perspective*. Lanham, Md.: University Press of America, 1985.

Denny, Brewster C. *Seeing American Foreign Policy Whole*. Urbana, Ill.: University of Chicago Press, 1985.

Hughes, Barry B. *The Domestic Context of American Foreign Policy*. San Francisco: W. H. Freeman & Co., 1978.

Johnson, Richard A. *The Administration of United States Foreign Policy*. Austin: University of Texas Press, 1971.

Kegley, Charles W., Jr., and Eugene R. Wittkopf. *American Foreign Policy: Pattern and Process*. New York: St. Martin's Press, 1991.

Kissinger, Henry. *American Foreign Policy: A Global View*. Singapore: Institute of Southeast Asian Studies, 1982.

Melanson, Richard A. *Reconstructing Consensus: American Foreign Policy Since the Vietnam War*. New York: St. Martin's Press, 1991.

Plischke, Elmer, ed. *Contemporary U.S. Foreign Policy: Documents and Commentary*. Westport, Conn.: Greenwood Press, 1991.

Snow, Donald M. *The Shape of the Future: The Post Cold War World*. Armonk, N.Y.: M. E. Sharpe, 1991.

# CHAPTER 2

# The President and the Executive Branch

Arriving in a foreign capital aboard Air Force One—a massive Boeing 747 emblazoned with the seal of his office—the president of the United States is greeted by the pomp and ceremony once reserved for monarchs. The outward symbols of great power are all there: swarms of security guards, a small army of aides and advisers, a doting band of news reporters, technicians who keep him in instantaneous communication with the White House, and a fleet of presidential limousines and helicopters that were flown in ahead of the president's arrival. These ornate trappings of power are merely the visible manifestations of the overriding fact of international life during the past half-century: The United States is the world's greatest superpower, and the president of the United States is its most powerful foreign policy-maker and a world leader.

It is a reality that would have startled the nation's Founding Fathers. In their deliberations over the new republic's constitution at the Philadelphia convention in 1787, the 55 delegates were all too aware of the dangers of excessive concentration of power—especially power over foreign affairs—in the hands of the executive. Their eighteenth-century world was filled with the object lessons of unaccountable European monarchs treating war and international intrigue as a personal amusement.

The resulting American Constitution, little altered for two centuries now, carefully divides formal policy-making authority between the executive and legislative branches. In the memorable words of the late Edward S. Corwin, "The Constitution . . . is an invitation to struggle for the privilege of directing American foreign policy." Each branch was given its own independent sources of authority, but the powers of each were carefully checked and balanced by countervailing powers given to the other. In the making of public policy, then, including foreign policy the Founding Fathers believed in *codetermination* by the two coequal elected branches, with neither branch dominant over or subordinate to the other. One of the most widely held myths about the American constitutional system is the notion that the Founding Fathers intended foreign policy to be the province of presidents, with Congress relegated to a decidedly secondary role. The point is of such fundamental importance that it bears repeating: what the Founding Fathers contemplated was a vigorous executive branch *and* a vigorous legislative branch whose separate views and powers would together set the nation's course in international affairs. Those who find a constitutional intent for presidential primacy or congressional primacy misread the nation's fundamental political charter.

The practice of the past two centuries, however, shows that the carefully calibrated balance envisioned by the Constitution's authors is difficult to maintain. The result has been a recurring swing of the pendulum between periods of presidential dominance of foreign policy and periods of congressional reassertiveness. The modern era of U.S. foreign policy, the period since World War II, has been one of presidential dominance, but that dominance has been challenged by the most recent phase of congressional assertiveness, which began in the 1970s.

Despite the Founding Fathers' vision of equal policy codetermination between the two elected branches, then, presidents are often able to dominate the foreign policy-making process. To understand why this is so, we need first to look at the formal powers granted to presidents and then to consider the informal powers and international circumstances that greatly enhance the president's formal authority.

## Formal Powers of the Presidency

The Constitution confers on presidents six formal roles and powers that together give him considerable, though hardly overwhelming, authority in foreign affairs. First, we simply list them, and then we turn to a brief discussion of each. Constitutionally the president is the United States' (1) chief executive, (2) chief of state, and (3) commander in chief; he is also granted enumerated powers in regards to (4) treaty making, (5) appointment of key personnel, and (6) the recognition of foreign regimes.

### Chief Executive

Article II, Section 1, makes the president the nation's chief executive. In this capacity, he presides over the vast array of federal agencies that carry out the business of government. Although few presidents devote much time or energy to the actual supervision of the sprawling federal bureaucracy, the fact that the president is chief executive means that all the agencies that possess the kind of specialized information and expertise essential to foreign policy-making report to the White House. Agencies such as the State Department, the Pentagon, the CIA, and the Office of the U.S. Trade Representative have incomparable resources, the most important of which is the large number of experienced and well-informed experts with unrivaled access to vital information. Although in recent years the Congress has strengthened its own institutional capabilities for independent analysis and foreign policy development, its staff cannot begin to compare to the rich lode of seasoned expertise residing throughout the sprawling executive establishment.

One challenge a president must meet is to develop a management and decision-making style that will ensure the mobilization of the executive agencies around presidential objectives rather than their pursuit of their own institutional interests. Presidents who successfully meet this challenge begin the foreign policy-making process with an advantage over Congress, which, as we have said, cannot match the analytic capabilities, specialized knowledge, and subject-matter expertise found in the foreign affairs bureaucracies. On the other hand, the growing proliferation of bureaucratic players in foreign policy-making, coupled with the fact that executive agencies often work against one another in seeking to influence foreign policy, somewhat lessens the older image of a president sitting securely atop an executive establishment reliably harnessed to his policy objectives.

### Chief of State

When acting in his capacity as chief of state, the president is the symbolic personification of the American nation. Although some writers sometimes dismiss this role as "merely" a ceremonial function, skillful presidents know how to use its powerful theatrical potential to enhance their political clout in the continual interbranch wrangling over defining U.S. foreign policy. Because he is a living symbol of the nation—just as the American flag or the national anthem symbolizes the shared legacy and ideals of the nation—the president is treated with extraordinary deference. His legal authority may indeed be comparable to that of Congress, but through his stature as national icon he is elevated to an entirely different plane than any member of Congress could ever enjoy. Both symbolically and emotionally, the public regards the president as the nation's leader, and not merely as the head of one branch of the national government. Because of his exalted symbolic stature, he is the one political leader whom everybody knows. He flies on his own airplane, he is chauffered in his own limousine, he resides in his own mansion, and he even has his own song, "Hail to the Chief."

Presidents who take the ceremonial role of chief of state lightly do so at their own peril. Jimmy Carter, for example, took office determined to get rid of the trappings of the "imperial presidency" of Richard Nixon, and so he made it a point to ride in ordinary sedans, wear cardigan sweaters while giving televised speeches from the Oval Office, and carry his own luggage when traveling. While initially refreshing, Carter's "plain folks" behavior eventually proved unsettling to the American people, who want leaders who are in many ways *not* like them but rather convey a certain theatrical sense of majesty. Carter's successor, Ronald Reagan, understood this desire perfectly well. He had, after all, been an actor, and he thoroughly enjoyed his new duties as ceremonial representative of the American nation embodied in the role of chief of state. Reagan's skill at playing the part of chief of state was an advantage when he turned to the more prosaic political tasks of dealing with Congress over the conduct of U.S. foreign policy.

### Commander in Chief

Article II, Section 2, makes the president the commander in chief of the nation's armed forces. While the constitutional language conferring this power to the president is clear enough, its deeper meaning is not. Two centuries of practice and precedent have established a presidential role that goes far beyond the merely ceremonial concept of civilian command. Successive presidents have sought to expand the concept to give the White House a policy-making authority to determine when, where, and for what purpose U.S. armed forces are committed abroad. While the Constitution clearly reserves to Congress the formal authority to declare war, modern presidents have asserted a decidedly expansive interpretation of their prerogatives to embark on armed hostilities without a formal declaration of war. Indeed, about 125 presidentially ordered conflicts in U.S. history were not accompanied by a declaration of war. Truman's commitment of large-scale forces to resist communist aggression in Korea in 1950, Johnson's invasion of the Dominican Republic in 1965, Reagan's invasion of Grenada in 1983, and Bush's invasion of Panama in 1989 are all examples of presidents relying on their capacious definition of their powers as commander in chief to commit the nation's armed forces to combat operations abroad.

Given the recent presidents' expanding interpretation of their independent authority to act in their capacity of commander in chief, Congress sought to reinstate the Constitution's intent and curb the president's independent ability to commit the nation to war. In 1973 Congress passed the War Powers Resolution over presidential veto. This legislation attempts to strike a balance between the need for presidents to respond to emergencies, on the one hand, and the constitutional design of joint executive-legislative codetermination of this most fateful foreign policy power, on the other. As we will see in Chapter 5, this act has been only partially successful in dissuading strong-minded presidents from adopting a highly permissive interpretation of their authority as commander in chief.

### Treaty Negotiator

The authority to commit the nation to legally binding international commitments is a major source of the president's power. It is significant, therefore, that the Constitution (Article II, Section 2) carefully divides this power between the president and the Senate in the well-known formulation that the president "shall have Power, by and with the Advice and Consent of the Senate, to make Treaties, provided two-thirds of the Senators present concur." While the president and his agents may thus have the initiative in negotiating treaties, they must be mindful of the ultimate need to win approval of two-thirds of the Senate.

President Woodrow Wilson's inability to win Senate approval of the Versailles Treaty and, with it, American participation in the League of Nations left a bitter aftertaste among successive presidents regarding the entire treaty-making process. Hence, the twentieth century has seen the growing presidential practice of relying on *executive agreements* to codify international agreements. Unlike treaties, executive agreements do not require congressional approval. The problem with executive agreements is that they are nowhere mentioned or legitimized in the Constitution. Their use evolved gradually, but until recently they represented a relatively non-controversial means of handling routine aspects of international dealings. Recent presidents, however, have increasingly used executive agreements to make major international commitments on behalf of the nation. This constitutes a sharp departure from the constitutional design that presidents should not be able unilaterally to determine the United States' foreign policy.

Today, executive agreements outnumber treaties by a ratio of nearly 20 to 1. Understandably, presidents want to have as free a hand as possible in what they have come to regard as "their" domain of foreign affairs. The danger is that both modern presidents and the American people appear to have forgotten the Constitution's clear intent and to have persuaded themselves instead that it is somehow a presidential right to determine the nation's international course.

### Nominator of Key Personnel

Article II, Section 2, of the Constitution authorizes the president to name senior executive officials and ambassadors "by and with the Advice and Consent of the Senate." Thus, his control over key foreign policy personnel is limited by the necessity to win Senate approval for his selections. Ordinarily, the Senate gives the president broad latitude in selecting his foreign policy team. Sometimes it swallows hard and confirms diplomatic appointees of dubious suitability. In recent decades about one-third of U.S. ambassadors have been political appointees (that is, they are not career diplomats). Of these, some are individuals with distinguished records of achievement in academic life (as was the late Edwin O. Reischauer, the United States' foremost Japan scholar who was named ambassador to Tokyo by President Kennedy) or political life (as was Robert Strauss, former Democratic party leader named by President Bush to head up the Moscow embassy). But others are wealthy campaign contributors who possess no apparent credentials for the challenging world of diplomacy. President Reagan's nominee for ambassador to Botswana, St. Louis businessman Theodore Maino, told the Senate Foreign Relations Committee that he was qualified for the job because he had a "commitment to public service, having a lifetime association with the Boy Scouts of America." The senators gulped hard but voted to confirm Maino anyway.

Occasionally, however, the confirmation requirement becomes the occasion for intense executive-legislative conflict. In 1981, for example, the Senate rejected President Reagan's first choice to be assistant secretary of state for human rights, Ernest W. Lefever. In part, the vote against Lefever reflected serious doubts about the nominee's suitability, but more fundamentally it registered the Senate's concern that the Reagan administration seemed insufficiently committed to the human rights agenda. More recently, President Bush's 1989 nomination of former Senator John Tower as secretary of defense triggered a pitched battle between the president and the Senate. Tower's rejection meant that Bush would have to name a secretary who enjoyed the confidence of members of Congress. The easy confirmation of Dick Cheney, an affable, well-liked congressman from Wyoming, showed once again that presidents are generally granted broad latitude in selecting key executive officials, as long as those officials have earned the respect of Congress.

### Recognizer of Foreign Governments

Derived from the constitutional grant, in Article II, Section 3, that "he shall receive Ambassadors and other Public Ministers," this power has been interpreted as enabling presidents to commence or terminate diplomatic relations with other nations by refusing either to receive their ambassador or appoint an American ambassador to their capital. Today it is difficult to recall the bitterly poisoned relations that existed between the United States and the communist regime that came to power in China in 1949. Chinese leaders denounced American "imperialism" and proclaimed their intention to encircle and defeat the United States by sponsoring anti-American revolutions throughout the Third World. The United

States, embittered by China's entry into the Korean War and racked by hysterical anticommunism at home, refused to recognize the Beijing regime for a quarter of a century, insisting instead that the defeated Chinese Nationalists on the island of Taiwan "represented" China. By the mid-1960s sentiment was growing in Congress and elsewhere for the U.S. government to acknowledge the reality that the Chinese communists did indeed govern China and should therefore be dealt with on a government-to-government level. The decision to alter U.S. policy, however, belonged entirely to the president. Not until Richard Nixon's historic trip to China in 1972 did the United States reverse its policy of isolating China diplomatically and begin the process of normalizing relations between the two nations. Similarly, the centrifugal forces of religion and ethnicity are today tearing apart many of the former communist nations of Europe and a number of multi-ethnic African countries. The decision to recognize new claimants to the mantle of statehood is an important question in U.S. foreign policy. Again, it is the president who alone determines if and when the United States will extend to them the legitimacy conferred by diplomatic recognition.

These six roles and powers comprise the formal powers available to any president in the shaping of U.S. foreign policy. Yet, as noted earlier, this is hardly an overwhelming cluster of constitutionally sanctioned authority. As we will see in Chapter 4, the Congress can point to an equally impressive array of constitutional powers in foreign policy-making. Indeed, American history displays about as many eras marked by congressional dominance in directing foreign policy as it does periods of presidential dominance. Given all these considerations, how are we to account for the fact that modern presidents are ordinarily able to dominate the foreign policy-making process? The answer lies in an assortment of informal sources of presidential influence. Theoretically available to any White House incumbent, they have been mastered by only a handful. Those who do master them, however, can transform the relatively modest formal authority of the presidency into a capacity to lead the nation in its dealings with the outside world.

## Informal Powers of the Presidency

### Presidential Singularity

The president's greatest advantage over the Congress is the fact that he is a single, universally known leader, while the Congress is inherently a rather faceless corporate body comprised of 535 members. Members of

Congress do not make it to Mount Rushmore; only presidents do. It is this presidential singularity, coupled with his designation as the nation's symbolic chief of state, that has so enhanced the modern presidency beyond its rather sparse constitutional foundations. In moments of crisis, the nation instinctively looks to the president for strength and reassurance about the future. His informal designation as the nation's "leader"—in ways that transcend his rather austere constitutional position—gives the president a built-in advantage over Congress in the ongoing institutional competition over who will define the nation's foreign stance. There are three other informal sources of presidential power—his role in molding public opinion, his dealings with foreign leaders, and his proclamation of presidential doctrines—in the foreign policy-making process, but note that all three flow from the basic fact that the presidency ultimately comes down to a single figure.

### Shaping Public Opinion

In his capacity to shape public opinion, again, the president enjoys the inherent advantage of being the people's focal point for leadership in a way that the "faceless" Congress is not. A president's ability to mobilize the public around White House policies is defined by his approval ratings and skill in using the media. With regard to the president's popularity at the moment, the public is always a fickle mistress. (Harry Truman underwent the widest swing in the opinion polls, receiving a record-high 87 percent approval rating at the beginning of his term and seeing that figure descend to a low of 23 percent.) Nonetheless, public support is a resource much prized by political leaders. Certainly, presidents who see their approval ratings drop sharply during their terms (both Johnson and Reagan bottomed out at 35 percent approval, Nixon hit a then-record low of 24 percent, and the hapless Carter plummeted to a dismal 21 percent approval) are less persuasive in rallying an already disapproving public around presidential objectives than are presidents who find themselves riding the crest of public affection. Truman, Kennedy, Johnson, and Bush all recorded approval ratings in excess of 80 percent; in each instance, however, the public's backing accompanied a grave international crisis and proved to be ephemeral.

Enhancing or inhibiting a president's ability to rally public support for his foreign policy objectives is his skill in using the media to reach the nation, define the policy agenda, and arouse the public to back him. The modern master at communicating directly to the people through the electronic media was Franklin D. Roosevelt, whose pretelevision "fireside chats" via radio created an unusually close bond between the public and its president and have been recreated by Bill Clinton with parallel intent. Similarly, John F. Kennedy and Ronald Reagan employed their natural eloquence and charm to great advantage in appealing directly to the people for support of their foreign policy objectives. Though much less graced by personal warmth, Richard Nixon often used prime-time televised addresses to go over the heads of Congress and the nation's opinion leaders in an effort to shore up public support for his foreign policies. Skillful presidents, then, are able to use their personal popularity and unrivaled access to the national media to generate popular support for their foreign policy preferences.

### International Diplomacy

Most modern presidents have developed a keen personal interest in the glamourous arena of international diplomacy and have devoted a great deal of their time and the prestige of their office to meetings with foreign leaders. During the domestic "budget summit" in 1990, President Bush made an unusually candid admission of his own preference for foreign policy over domestic policy: "When you get a problem with the complexities that the Middle East has now . . . I enjoy trying to put the coalition together and . . . seeing that this aggression doesn't succeed. I can't say I just rejoice every time I go up and talk to [Congressman] Danny Rostenkowski . . . about what he's going to do on taxes." Presidents can claim credit for dramatic foreign policy successes, whereas domestic problems seldom lead to clear-cut victories and, when they do, presidents can less plausibly claim credit for themselves.

Televised images of U.S. presidents traveling abroad enhance the notion that it is "natural" for presidents to determine the nation's external posture, while comparable efforts by members of Congress are dismissed as mere "meddling." Certainly, all recent presidents have devoted a large proportion of their time and energies to foreign affairs and are commonly associated with their international adventures: Truman at Yalta, Eisenhower escorting Nikita Khrushchev on his historic visit to the United States, Kennedy meeting Khrushchev in Vienna and later electrifying the people of Berlin, Johnson visiting American soldiers in Vietnam, Nixon on his historic 1972 visits to Beijing and Moscow, Ford's arms control mission to Vladivostok, Carter's Middle East peacemaking at Camp David, Reagan's Berlin exhortation, "Mr. Gorbachev, tear down this wall!," George Bush's visit to American troops in Saudi Arabia during Operation Desert Shield/Desert Storm, and Bill Clinton's meeting with Mexican President

Carlos Salinas even before Clinton's inauguration as president. These settings allow presidents to feel most in control of the national interest and to bask in international acclaim for policy triumphs associated with them.

### Presidential Doctrines

The fourth informal source of presidential power is the president's ability to put his distinctive stamp on policy by unilaterally proclaiming doctrines bearing his name. Though not, strictly speaking, binding on the nation, presidential doctrines carry great weight, both at home and abroad. Domestically, they constitute the framework within which policy debate occurs and are typically accepted — with varying degrees of enthusiasm — by the public and policy elites because to repudiate them would be to present an image of national disarray to the rest of the world. Abroad, presidential doctrines are carefully noted in official circles and treated as authoritative pronouncements of U.S. policy.

Hearkening back to the historic Monroe Doctrine, the names of five recent presidents have been attached to foreign policy doctrines. The Truman Doctrine, unveiled in a speech to Congress in 1947, set the tone of ideological anticommunism in postwar U.S. foreign policy. The Eisenhower and Carter doctrines asserted the United States' vital interests in the Middle East. The Nixon Doctrine, introduced in a rambling chat with reporters on Guam Island during a refueling stop in 1969, announced the United States' unwillingness to become mired in protracted Third World wars, as it had done in Vietnam. Finally, the Reagan Doctrine, a term coined by a journalist in 1986, captured Reagan's determination to go beyond the containment of communism and instead seek its undoing in Third World outposts such as Nicaragua and Afghanistan. In each instance, the president seized the policy-making initiative and defined the essential direction of the nation's foreign policy through his capacity to command wide attention, speak with a single voice, and conduct himself as the broadly defined national leader that so many now expect our presidents to be. Next we examine how recent presidents have approached the formidable task of directing the foreign policy bureaucracy and making decisions about the actual content of U.S. foreign policy.

## Styles of Presidential Decision-Making

Bill Clinton is the forty-first American president (though his presidency is the forty-second, a function of Grover Cleveland's two terms — the twenty-second and twenty-fourth presidencies — being interspersed with that of Benjamin Harrison). Like all his predecessors, Clinton wears the hat of chief executive, and in this role, he sits at the pinnacle of the executive branch. His formal authority over executive agencies is assured him by the same constitutional language that made George Washington the first chief executive.

Even though the Constitution has changed little during the past two centuries, the realities of the federal establishment have been altered beyond recognition since the early days of the Republic. The executive branch has grown so vast and complex that it inherently resists central direction. The sheer scale of the president's job of running the executive branch is nearly overwhelming, whether measured by employees (over 4 million civilians and members of the armed forces) or budget (in excess of $1 trillion annually) or administrative structure (14 cabinet departments and 60 noncabinet executive agencies). Sixty years ago President Hoover could direct his executive domain with a White House staff of 3 secretaries, 2 military aides, and 20 clerks; Bush's White House staff of 500 seemed as swollen as the executive apparatus it sought to direct; President Clinton promised to reduce staff by 25 percent, still leaving a sizable number.

Given the elephantine dimensions of the federal bureaucracy, it is difficult for any president to get a handle on it. The kind of specialized information, policy expertise, and analytical skills necessary for policy formulation are broadly dispersed throughout the executive branch. So the president needs to attain command over his branch so that that talent and information will be mobilized around presidential purposes. Thus, each president needs to select and institute a management system that will get the executive establishment to serve *his* ends of presidential decision-making rather than degenerating into an array of competing and unelected fiefdoms.

There is, of course, no one best way for a president to manage the bureaucracy. Rather, each president must set in place a decision-making management system that best fits his own experience and personality. So we begin here by focusing on the personality characteristics and idiosyncrasies of recent presidents. They do make a difference.

To start us thinking about the considerable variance among presidents in terms of traits like intellectual capacity, how they relate to other people, their sense of themselves, and the like, here are eight quotations from post–World War II presidents. See if you can match the presidents— Truman, Nixon, Ford, Reagan, and Bush—with the quotations (answers are on page 70), and as you do so, try to specify the personality traits that you think are most important in shaping the way presidents approach the task of foreign policy decision-making.

1. "I'm afraid that I let myself be influenced by other's recollections, not my own. . . . The only honest answer is to state that try as I might, I

cannot recall anything whatsoever about whether I approved an Israeli sale in advance or whether I approved replenishment of Israeli stocks around August of 1985. My answer therefore and the simple truth is, 'I don't remember, period.'"

2. "I don't pretend to be a philosopher. I'm just a politician from Missouri and proud of it."

3. "There is no Soviet domination of Eastern Europe and there never will be any under (my) administration."

4. "I guess it just proves that in America anyone can be president."

5. "Now, like, I'm president. It would be pretty hard for some drug guy to come into the White House and start offering it up, you know? . . . I bet if they did, I hope I would say, 'Hey, get lost. We don't want any of that.'"

6. "When the president does it, that means it is not illegal."

7. "Once a decision was made, I did not worry about it afterward."

8. "I have often thought that if there had been a good rap group around in those days I might have chosen a career in music instead of politics."

## Typology of the Presidential Personality

In order to help us move beyond the merely quirky aspects of presidential personality and begin to get an analytical grasp of how personality affects foreign policy decision-making, we need to establish a conceptual framework that reveals what the important factors are and how those factors can help or hinder presidents as they seek to manage the immense resources available in the federal agencies. Probably the best work done on this subject is that of Professor Alexander George of Stanford University. In his writings, George alerts us to the importance of three key personality variables that affect the ways presidents approach the tasks of management and decision-making. In the exercise above, perhaps you came up with a different set of personality traits that you regard as prime movers in presidential decision-making. If so, see if you agree with George or if you feel that his framework omits some important factors. In any case, we use George's typology here as a way of stimulating thought on this important topic.

The first variable is what Professor George calls a president's cognitive style. It refers to how a president processes information, how he defines his information needs, and how he gets the information he wants. Some presidents are information minimalists. A good example is Ronald Reagan, who seldom read serious material, displayed minimal intellectual curiosity about the details of the policy issues he was deciding, and had a limited attention span that required his aides to keep their briefings truly brief lest he nod off in midpresentation. Other presidents like to receive as much information as possible on policy issues. Kennedy, for example, immersed himself in the intricacies of policy questions, as Nixon did and Clinton does. All three were voracious readers with remarkable memories. Similarly, Jimmy Carter tried to master the most minute detail, even going so far as supervising the scheduling of the White House tennis court.

The concept of cognitive style also alerts us to the ways presidents prefer to get their information. Some (e.g., Nixon) are more comfortable with the written word, while others (e.g., Bush) prefer the interactions of oral briefings and discussions with senior aides and subject-matter specialists.

The second key personality variable is a president's personal sense of efficacy and competence. This trait simply refers to what the president himself feels he is good at and what he regards himself as less competent in doing. Ronald Reagan, for example, knew his limits as a thinker and a hands-on manager, but as we have said, he thoroughly enjoyed the ceremonial role of chief of state. He was unusually effective in the symbolic uses of the presidency to reach out and communicate to the nation. Jimmy Carter, by contrast, was not an uplifting orator but was much more at home immersed in the details of policy issues. Both Bill Clinton and George Bush are renowned for their interpersonal skills, which have enabled them to work amicably with political supporters and opponents alike. Richard Nixon, perhaps our most complex and troubled president, was most comfortable grappling with complex foreign policy issues that required the mastery of a great deal of information and strong analytical abilities. However, he was chronically uncomfortable around other people, especially in unstructured settings. He was awkward and ill at ease, and had almost no knack for making small talk. Standing atop China's Great Wall in 1972, during his historic trip that restored the United States' relations with that gigantic nation, Nixon could only remark, "This sure is a great wall." So presidents, like the rest of us, are well suited by their particular skills and temperament to do some aspects of their job and feel much less at home performing other parts of their complex job.

The third key personality variable is the individual president's orientation toward political conflict. The conflict of competing ideas and interests is, of course, the essence of political life, but political leaders vary enormously in how they react to conflict. Some, like Franklin Roosevelt, thrive on it. Roosevelt never saw politics as dirty or unsavory, but instead viewed it as the untidy reality of democratic life. Other presidents dislike disagreements, debate, and conflict, and so try to avoid them. Nixon, despite his aggressive and contentious political oratory, was uncomfortable when personally facing conflict. He did not enjoy hearing his advisers debate one another nor did he like being in situations where he could be contradicted. Therefore, as president, Nixon would often withdraw into private solitude where he could mull over his own ideas without the tensions of interpersonal disagreement. Nixon relied on a handful of powerful White House assistants to filter out face-to-face dealings wherever possible.

These three personality traits—cognitive style, sense of personal efficacy, and orientation toward political conflict—influence presidents as they attempt to create a decision-making management structure that will best suit them and help them master the vast federal bureaucracy and assure presidential dominance of the foreign policy-making process. As Richard Johnson (in his book, *Managing the White House*) has shown, each president's personality then leads him, whether self-consciously or intuitively, to select one of three alternative management and decision-making styles. Here we will briefly describe the three models and then illustrate each with case studies of recent presidencies.

The first is the *competitive model*. This management style places great stress on the free and open expression of diverse advice and analysis within the executive branch. Individuals, departments, and agencies openly compete with one another to influence presidential policy-making. The competition of personalities and agencies is inherent in any bureaucracy, but this decision-making style both tolerates and encourages it. Presidents who employ this style want to ensure that as many options as possible reach them and as few decisions as possible are resolved through bureaucratic bargaining at lower levels. In practice, this model is anything but tidy. Multiple channels of communication to and from the president are tolerated, and a good deal of overlap in agency jurisdiction occurs.

The second style is the *formalistic model*. Presidents who opt for this approach emphasize an orderly decision-making system, one with structured procedures and formal, hierarchical lines of reporting. Presidents who choose this style prefer the orderly adherence to well-defined procedures and formal organizational structure to the open conflict and bureaucratic bargaining inherent in the competitive model.

The third style, the *collegial model*, seeks to retain the advantages of the other two models while avoiding their drawbacks. Presidents using this model try to bring together a team of key aides, advisers, and cabinet officers who will truly function as the president's team. Ideally, this model encourages a diversity of outlook, competition among policy alternatives, and group problem-solving within the presidential team. Department and agency heads are expected to regard themselves more as members of the president's team than as spokespersons for their organization's perspective, but by stressing the collegial character of decision-making, the extreme bureaucratic infighting associated with the competitive model is avoided.

Now that we have identified the three key personality variables associated with presidents and the three alternative presidential management styles, we will present a brief survey of the foreign policy decision-making styles of recent presidents. We begin with Franklin D. Roosevelt, who presided over the United States' gravest crisis in World War II and move chronologically to the Clinton administration. This sample of 11 presidents will give us some insight into which management styles have led to good foreign policy-making and which have spawned policy failures.

### Franklin D. Roosevelt

Franklin D. Roosevelt (1933–April 1945) offers the only successful example of the competitive model of presidential decision-making management. Roosevelt's choice of this style was rooted squarely in his personality. Supremely self-confident and entirely at home as president, Roosevelt delighted in the game of politics and viewed it as a means of achieving beneficial policies for the nation. In terms of cognitive style, he had an insatiable appetite for detail and preferred to learn in face-to-face encounters. His sense of efficacy and competence was exceptionally strong, for he believed himself to be uniquely qualified to lead the nation through the twin crises of the Great Depression and World War II. Finally, as noted, Roosevelt was comfortable in the presence of political conflict, which he viewed as a necessary, inevitable side-effect of democratic life.

Given his personality, the competitive model made sense for Roosevelt. As president, he deliberately stirred up competition and conflict among the various executive agencies and cabinet officers. This was his way of ensuring that the important issues wound up in his own hands. Roosevelt would often bypass cabinet heads and deal directly with lower level officials in order to get the information he needed. Sometimes he would assign several departments the same task of developing alternative policy options, thus assuring that the bureaucracy would not settle issues itself and present the president only bland proposals representing the lowest common denominator of bureaucratic bargaining.

The unorthodoxy of Roosevelt's style looked chaotic to outsiders and to management specialists, but it generally worked for him because of his unique combination of personality traits, not the least of which was his extraordinary self-confidence. A clear danger of the competitive management style is that the president can become overloaded with information and by the need to make decisions that would ordinarily be resolved at lower levels. Roosevelt usually avoided this pitfall by using the competitive approach selectively; in a number of issue areas, he insisted that the pertinent agencies and his subordinates resolve policy disputes among themselves.

### Harry Truman

Harry Truman (April 1945–January 1953) was in many ways an improbable man to become the nation's chief executive. A plain man of modest background, little about him suggested a capacity for exceptional leadership, but historians today give him high marks for his courage and steadfastness in making exceedingly difficult decisions. It fell to Truman, for example, to decide whether or not to use the secret new atomic bomb against Japan to end World War II. The historic U.S. response to the Soviet challenge in the aftermath of the war was also the result of Truman's unblinking resoluteness. It was Truman, too, who negotiated the Marshall Plan, who presided over the formation of NATO, and who committed U.S. forces to counter communist aggression in Korea.

Determined to carry on Roosevelt's legacy of internationalism, Truman was equally resolved to rein in the turbulent bureaucratic politics that Roosevelt so thoroughly relished. Truman did this by instituting a formalistic management and decision-making system. Under Truman, the authority of department heads within their respective policy domains was strengthened and a more traditional, hierarchical chain of reporting and command was instituted. The president would no longer dilute the authority of cabinet officers by dealing directly with their subordinates, nor could those subordinates kick over the traces of formal authority and gain easy access to the president.

Though personally modest and unassuming, Truman had an acute sense of the dignity of the office he inhabited and was adamant that presidential authority be respected within his administration. Accordingly, his approach was to delegate heavily to his agency heads on routine issues while insisting that the president alone must make the major decisions. Truman did not particularly welcome the National Security Council system established in 1947, viewing it as a potential intrusion on presidential prerogatives. He therefore kept the NSC machinery at arm's length, and for advice, he relied heavily on his secretary of state, Dean Acheson. In the end, however, it was Truman himself who charted the United States' course during the turbulent, formative years of the Cold War.

## Dwight D. Eisenhower

Dwight D. Eisenhower (January 1953–January 1961) brought to the presidency the long-standing assumptions and practices he had acquired during his distinguished military career. Accustomed to clearly delineated lines of authority and solid staff work, it is not surprising that Eisenhower, like Truman, opted for the formalistic management model. His well-known insistence that aides distill issues requiring presidential decision into one-page memos has led to some misunderstanding of Eisenhower's cognitive style. He was, in fact, uncommonly well informed on international affairs but preferred to receive much of his information through staff briefings. In terms of sense of efficacy, Eisenhower's command of allied forces in Europe during World War II left him self-confident about his abilities to deal with complex organizations and strong-willed figures. He was less at home in the rough-and-tumble world of political conflict than presidents who have risen through the political ranks, however, and so the formalistic model was well suited to his personality, experience, and leadership style.

Eisenhower's policy-making style differed from Truman's principally in Eisenhower's greater reliance on centralized staffing to channel the flow of information, options analyses, and the like. Where Truman had made minimal use of the NSC machinery, Eisenhower more eagerly embraced it as a way of routinizing policy analysis and debating policy options. It was Eisenhower who first created the position of assistant to the president for national security affairs. The first person to hold the job was Robert Cutler, a Boston investment banker, who both coordinated the activities of the NSC and, when asked, advised Eisenhower on foreign policy issues.

Although many historians have depicted John Foster Dulles, Eisenhower's secretary of state, as an exceptionally influential figure in the shaping of Eisenhower's foreign policy, more recent interpretations find Dulles's role to have been much exaggerated. As the newer "revisionist" accounts argue, it was Eisenhower who orchestrated his administration's policy stance, albeit often through indirect, hidden-hand methods.

## John F. Kennedy

John F. Kennedy (January 1961–November 1963) brought to the White House a youthful vitality, a commitment to foreign policy activism, and a determination to be more personally involved in the details of policy-making than he (perhaps erroneously) believed Eisenhower to have been. This determination was intensified early in his administration by the humiliating failure of the U.S.-sponsored effort to topple Cuba's Fidel

Castro in the Bay of Pigs fiasco. In his own postmortem of the disaster, Kennedy concluded that the operation's poor planning and execution were due in large part to faulty assumptions embedded in the executive agencies, especially the CIA, which had gone largely unchallenged. Henceforth, Kennedy concluded, foreign policy would be closely directed from the White House. That, in turn, required a team of policy-makers who were more loyal to the president than to their agencies' parochial outlooks. The result was a collegial style of policy-making, which placed Kennedy at the hub of a team that included Secretary of State Dean Rusk, Secretary of Defense Robert McNamara, and National Security Adviser McGeorge Bundy.

The collegial style, with its freewheeling give and take among a close-knit team in which the president is first among equals, was a good match for Kennedy's personality. As noted, he had an unquenchable appetite for information. In terms of sense of efficacy and competence, he had displayed a serene self-confidence throughout his fabled life. Finally, he was a thoroughly political creature who delighted in spirited political discourse. His personality, then, combined with his determination to be intimately involved in the details of foreign policy-making, made the collegial model a good choice for him.

Kennedy's crowning achievement in foreign affairs was his skillful and successful direction of the Cuban missile crisis of October 1962. A number of writings have chronicled the close teamwork and thoughtful debating of policy options among Kennedy's foreign policy circle. When Soviet leader Khrushchev backed down and agreed to withdraw Soviet missiles from Cuba, it marked a signal victory for U.S. policy. Nuclear war had been averted, and Kennedy's collegial decision-making management style had been vindicated.

### Lyndon B. Johnson

Kennedy's assassination in November 1963 elevated Lyndon B. Johnson to the presidency, which he occupied until January 1969. Johnson idolized Franklin D. Roosevelt ("He was like a daddy to me," he would often note) and sought to emulate both his philosophy of governmental activism and his competitive management style. Like FDR, Johnson did possess a legendary ability to persuade and manipulate other leaders in one-on-one dealings, a skill that he had employed masterfully as Senate majority leader during the Eisenhower years.

But Johnson differed from Roosevelt in two crucial ways that would ultimately doom his presidency. First, where Roosevelt had been supremely self-assured, Johnson was a deeply insecure man. He often

masked his insecurity with an outward show of forcefulness and dominance, but he was remarkably thin-skinned, easily wounded by real or
imagined slights, and constantly seeking to win the approval of others
through his immense political gifts. One biographer traces Johnson's
relentless drive to achieve greatness to his chronic need to shore up a
congenitally fragile self-esteem. Second, where Roosevelt was a committed
internationalist, Johnson remained unusually parochial for a national
leader. His deep ignorance of international issues, coupled with his
unrequited craving for the approval of Kennedy's elegant loyalists, left him
exceptionally dependent on the foreign policy team he had inherited from
the slain Kennedy.

For a time, Johnson's presidency worked wonderfully well. His
promise of a golden age for the United States, captured in the soaring
rhetoric of a "great society," led to a landslide victory over conservative
Republican challenger Barry Goldwater in 1964. After 1965, however,
Johnson became ever more deeply mired in the nightmare of Vietnam.
Warmly expansive when his relentless activism won him public praise,
Johnson reacted with petty defensiveness as his war policies came under
increasing attack in Congress, on college campuses, in the media, and
among the general public.

By the late 1960s Johnson was a besieged president. Reviled by antiwar
protesters ("Hey, hey, LBJ, how many kids did you kill today?" went one
of their more printable chants), abandoned by his fellow liberal Democrats, scorned by the media, backed by a shrinking constituency, and
criticized even within his own executive branch by figures such as
George Ball, Roger Hilsman, and Townsend Hoopes, Johnson endured a
firestorm of criticism over his failed militarization of the conflict in
Vietnam. Denied the public approval he craved, Johnson increasingly
retreated into a closed circle of trusted loyalists. As he did so, he
abandoned the competitive model of decision-making in favor of a variant
of the collegial model in which he was shielded from face-to-face dealings
with his critics.

As early as 1966 Johnson was relying on a foreign policy coordinating
mechanism known as the "Tuesday lunch," in which he met regularly with
Secretary of State Rusk, Secretary of Defense McNamara (and, in 1968,
his successor, Clark Clifford), Richard Helms of the CIA, and National
Security Adviser Walt Rostow. By confining discussion of Vietnam policy
to this tight band of loyalists, Johnson was somewhat able to seal himself
off from conflicting views and from the painful reality that his policies
were not working. By 1968 Johnson was so thoroughly unpopular that he
could safely make public appearances only at military bases. After an
embarrassing near-defeat in the New Hampshire primary, Johnson took

himself out of the race for reelection and withdrew to his Texas ranch, a tragic figure brought down by a disastrous foreign policy in a peripheral land.

### Richard M. Nixon

Johnson's political disgrace, as well as a broad public revulsion against the excesses of the 1960s, made possible the improbable political comeback of Richard M. Nixon, who had narrowly lost to John F. Kennedy in 1960 and was written off as a national figure after his humiliating defeat in the 1962 California gubernatorial race. Nixon, who would occupy the Oval Office from January 1969 until his resignation under the cloud of Watergate in August 1974, brought to the presidency an extraordinarily complex personality. Throughout his political career, he seemed to remain an oddly private person in the most public of professions. Driven by deep-seated insecurities and inordinately sensitive to criticism, Nixon appeared to form few lasting friendships. Given his difficulties in inter-personal relationships, both the competitive and collegial models were ruled out.

At the same time, Nixon came to office determined to dominate the foreign policy-making process. Caring little about domestic issues, Nixon had a passionate interest in foreign affairs and regarded himself as an expert on the subject. However, he also harbored a deep distrust of the very foreign policy bureaucracy he now headed. His deepest contempt was reserved for the State Department, which he viewed as a hotbed of liberal Democrats likely to be hostile both to him personally and to his policies.

The upshot of this peculiar mix of personal vulnerability and political will was a decision-making management system unlike anything seen before or since. Creating his own variant of the formalistic system, Nixon sought to centralize White House control over foreign policy by vastly expanding the role and stature of the National Security Council staff, whose loyalty to the president was more certain. Pivotal to the new system was the head of the NSC staff, the national security adviser. For this position Nixon selected Harvard political scientist Henry Kissinger, even though the two had not met prior to Nixon's election. The trend toward a strengthened role for the national security adviser had begun under Kennedy, who had similarly turned to Harvard, selecting McGeorge Bundy for the job. But whereas Bundy had a staff of 12, Kissinger would create a formidable White House operation with a staff of 100.

Despite their differences in background (Nixon was raised a Quaker and had spent his adult life in the tumultuous world of national politics, whereas Kissinger was a Jewish refugee from Hitler's Germany and had spent his adult life in the elite environs of Harvard), the two men shared a number of key traits and assumptions. Kissinger reinforced Nixon's disdain for the bureaucracy, which both regarded as typically stodgy, mediocre, incapable of creativity, and unable to rise above narrow agency perspectives. Like Nixon, Kissinger was a believer in unsentimental *realpolitik* grounded in an impersonal calculus of national interest and the balance of power. Finally, the two men shared a penchant for secrecy and dramatic surprise.

Academic treatments of the Nixon years often give Kissinger credit for the administration's shrewd diplomacy and blame Nixon himself for the era's political and diplomatic reversals. A better reading of the available evidence suggests that Nixon deserves at least as much credit as Kissinger for such strategic innovations as the opening to China and the relaxation of tensions with the Soviet Union. Despite Kissinger's stature as a media celebrity, there is no reason to doubt that Richard Nixon was fully in control of his own administration's inventive foreign policy.

It was entirely Nixon's idea to create the most centralized and structured White House foreign policy apparatus ever. The essence of his creation was the well-known system of six interagency committees, each of which was chaired by Kissinger and so was attuned to presidential perspectives. They were (1) the Vietnam Special Studies Group, which dealt with the most pressing policy issue of the day; (2) the Washington Special Actions Group, which was concerned with international crises; (3) the Defense Programs Review Committee, which added a White House layer to the executive branch's development of military and security policy; (4) the Verification Panel, which dominated administration policy-making on strategic arms control; (5) the so-called 40 Committee, which imposed White House control over covert operations abroad; and (6) the Senior Review Group, which treated policy development on all other issues. These six committees were clearly the locus of foreign policy-making within the executive branch, thus ensuring that lower level officials in the various agencies would either strive to have their voices heard within the White House system or would be frozen out of the policy-making action. In addition, the committees could reach down into agencies such as State, DOD, and the CIA, absorbing key personnel and defining the parameters of policy discussion. Keeping the career foreign policy bureaucrats constantly off balance, in the dark, and out of the policy-making loop was most definitely an intentional byproduct of the Nixon-designed operation so skillfully implemented by Henry Kissinger.

To further ensure that the White House would encounter minimal resistance from the entrenched foreign affairs bureaucracy, Nixon named his former law partner, William Rogers, to be secretary of state during his first term. Nixon had cunningly calculated that Rogers's lack of foreign policy expertise or stature would render him a weak advocate of State's institutional perspective, thus enhancing Nixon's strategy of maintaining tight White House dominance of the foreign policy process.

By ensuring that all information, analysis, and policy advocacy went through Kissinger, Nixon thereby assured his own primacy in foreign policy-making. Discussions of whether or not Kissinger was a too-powerful figure miss the point that he was only as powerful as Nixon determined would serve his own presidential interests. It is true that Kissinger understood all too well Nixon's craving for secrecy and seclusion and that Nixon typically made major decisions in lonely isolation using the cogent options analyses prepared by Kissinger. As noted, however, descriptions of Nixon as an unwitting captive of Kissinger's dominating intellect are generally mistaken. In essence, Nixon used Kissinger, not the other way around.

The dangers of Nixon's extreme policy-making centralization are readily apparent. In the first place, however cautious and unimaginative the State Department and other agencies may be, they are the repository of valuable subject-matter expertise and diverse points of view. Little is gained by deliberately ignoring their assessments, and a great deal of expert opinion is wasted in demoralizing schemes to bypass conventional channels. Second, Nixon's utilization of Kissinger for operational missions (as in his secret 1971 trip to China and his role as presidential emissary to the Vietnam peace talks held in Paris) altered the role of national security adviser from that of policy analyst and presidential counselor to that of foreign policy executor. Since the national security adviser is neither confirmed by Congress nor compelled under ordinary circumstances to report to Congress, his involvement in the actual conduct of foreign policy raises serious questions regarding accountability and the constitutional prescription of checks and balances. Finally, there is some merit to the argument that in isolating himself from his own executive establishment, Nixon was dependent not only on the information and analysis provided by Kissinger, but also on Kissinger's forceful advocacy of specific policy options. Nixon's very success in keeping the foreign affairs bureaucracy at arm's length meant that there was seldom a serious counterweight to Kissinger in urging the president to adopt one policy initiative over another.

In light of Nixon's unusual personality as well as his determination to personally dominate U.S. foreign policy-making, his White House-centered decision management system was perhaps the model most appropriate for him. Whatever the ultimate verdict of historians regarding his character and leadership, most observers credit Nixon with achieving remarkable breakthroughs in relations with the then-menacing communist giants, China and the Soviet Union. But the very contempt for established institutions and penchant for secrecy that served him so well in international affairs had also spawned a White House culture of deceit, evasion, and criminality that made Watergate an ever-present possibility. As Nixon became ever more hopelessly ensnared in an illegal coverup of his own making, his political legitimacy was so eroded that, in the end, he had little choice but to resign the presidency he had fought to attain all his life.

### Gerald R. Ford

Nixon's successor, Gerald R. Ford (August 1974–January 1977), can be dealt with briefly because of the brevity of his tenure. Sharing Harry Truman's unpretentious modesty but not his capacity for transcendent greatness, the hapless Ford presided over a demoralized nation and is best remembered for helping restore the nation's faith in the elemental decency of its president. In the wake of Watergate and the definitive failure of U.S. policy in Vietnam in 1975, the American people were broadly suspicious of political leaders and wished to turn away from strenuous exertions in foreign affairs. Faced with such strong public sentiments and acknowledging his own limitations as an international statesman, President Ford essentially retained the Nixon foreign policy team and continued Nixon's policies, but he rejected Nixon's obsessive secrecy and insistence on exclusive White House control of the policy process.

Ford's formalistic management system was closer to the Truman and Eisenhower model than to Nixon's. Matters were made easier by the fact that Henry Kissinger had become secretary of state in 1973 and had, unsurprisingly, "discovered" the merits of the department's professional corps. In his place as national security adviser was Air Force Lieutenant General Brent Scowcroft, himself a Kissinger protégé but nonetheless very much his own man. In Scowcroft's hands, the NSC staff reverted to its traditional role of coordinating the flow of information and analysis of competing policy options, but its operational mission was virtually eliminated. Unlike Kissinger, Scowcroft was a self-effacing man who was more interested in assuring that the president was apprised of pertinent information and aware of diverse points of view than in using his position to press his own preferred policies.

From the mid-1960s to the mid-1970s, the nation was convulsed by the twin disasters of Vietnam and Watergate. Taken together, they left a deeply demoralized public shorn of its earlier innocence and faith in its political leaders. Though ideological and partisan opposites, Johnson and

Nixon shared a dangerous combination of deep personal insecurity and overwhelming political ambition. Their combined political legacy was poisonous to the body politic, corroding the moral legitimacy of government and the bond of trust between leaders and the led which is essential in a democracy. Thus, in the presidential election of 1976 the American public vented its anger against "Washington politicians" by turning to an outsider, a former Georgia governor who emphasized his personal integrity and made his lack of Washington experience seem like a virtue.

### Jimmy Carter

Jimmy Carter (January 1977–January 1981) arrived in Washington as head of the political establishment he had successfully run against. He brought to the task an array of personal traits that were so attractive that they make the disappointments of his term all the more keenly felt. Nearly everyone admired Carter for his strength of character, high intelligence, abiding decency, personal discipline, exceptional work ethic, and extraordinary appetite for detailed mastery of complex issues. To compensate for his lack of experience in foreign affairs, as president he further intensified his long-established workaholism, immersing himself in endless books, documents, and reports on the intricacies of international matters.

Carter's voracious capacity for detail and his insistence on being involved during the early stages of policy development—rather than reviewing options presented to him by the bureaucracy and NSC staff—accounts for a great deal of his foreign policy decision-making style. Moreover, his robust self-confidence and personal comfort in the give and take of policy debate meant that the formalistic model would not suit him particularly well. Aware that perhaps no one besides Franklin Roosevelt could juggle the burdens of the competitive model, Carter settled on the collegial model as his typical approach to foreign policy decision-making.

Carter was critical of the extreme centralization of power in the White House under Nixon. He believed that it had too often left Nixon isolated from diverse points of view. The collegial model, he felt, would avert a similar isolation in his own administration by regularly exposing him to policy debate with the members of his foreign policy team. At the same time, he wanted to make greater use of the formalized capabilities of the NSC staff than Kennedy had done and to restore the authority and stature of cabinet heads. Thus, Carter's version of the collegial model also contained some ingredients of the formalistic model.

Given Jimmy Carter's ambitious cognitive style, his high sense of personal efficacy and competence as a decision-maker, and his comfort amid the tumult of political conflict, the collegial model best suited his personality and policy-making style. Unfortunately, the reverse was not true: Carter was not the best person to attempt the collegial system. In order to understand why this is so, we need to examine more closely the preconditions for successfully utilizing this model.

If decision-making collegiality is to work, at least one of two conditions must be present. First, while remaining receptive to diverse points of view, the president must be a commanding figure who articulates a clear sense of vision from which the collegial deliberation of policy specifics takes its bearings. Without that condition, the second prerequisite for successful collegiality is an essential commonality of outlook among the key players. A shared worldview, then, whether imposed by the president or arising voluntarily among the chief actors, is the essential glue that holds collegial deliberations together and permits the development of policy coherence. In time it would become painfully apparent that neither of these conditions was present in the Carter White House.

Trained as an engineer at the U.S. Naval Academy and later displaying a talent for the pragmatics of business, Carter was most at home dealing with the nuts and bolts of problem-solving. His career in Georgia state politics was characterized by high personal integrity and diligent attention to the details of day-to-day problems. Never much of a conceptualizer, and almost entirely without foreign policy credentials, Carter found it difficult to articulate a coherent foreign policy strategy that went beyond earnest platitudes. Apart from his laudable insistence that concern for human rights must be one of the United States' international objectives, Carter's foreign policy "vision" seldom amounted to more than well-intended bromides. So there would be no top-down grand design to shape the efforts of Carter's collegial decision-making team.

At the same time, the very composition of that team ensured the lack of a spontaneous commonality of worldview among the men charged with clarifying policy for the nation. Besides Carter, the major players were Secretary of State Cyrus Vance, Secretary of Defense Harold Brown, and National Security Adviser Zbigniew Brzezinski. Brown, like Carter, was a talented pragmatist who neither created nor obstructed the kind of overarching sense of purpose and vision necessary for policy coherence. Vance and Brzezinski, on the other hand, held deep convictions about the overall strategic design the United States should be pursuing in the post–Vietnam era. Those convictions, however, were fundamentally incompatible. In essence, Jimmy Carter's foreign policy foundered on his own inability to embrace definitively either the worldview articulated by Cyrus Vance or that of Zbigniew Brzezinski.

Vance had held Pentagon positions during the Johnson administration and became personally haunted by what he came to regard as the senseless militarization and violence of our tragic involvement in Vietnam. By the time he became secretary of state in 1977, he was a committed "dove" advocating a diplomacy of humane globalism. Vance believed that the Cold War standoff with the Soviet Union had lost its vitality and could be virtually ended through conciliatory U.S. efforts. To Vance, it was in the United States' own interest to reduce Cold War tensions, press for further arms control agreements, and place a new emphasis on Third World development and on the enhancement of universal human rights.

Brzezinski, by contrast, proceeded from a worldview that emphasized the necessity of remaining firm against what he regarded as a Soviet Union still committed to expanding its sphere of global influence and propagating totalitarian communism in Third World nations. To a "hawk" like Brzezinski, strategic arms limitations agreements were more in the Soviets' than in our own interests. We could afford the stiff costs of a prolonged arms race, he reasoned, whereas the Soviets could not. Therefore, Brzezinski argued, the United States should take a hard line against Soviet adventurism in such Third World locales as Angola, Ethiopia, and Afghanistan. He advocated a policy known as "linkage," whereby progress on arms control and other aspects of East-West détente would be linked to Soviet restraint abroad, particularly in the Third World.

Given the fundamental incompatibility of his two most important foreign policy advisers, and lacking a clear strategic vision of his own, President Carter practiced the politics of equivocation. Unwilling—and perhaps unable—to choose between the worldview of Vance and the worldview of Brzezinski, he tried to resolve the split in his foreign policy team by embracing elements of both positions. On one memorable occasion in 1978, Carter asked Brzezinski and Vance each to prepare recommendations for a major speech he was scheduled to give on Soviet-American relations. As expected, the two memos contained contrasting and incompatible views. In essence, Carter simply stapled the two papers together and gave a speech filled with embarrassing contradictions and mixed messages about the United States' true stance.

Two events in late 1979—the Iranian hostage crisis and the Soviet invasion of Afghanistan—swung Carter decisively toward Brzezinski's hard-line stance. Vance's resignation in the spring of 1980 meant that, at long last, Carter's collegial foreign policy-making system could proceed from the unity of outlook essential for it to function. But for Carter, foreign policy coherence came too late. Disillusioned by his stewardship both at home and abroad, the people rejected Carter in the 1980 election in favor of his Republican challenger.

## Ronald Reagan

As Ronald Reagan began his two terms (January 1981–January 1989) he was, at age 69, the oldest man ever inaugurated as president. But his advanced age was only one of the characteristics that made him seem an unlikely occupant of the White House. He had spent most of his adult life as an entertainer, beginning in radio and advancing to the movies and to television roles. Foreign observers were perplexed and bemused to find that a man who had once co-starred in a movie with a chimpanzee (in *Bedtime for Bonzo*) was now the leader of the free world. Even more troubling than his advanced age and his unusual background were his casual work habits. During his two terms as governor of California, Reagan had displayed the intellectual and management traits that he would bring to his new role in Washington: (1) a near-absence of intellectual curiosity and a disinclination to grapple with the complexities of policy matters and (2) a casual, nine-to-five management style that required delegating extensive authority to subordinates.

As noted earlier, Reagan's cognitive style was that of a minimalist. He rarely read works of nonfiction, preferring to acquire information through short briefings from his aides on the essentials of policy issues. Reagan's command of the complexities of substantive matters was so uncertain, and his memory so unreliable, that his aides regularly equipped him with prepared remarks on 3 × 5 cards for use in "conversations" with foreign leaders.

In terms of personal sense of efficacy and competence, Reagan cared little about the rigors of hands-on management of the executive establishment, nor was he particularly at home engaging in freewheeling debate over alternative policy proposals. Rather, he enjoyed the symbolic uses of the presidency to communicate with the nation in carefully staged events. Dubbed the "Great Communicator," Reagan was well served by an uncommonly smooth and effective delivery style he had honed during his many years as an actor and as a corporate spokesman for General Electric. Perhaps his greatest leadership strength was his exceptional knack for connecting emotionally with the mass public through televised addresses prepared by his talented team of speechwriters.

His often-powerful speeches were not merely a case of a trained actor effectively delivering his lines. In Reagan's case, two factors made his rhetoric an uncommonly powerful instrument in rallying public support around presidential objectives. The first was his apparent sincerity. Though intellectually uncomplicated, Reagan was genuinely committed to a core set of conservative principles. He believed ardently that by reducing governmental regulation of business and reducing taxes, "the miracle of the market" would produce expanded economic growth and opportunity at home. Internationally, he believed that the United States should aggressively confront totalitarian communism and seek to defeat it, not accommodate it. He believed that the United States had retreated from international leadership in a wave of post–Vietnam self-doubt. To reassert its rightful role, the United States would need to enhance its military capability and, more importantly, to assert its values forcefully and confidently, whether that meant condemning the Soviet Union as an "evil empire" or standing up to leftist Third World autocrats. U.S. reassertiveness, then, was Reagan's irreducible foreign policy principle.

The second trait that made Reagan more than a mere orator was his genuinely warm and serene disposition. If he did not possess the furious energy of Lyndon Johnson or the intellectual prowess of Richard Nixon, neither was he possessed of the inner demons that haunted both men. His sunny outlook and personal warmth made it difficult for anyone actually to dislike Reagan. Even his harshest political critics shared in the pervasive aura of good feelings that surrounded the genial Californian. Reagan's generally high approval ratings in opinion surveys helped strengthen his hand in dealing with the Congress and with foreign leaders.

Given his blend of deeply held core values, lack of personal expertise on international matters, and a disengaged executive style, it is not surprising that Reagan adopted a formalistic decision-making management style. Reagan intended that his administration would derive its foreign policy bearings from his own clearly stated principles. For developing concrete policy stances and overseeing the actual conduct of U.S. diplomacy, Reagan intended to (1) delegate broad authority to cabinet officers and (2) count on his national security adviser and the NSC staff to ensure overall coordination.

This last-named intention continually bedeviled the Reagan presidency. In seeking to restore the authority of cabinet officers, Reagan permitted the pendulum to swing too far away from the Kissinger-Brzezinski model of strong presidential assistants. During his eight years as president, Reagan went through a record six national security advisers. Of the six, the first four were arguably out of their element. The first, Richard Allen, was a rather peripheral figure in foreign policy circles. Reagan had so thoroughly downgraded the NSA's role that Allen did not even have direct access to the Oval Office but reported instead through the White House chief of staff, Edwin Meese.

In 1982 Allen was replaced by William Clark, a former California rancher and state judge who had no foreign policy credentials whatever. Reagan selected him for the sensitive position because the two men were old friends and because Reagan trusted Clark and felt comfortable in his presence. From late 1983 to 1985 the NSA chief was Robert "Bud" McFarlane. A Marine colonel and protégé of Henry Kissinger, McFarlane was a decided improvement over his two predecessors and performed generally well except for presiding over the Iran-Contra fiasco (which is, after all, a rather significant "except for," as in "Except for that, Mrs. Lincoln, how did you enjoy the play?"). In 1985 McFarlane was succeeded by John Poindexter, a Navy admiral of substantial technical skills but almost wholly lacking in foreign policy or political competence.

By 1985 and 1986 the NSC staff occupied the worst of two bureaucratic worlds: on the one hand, its downgraded leadership was a pale imitation of the policy-making role exercised by Kissinger and Brzezinski; on the other hand, Reagan's hands-off managerial style delegated so much autonomy to the NSC staff that the excesses of Oliver North were given free play. The resulting Iran-Contra scandal was a foreign policy disaster for the nation and a severe blow to Ronald Reagan's reputation.

Not until late 1986, with the naming of Frank Carlucci, did Reagan have a national security adviser of adequate knowledge and competence. When Carlucci was shortly thereafter named as secretary of defense, he was replaced at the NSC by the equally intelligent and pragmatic Colin Powell, an Army general. Unfortunately for them and for Reagan, too, they arrived at their posts in the autumn of the Reagan presidency, well beyond the point when the administration's essential identity was formed.

Thus, Reagan's original wish to establish a smoothly functioning formalistic decision-making system, one that would fill in the policy specifics outlined by his broad-brush core convictions, was severely undercut by the constant personnel changes, incompetence, and — in the case of the Iran-Contra scandal — illegal conduct within the NSC staff. And yet it would be a mistake to conclude that the Reagan administration was unable to attain coherence in its foreign policy-making. However one judges the merits of his foreign policy, it was indeed more often than not reasonably coherent. We thus confront the irony that Jimmy Carter, for all his high intelligence and personal attention to substantive detail, seldom obtained foreign policy coherence, while his nemesis, Ronald Reagan, for all his vagueness and disengaged leadership style, frequently did.

How can this seeming paradox be explained? The answer lies largely in other aspects of Reagan's formalistic policy-making system that we have not yet discussed. In order to achieve foreign policy coherence in a formalistic decision-making system, at least one of three conditions must be met. The first is firm, hands-on policy-making management at the top, as was the case with Truman and Nixon. As we have seen, this condition was most assuredly not present in the somnolent Reagan presidency. Second, coherence can be enhanced through strong coordinating leadership from the national security adviser. As we have seen, four out of Reagan's six NSAs were of dubious competence. The third and final possibility is a policy coherence that arises naturally from an essentially common worldview among the key policy-makers. This, precisely, was the strength of the Reagan team.

Though differences occurred, they were seldom of a fundamental nature as were the irreconcilable differences between Secretary of State Vance and National Security Adviser Brzezinski during the Carter years. Under Reagan, the differences among the major policy-makers were matters of style (seen in the short-lived tenure of the abrasive Alexander Haig, Reagan's first secretary of state) or involved secondary matters. The principal members of Reagan's formalistic policy-making team were Secretary of State George Shultz, Secretary of Defense Caspar Weinberger, and CIA Director William Casey. Shultz and Weinberger were old friends; both had held important positions in the Nixon administration and had worked together as senior officers in the Bechtel Corporation. Both shared the essentials of Reagan's conservative outlook, though neither was as ideologically driven as their chief. On most major issues, the two men saw eye to eye, the significant exception being Shultz's advocacy of the use of force to counter terrorism in the Middle East and Weinberger's opposition to it. By presenting Reagan with agreed-upon policy recommendations on specific issues, the Shultz–Weinberger–Casey team made it possible for Ronald Reagan to preside over a reasonably coherent foreign policy. To the extent that his formalistic decision-making system worked, it is due to the shared worldview among his principal agency heads.

### George Bush

Reagan was succeeded by his vice president, George Bush (January 1989–January 1993). Bush's election was greeted with the expectation that he would devote himself heavily to his favorite subject, foreign affairs. Unlike Reagan, Bush had had extensive foreign policy experience prior to becoming president. He had represented the United States in China and at the United Nations and had served as head of the CIA. Where Reagan was heavily ideological but intellectually casual, Bush was more pragmatic and exceptionally well informed on complex international issues. In contrast to Reagan's disengaged policy-making style and extensive delegation to subordinates, the energetic Bush relished a hands-on management style and personal immersion in the details of foreign policy-making.

Given his deep interest in international affairs, his self-confidence in dealing with other people, and his extensive experience in the policy-making process, the collegial model represented a natural decision-making style for Bush. Like Kennedy and Carter, the two prior practitioners of collegial decision-making, Bush was thoroughly engaged, hard-working, energetic, and intelligent. He came to office much more steeped in world issues than was Carter, a one-term Georgia governor. In addition, Bush had held a variety of positions in the foreign policy agencies, unlike Kennedy, whose prior experience had been as a congressman and senator. In terms of personality traits and prior experience, then, Bush seemed the ideal president to make successful use of the collegial decision-making system.

The makeup of the collegial team President Bush assembled was also encouraging. James Baker, the secretary of state, had been a close personal friend of the president for 30 years. He had served in the Reagan administration as White House chief of staff and as secretary of the treasury. His intelligence, political shrewdness, and close relationship with the president ensured that he would be both a strong secretary of state and a team player within the administration. For secretary of defense, Bush turned to Dick Cheney, a former White House chief of staff under Gerald Ford and later congressman from Wyoming. One of Washington's most respected and well-liked figures, Cheney—like Baker—promised to be both a strong head of his agency and an effective player within the White House team. Finally, as national security adviser, Bush turned to Brent Scowcroft, who had previously held the position in the Ford administration. Widely admired for his scholarly grasp of international issues (he holds a Ph.D. in Russian history) and his unpretentious demeanor, Scowcroft looked like an ideal NSA: more competent than most of Reagan's men had been, yet less abrasive and self-serving than Kissinger and Brzezinski had been.

A number of factors made this an unusually cohesive collegial team. All had held positions in the Ford administration, all shared a worldview of pragmatic, moderate conservatism, and all were congenial personalities who gave little evidence of undue egoism or arrogance.

In more stable times, the Bush policy-making team almost certainly would have been a striking success. Their ability to work well with one another was a decided plus, as was their undeniable intellectual command of Cold War international politics. Their problem was that the world they all knew so well was collapsing around them, and, as it did so, the Bush team too often seemed to be a half-step behind the march of history. For 45 years, the Cold War had provided the fixed compass points of world affairs. It defined the givens within which American policy-makers were forced to operate. The bipolar schism between two ideologically incompatible superpowers, each heavily armed and each presiding over its subordinate bloc of allies—this had been the foreign policy playing field that George Bush and his talented colleagues had known so well. But in the very year he took the presidential oath of office, the Cold War edifice collapsed amid the ruins of communism.

It was thus George Bush's fate to reach the presidency with his instinctive caution, pragmatism, and considerable talent for problem-solving at the precise historical moment when revolutionary upheavals were rendering those traits less useful. Certainly, his presidency was an eventful one: 1989 saw the brutal crackdown on student protesters in China, the collapse of communism in Central Europe, and the U.S. invasion of Panama. The years 1990 and 1991 were dominated by the U.S.-led effort to expel Saddam Hussein from Kuwait and the definitive failure of communist rule in the Soviet Union. The year 1992 saw the eruption of ancient ethnic hatreds in the formerly communist controlled republics that had comprised the Soviet Union and Yugoslavia, as well as the promise of a single North American trade bloc and a new global emphasis on the environment.

In fairness, perhaps no president, and no decision-making model, could have performed any better amid the dizzying pace of events of Bush's term. In addition, the revolutionary changes confronting Bush were the result of an historic triumph of the United States' Cold War foreign policy. Containment of the Soviet Union and of communism, waged for so many years and at such high cost to the American people, had worked; communism, the twentieth century's boldest social experiment, had failed spectacularly. In a very real sense, then, whatever problems the Bush presidency encountered in developing a foreign policy appropriate to the times were the most welcome problems of the nation having succeeded in its central foreign policy objectives of the past 45 years.

And yet there was an inescapable sense that Bush's foreign policy-making team constituted the right group of players assembled for the wrong game. Three of their best known decisions capture both their very real strengths and the vulnerabilities of Bush's collegial foreign policy-making approach. The first was his dramatic proposal for conventional force reductions in Europe unveiled at the Brussels NATO summit in May 1989. Frustrated by the blandness of an early interagency study of the best approach to use with the Soviet Union, and piqued that Mikhail Gorbachev was widely hailed in the West for his bold measures aimed at ending the Cold War, President Bush retreated to his Kennebunkport, Maine, vacation home with his foreign policy inner circle and tasked the group to help him develop a dramatic gesture that would take the spotlight off Gorbachev. The result was a sweeping proposal for deep, asymmetrical cuts in conventional troops and equipment stationed in Europe. Bush made it a point to exclude the regular foreign policy bureaucracy in his

Kennebunkport discussions, deeming such departments and agencies as State, DOD, and the Arms Control and Disarmament Agency too cautious for the sort of dramatic surprise he wished to spring. In the end, Bush's proposal achieved its short-term public relations objective and its medium-term arms control objectives, serving as the basis for the 1990 Conventional Forces in Europe (CFE) arms reduction agreement. But its very preoccupation with the mesmerizing figure of Mikhail Gorbachev was symptomatic of Bush's slowness in grasping the profoundly centrifugal forces at work in the Soviet Union that would ultimately make Gorbachev irrelevant. As late as 1991, Bush and his collegial policy-making team were preoccupied with how to cope with Gorbachev and the Soviet Union and were surprisingly late in acknowledging that the future lay with Boris Yeltsin and the other heads of a post–Soviet, noncommunist assortment of republics, not with Gorbachev and a centralized state known as the Soviet Union.

Similarly, Bush and his foreign policy inner circle won wide praise for their skillful response to Saddam Hussein's invasion of Kuwait in August 1990. In his handling of Operation Desert Shield/Desert Storm in 1990 and 1991, Bush went to great lengths to confine critical information and the consideration of policy options within his tight collegial circle of Baker, Cheney, Scowcroft, and General Colin Powell, now chairman of the Joint Chiefs of Staff (see the detailed account in Chapter 8). In the war's aftermath, however, serious questions were raised about the Bush administration's indulgent attitude toward the Iraqi dictator prior to his fateful invasion and annexation of Kuwait. However brilliant the campaign to eject Saddam from Kuwait had been, it became apparent that earlier U.S. policy itself had sent Saddam Hussein the wrong signals regarding U.S. intentions.

Finally, at the Earth Summit held in Brazil in the summer of 1992, the Bush administration staked out an American position on environmental issues that was seriously at odds with the overwhelming sentiment among the assembled nations of the world. Particularly controversial was the U.S. decision not to sign a treaty aimed at protecting the earth's biodiversity. Once again, Bush had arrived at his policy within the collegial confines of his foreign policy-making team. In doing so, however, he had excluded important voices within his own administration — including William Reilly, director of the Environmental Protection Agency — who was advocating U.S. support for the biodiversity treaty and other international environmental measures.

Each of these decisions (1) was made within a closed circle comprised of Bush's foreign hand-picked policy-making team and (2) was essentially reactive in character rather than arising from a coherent vision of how the

United States intended to lead the post–Cold War world. A good case can be made that in attempting to address such newly important issues as international environmental protection, the closed-circle nature of Bush's foreign policy-making style left him vulnerable to the syndrome of *groupthink*. This term, coined by the Yale psychologist Irving Janis, refers to the tendency within small groups to minimize conflict and screen out ideas that threaten the cohesiveness of the group. A more fundamental problem for George Bush, however, was his congenital inability to think through, articulate, and act on a coherent vision of the larger purpose behind his frenetic activity. "The vision thing," as he once called it, would have been less of a problem in an era of stability which prized pragmatic problem-solving. But amid the revolutionary pace of global events during his administration, Bush's lack of a clear sense of overarching purpose too often left him and his admirable team of foreign policy associates adrift without a conceptual compass.

### Bill Clinton

The election of Bill Clinton in 1992 reflected a pervasive national yearning for change. Polls routinely revealed a deep public anxiety that the nation had in some fundamental sense lost its way and that the incumbent George Bush and his fellow Republicans had all too little sense of how to get the country back on track. Although all new presidencies send the nation's pundits into predictable declarations that "historic change" is at hand, the elevation of Bill Clinton did indeed seem to betoken a genuine turning point in American life. This was due largely to the restoration of Democratic control of both elected branches of the federal government and the presumed end of the paralytic syndrome known as "gridlock"; Clinton's youth and the related phenomenon of generational change; and the widely held—if naive—belief that the end of the Cold War would permit America a respite from international exertions and allow a less distracted focus on a host of domestic needs, ranging from education to race relations to health care to the rebuilding of the nation's industrial prowess.

The end of governmental gridlock, it soon became apparent, had relatively little to do with Congress and the presidency being in the hands of different political parties. (The Republican Eisenhower had enjoyed cordial relations with the Democratic Congress, while the Democrat Carter had a turbulent relationship with an even more Democratic Congress.) Rather, what was needed was a new degree of common purpose among the American people and a president who frankly relished the give and take that is the essence of political life. On both counts, the Clinton years promised a noticeable reduction—though most assuredly not the end—of policy gridlock. The 1992 campaign had reflected a new seriousness within the electorate that the nation's frayed social fabric must be repaired, and the elected leadership in both branches mirrored the new sobriety concerning matters such as education, global competitiveness, and the runaway national deficit. Moreover, Clinton's much-advertised political skills assisted him in working with a Congress that had grown overly adversarial towards an executive branch that had for 12 years, under Reagan and Bush, made it the nation's scapegoat for every conceivable ill besetting the republic.

The second harbinger of change was the theme of youth and generational succession. At age 46, Clinton was the second youngest elected president. John Kennedy had been elected at age 43, but—as noted above—Kennedy's celebrated rhetoric of change was essentially a summons for an intensification of the Cold War, not a call for a drastic change of national purpose. Clinton was the first president born after World War II, and his ascendancy to the nation's top job cast into bold relief how little he and his fellow "baby boomers" had in common with the life experiences and shared worldview of the generation of Cold War leaders. Despite the great range of their ages at the time they were inaugurated (Kennedy was 43, Reagan was 69), all the post–World War II presidents prior to Clinton had shared two traits. First, all had been preoccupied with the central struggles against totalitarianism in World War II and the protracted Cold War and, second, all had served in the nation's armed forces. Truman had served in Europe in World War I, Eisenhower, Kennedy, Johnson, Nixon, Ford, Reagan, and Bush had served in World War II, while the Annapolis-trained Carter alone wore the uniform during peacetime. Clinton's much-discussed avoidance of the draft during Vietnam—and his difficulty in presenting a consistent and straightforward account of the circumstances surrounding his evasion of military service—meant that the new commander in chief would be watched closely for any signs of undue "softness" in military matters or, perhaps more dangerously, of a tendency to resort too readily to force to dispel the lingering doubts that wartime draft evasion inevitably create.

More fundamentally, however, Clinton's would be the first truly post–Cold War presidency. While the protracted conflict had ended during the Bush years, the essential character of the Bush foreign policy was grounded in the 40-year political, ideological, and military struggle against the Soviet-led coalition. Even with the Cold War won, Bush's difficulties in adapting both the nation's institutions and its policy premises to a post–Cold War environment were all too apparent. Clinton, by contrast, had been little affected personally by the nation's geostrategic exertions and would take office unencumbered by Cold War imperatives. In addition, Clinton liked to surround himself with fellow 40-something "boomers." To this age cohort, the Great Depression, Hitler, and Stalin were the stuff of history lessons, while their common defining experiences were the youthful charms and terrors of the 1960s, including a broad opposition to U.S. policy in Vietnam, obligatory experimentation with hallucinogenic drugs (whether or not one inhaled), a heightened sensitivity to racial and gender discrimination, and—following the disillusionment with the liberal Lyndon Johnson and the conservative Richard Nixon—an early loss of political innocence and the near-absence of credible heroes. Shorn of the heroic foreign crusades of their parent's generation and skeptical of the perceived verities of their society, Bill Clinton and his youthful colleagues did indeed represent a departure from the generation that had endured the Great Depression, defeated the Axis powers in World War II, and maintained a firm and, ultimately, successful containment against totalitarian communism.

Another source of the broad expectation that the Clinton era would mark a genuine turning point was the hope—shared by Clinton and the public alike—that the demise of the Cold War would permit a sharp downgrading of foreign affairs and a corresponding renewal of attention to the nation's domestic requirements. To Clinton, the hoped-for respite from international matters was a product of both experience and conviction. In terms of experience, Clinton assumed the presidency almost wholly lacking in foreign policy credentials. A career politician, he had served an unprecedented five terms as governor of Arkansas, a small, poor, southern state. Aside from participating in three foreign trade expeditions, Clinton had devoted virtually none of his professional life to international matters. In terms of personal conviction, Clinton ardently believed that the nation's most pressing needs involved domestic policy. His 1992 campaign manager, James Carville, had posted a hand-lettered sign in the Little Rock campaign headquarters which was meant as a daily reminder to the campaign staff of their central issue. "The economy, stupid," it read, but it could as easily have served as a concise summation of Clinton's abiding passion. He deeply believed that the most fundamental prerequisite to great power status was a healthy economy at home, and he was equally persuaded that the debt-riddled U.S. economy of the early 1990s would slowly erode the nation's capacity both to offer its own people a better future and enable the nation to continue to function as a world leader. Both by background and intellectual conviction, then, Clinton took office hoping to be able to concentrate on the nation's economic and social ills.

Whatever his hopes, it was soon apparent that the post–Cold War world would not be a tidy world from which the United States could disengage. Economic interdependence, ethnic conflicts, the collapse of state authority in much of the former communist world, the proliferation of weapons of mass destruction and missile technology, and the challenge to order posed by regional aggression all meant that Clinton would be denied the foreign policy "breather" he had hoped for.

Despite Clinton's lack of foreign policy credentials, and despite the fact that the world confronting him was one in which the familiar signposts of the Cold War were now entirely gone, thus requiring uncommon astuteness in analyzing global currents, it was clear from the beginning that Bill Clinton would be the hands-on manager and architect of his administration's foreign policy. In order to understand why this is so, it is worth reviewing the three critical personality variables identified by Professor George and noting Clinton's characteristics on each.

In terms of cognitive style, Clinton himself has accepted the label of "policy wonk," reflecting his superb intellect and his insatiable appetite for policy-relevant details. Raised in rural Arkansas, never personally far from the state's pervasive poverty, Clinton experienced a meteoric rise that was a classic demonstration of merit fueled by ambition. Following undergraduate work at Georgetown University, he studied at Oxford on a coveted Rhodes Scholarship and capped his formal training by earning a law degree at Yale University. A quick study with a prodigious memory, Clinton relished the most arcane aspects of public policy matters. So, despite his lack of formal experience in world affairs, Clinton assumed the American presidency confident that his customary diligence and intelligence would permit him quickly to come up to speed on the intricacies of global politics.

Similarly, Clinton brought to the presidency an exceptional sense of his own political efficacy. An inveterate "people person," he had nurtured a gift for persuasion and coalition building during his long political ascent. Supremely self-assured in face-to-face dealings and blessed with perhaps the most thoroughly honed political skills of any U.S. president since Franklin Roosevelt, Clinton bore the "can-do" air of a man who is convinced that with enough effort and persuasion he can bring together political adversaries in support of sound policy objectives.

It is the third personality variable—orientation toward political conflict—that is most problematic in Clinton's case. Justly celebrated for his skill in finding common ground between widely divergent positions, Clinton is a genuine people-pleaser who goes to great lengths to avoid or minimize political conflict. While psychological interpretations of political behavior can easily be overdone, Clinton himself has acknowledged that growing up in a household dominated by an abusive, alcoholic stepfather left its mark on him in the eagerness to please that is the common lot of children of alcoholics. Clinton's relentless efforts to act as a peacemaker and an uncommon knack for finding common ground between political enemies can be a source of strength as the United States attempts to dampen the bloody ethnic and national hatreds of the post–Cold War world. It is also true, however, that his reluctance to take a firm stand and alienate others (i.e., standing up to domestic interest groups on trade issues) may lead to a dangerous policy drift in a chaotic world requiring decisive leadership.

Clinton's confidence in his own political skills and intellect meant that he would place himself at the center of a collegial foreign policy-making team. Joining Clinton's inner circle are Secretary of State Warren Christopher, Secretary of Defense Les Aspin, and National Security Adviser Anthony Lake. Sixty-seven years old at the time he took office, Christopher was a link to the generation of American leaders that Clinton and his fellow baby-boomers were supplanting. A Los Angeles lawyer by profession, Christopher had served as deputy attorney general in the Johnson administration and as deputy secretary of state in the Carter administration. In both his public service and his private practice, Christopher was broadly admired for his intelligence, his meticulous grasp of precise details, his skill as a quietly effective negotiator, and his determinedly noncharismatic discretion and loyalty. While these traits serve him well as a tactician and as a trusted presidential confidant, great secretaries of state have demonstrated two additional traits: a capacity to conceptualize and to communicate. Christopher's preferred world is that of mastering detail, not the development of overarching vision. And while his private communication reflects lawyerly precision, he is notably not a commanding public orator. His loyalty as a team player and his keen intelligence make him a valuable member of Clinton's collegial team, but the administration's development of a coherent global strategy will call for skills that Secretary Christopher has not displayed.

Clinton's secretary of defense, Les Aspin, matches Clinton's own academic accomplishments, with degrees from Yale, Oxford, and MIT. A former Pentagon analyst, Aspin emerged as the House of Representatives' leading defense intellectual during his two decades in Congress. Renowned both for his analytical flair and for his knack for generating publicity, Aspin helped move the Democrats away from their reflexive post–Vietnam opposition to a strong national defense and the use of force. A moderate Democrat, Aspin alienated his more liberal House colleagues by supporting aid to the Nicaraguan Contras and funding for the MX missile during the Reagan years and for supporting the Persian Gulf War during the Bush administration. Where Secretary of State Christopher places greater emphasis on the efficacy of quiet diplomacy, Aspin has criticized the post–Vietnam "all or nothing" approach toward the use of force and is the most likely member of Clinton's inner circle to advocate limited U.S. force for purposes such as humanitarian relief, drug interdiction, counterterrorism, peacekeeping, and the protection of vulnerable minorities such as the Kurds of Iraq or the Bosnians in the former Yugoslavia. As forceful and extroverted as Christopher is reserved and taciturn, Aspin is perhaps the most influential member of Clinton's collegial team in terms of articulating strategy and initiating policy.

Anthony Lake, Clinton's national security adviser, entered the Foreign Service following schooling at Harvard, Cambridge, and Princeton. He rose quickly to become Henry Kissinger's principal assistant for Vietnam during the Nixon years and later directed the State Department's policy planning during the Carter administration. Unlike such predecessors as Brent Scowcroft, Colin Powell, Robert MacFarlane, and John Poindexter, Lake has little first-hand experience in military matters. And unlike Kissinger or Brzezinski, Lake is not a prominent academician with well-developed policy prescriptions spelled out in numerous books and articles. But in a book he co-authored in 1984 Lake argued that the proliferation of foreign policy players and the erosion of consensus over what our policy should be severely hampered the nation's ability to forge a coherent and effective foreign policy. He has been an especially forceful advocate for placing greater weight on the expertise and views of career Foreign Service officers.

To Lake, the end of the Cold War renders the old debate between interventionist "hawks" and conciliatory "doves" meaningless. Rather, he believes, the principal policy schism within the United States is between traditionalists who believe that the nation's interests are protected by the maintenance of a balance of power and modernists, like himself and President Clinton, who believe in the Wilsonian principle that U.S. interests are best protected by using the nation's overwhelming power to promote democracy around the world. Lake's grasp of the intricacies of world affairs exceeds that of the other members of Clinton's foreign policy inner circle. His self-effacing demeanor, however, further cedes the role of chief strategist to the forceful Les Aspin.

The relative lack of conceptual flair among Clinton's team assures that Clinton himself will remain at the center of his administration's foreign policy development. This presents two potential dangers. First, as with Jimmy Carter, Clinton's lack of foreign policy experience and absorption with the details of policy issues could leave him overburdened and paralyzed by the enormity of presidential decision-making. Second, Clinton's collegial team might fail to cohere either personally or in terms of developing a consensual worldview. Recall that for collegial decision-making to work well, at least one of two conditions must be present: (1) a commanding president who articulates a clear strategic vision from which the collegial deliberation of policy specifics takes its bearings, or (2) an essential commonality of outlook among the principal players. Clearly, Bill Clinton is trusting that the intelligence and diligence that won him the presidency will serve him well as he orchestrates the United States' approach to the uncharted international waters of the 1990s.

From this survey of the foreign policy decision-making styles of our 11 most recent presidents, three conclusions emerge. First, the competitive decision-making model is the most problematic of the three, having been used successfully only once (by Roosevelt) and attempted unsuccessfully by one other president (the early phase of Johnson's term). Given the overwhelming complexity of contemporary government and the enormous demands on a president's time and attention, the challenges of the competitive model are simply too daunting to make it a recommended presidential practice.

Second, the collegial model has worked well under optimal circumstances (Kennedy's), but in the absence of a coherent presidential vision (as in the cases of Carter and Bush) or presidential expertise in foreign affairs (as in the case of the late Johnson administration), collegial White House decision-making runs the risk of excluding outside views and miring the president in the "trees" of specific issues without providing an overall map of the foreign policy forest he intends to nurture.

Finally, the formalistic model is the favorite among recent presidents, with five of our most recent presidents opting for it (Truman, Eisenhower, Nixon, Ford, and Reagan). Not only has it been used most frequently, but it has often been associated with successful presidential leadership, as in Truman's visionary policies at the inception of the Cold War, Eisenhower's avoidance of major war during the tense crises of the 1950s, and Nixon's celebrated opening to China and policy of détente with the Soviet Union. While the choice of decision-making management system is up to the individual president, and naturally reflects his long-established personal traits and style, the formalistic model is the one that has most reliably led to successful policy-making during the past 50 years.

*ANSWERS TO PRESIDENTIAL TRIVIA QUIZ, PAGE 41:*

1. Ronald Reagan, Letter to Tower Commission, February 20, 1987.
2. Harry Truman, *Quote Magazine*, October 23, 1955.
3. Gerald Ford, in second Ford-Carter debate, October 6, 1976.
4. Gerald Ford, cited in Richard Reeves, *A Ford Not a Lincoln.*

5. George Bush, to schoolchildren in Amish country, 1989.

6. Richard Nixon, TV interview with David Frost, May 20, 1977.

7. Harry Truman, *Memoirs*, Vol. II, Ch. 1.

8. Richard Nixon, quotation cited in *Newsweek*, 1990.

## SUGGESTED READINGS

Barilleaux, Ryan J. *The President as World Leader*. New York: St. Martin's Press, 1991.

Clark, Keith C., and Laurence J. Legere, eds. *The President and the Management of National Security*. New York: Praeger, 1983.

Corwin, Edward Samuel. *The President's Control of Foreign Relations*. Princeton N.J.: Princeton University Press, 1917.

Falkowski, Lawrence S. *Presidents, Secretaries of State, and Crises in U.S. Foreign Relations: A Model and Predictive Analysis*. Boulder, Colo.: Westview Press, 1978.

George, Alexander L. *Presidential Decisionmaking in Foreign Policy: The Effective Use of Information and Advice*. Boulder, Colo.: Westview Press, 1980.

Hilsman, Roger. *The Politics of Policy Making in Defense and Foreign Affairs: Conceptual Models and Bureaucratic Politics*. 2nd ed. Englewood Cliffs, N.J.: Prentice Hall, 1990.

Hoxie, R. Gordon. *Command Decision and the Presidency: A Study in National Security Policy and Organization*. New York: Reader's Digest Press, 1977.

Johnson, Richard T. *Managing the White House*. New York: Harper & Row, 1974.

Kellerman, Barbara. *The President as World Leader*. New York: St. Martin's Press, 1991.

Mosher, Frederick W., David Clinton, and Daniel G. Lang. *Presidential Transitions and Foreign Affairs*. Baton Rouge: Louisiana State University Press, 1987.

Neustadt, Richard E. *Presidential Power and the Modern Presidents: The Politics of Leadership from Roosevelt to Reagan*. New York: Free Press, 1990.

Nuechterlein, Donald Edwin. *National Interests and Presidential Leadership: The Setting of Priorities*. Boulder, Colo.: Westview Press, 1978.

Rubin, Barry. *Secrets of State: The State Department and the Struggle over U.S. Foreign Policy*. New York: Oxford University Press, 1985.

# CHAPTER 3

# The Role of Executive Agencies

The personal style and priorities that the Clinton administration has brought with them to the presidency will affect the relative importance and use of the executive branch agencies that recommend and implement presidential foreign policy decisions. The end of the Cold War and the consequent changes in the international environment would have caused institutional change even if Bush had taken the presidential oath of office on January 21, 1993. A new president with a different background and set of priorities is likely to accelerate that change.

Already, it has become commonplace to describe the Clinton regime as the first post–Cold War presidency. But what does that phrase really mean? In a literal and chronological sense, of course, the 1992 election was the first presidential election since the revolutions of late 1989 began to tear down the Cold War structure. If that were the sum total of what the concept of a post–Cold War presidency meant, it would not tell us very much. However, it means a lot more.

The election of Bill Clinton and Al Gore was important for two other reasons that will contribute to likely change. First, the change was generational: the Bush administration, from the president down through his closest advisers, was dominated by men in their fifties and sixties whose intellectual roots were in the Cold War international system. Clinton and Gore, of course, belong to the baby-boomer generation that first confronted foreign and defense matters through the distorting eye of Vietnam. The deep Cold War experiences of the late 1940s (the fall of Eastern Europe, the Berlin Blockade, the communization of China), the 1950s (Korea, Hungary, Quemoy and Matsu), and the early 1960s (the Cuban missile crisis) forged the worldviews of most of the Bush team; as noted earlier, they were history lessons to the new leaders.

Second, the change of administrations also brings the presidency back to the Democratic party for the first time since 1981. Although too much can be made about how Democrats and Republicans differ in their approaches to policy generally or to foreign and defense policy, we can make two observations with some surety. On one hand, Democratic activists tend to be somewhat younger than their Republican counterparts; the generation of political appointees who will fill positions in the Clinton administration will probably be contemporary to or younger than the president and thus their orientations will also be post–Cold War. On the other hand, the people who are coming into the government have been on the outside of government power for 12 years and have spent some of that time concocting different solutions to problems than those to which we have become accustomed.

The changes that can be expected are likely to be both procedural and institutional as well as substantive, and in many cases they will be closely related. The first institutional change that Clinton announced during the transition was his intent to form an Economic Council parallel in function to the National Security Council which would facilitate a substantive change toward a more prominent, activist position in the economic area.

The remainder of this chapter will discuss the most prominent executive branch departments and agencies that serve the president in the general area of defense and foreign policy. In each case, we will begin by describing the traditional role of the agency and how it has been organized to fulfill that role. We will then examine how that role is likely to change and how change is likely to be reflected institutionally. Because the administration is so new, much of this discussion must be speculative. Since the Clinton administration's announcements in the economic area so closely paralleled its recommendations, the Carnegie Endowment for International Peace-Institute for International Economics' "Special Report: Policymaking for a New Era" (hereafter cited as Carnegie-IIE; see suggested readings for a complete citation) has formed the base for several of our suggestions.

We will begin by discussing the two agencies whose functions will likely undergo the greatest change—the Department of Defense and the intelligence agencies. The DOD has been an obvious candidate for change and contraction because it is a unique artifact of the Cold War. Nonetheless, early indications suggest a revived role for the agency in the area of peacekeeping and peace enforcement. The intelligence community, too, as a product of the Cold War, is a prime candidate for restructuring and contraction.

Our discussion will then move to the Department of State. Traditionally, State was the preeminent and virtually the only actor in foreign policy, but the national security tenor of the Cold War eroded its dominance. Its role now that the Cold War is over is a matter of great interest. Finally, an emerging concern is the complex of institutions that attempt to influence both domestic and international economic policy—two areas that are increasingly difficult to separate. Using the Economic

Council structure as an organizing device, we will examine how the administration is planning to deal with this obvious priority.

## The Defense Department (DOD)

Across the Potomac River from Washington sits the five-sided building housing the Department of Defense. Those who work there have given its headquarters, descriptively called the Pentagon, many nicknames. To some critics, it joins the National Security Agency in being called the puzzle palace; to most, and especially the uniformed officers who bustle about in its stark hallways, it is simply "the Building."

Physically, DOD's most notable characteristic is its size. The Pentagon, its main headquarters, is the largest office building in the world. Size, however, is also measured in terms of the number of people who work for the department and the share of national resources that defense commands. In terms of employees, the Department of Defense is the largest single agency of the federal government. Before so-called downsizing of the force began in 1990, DOD employed roughly 3 million people, 2 million in uniform and 1 million civilians in a variety of roles. Currently planned cuts in the defense area made possible by the end of the Cold War will reduce those numbers by over 25 percent when Clinton-mandated reductions are implemented. Within the armed services themselves, these cuts will be somewhat differential: the Army, for instance, will lose the most personnel, while the Marines will lose the least. At issue for the Clinton administration is how many more cuts can be made without undercutting the national defense. Early projections suggest a further combined military-civilian reduction of about 200,000 positions beyond those scheduled by the Bush administration.

The other dimension of size, which creates great leverage for DOD, is the extent of its claim on budgetary resources. Before the end of the Cold War, DOD's budget was the second largest (behind entitlement programs such as social security and medicare) within the federal budget, claiming upward of one-quarter of all appropriated dollars. Moreover, two-thirds of the budget is controllable, which means that it must be appropriated annually by Congress. The other category, the uncontrollable budget, consists of items that are automatically appropriated in the absence of interfering legislation; social security and interest payments on the national debt are examples. This controllable portion of the DOD budget is by far the largest single discretionary element in the overall federal budget, making defense dollars the target of those seeking new policy priorities for which dollars are not currently available.

The defense budget, like personnel levels, is scheduled to decline gradually; in fact, by 1996 defense will command less than 20 percent of the budget and will have been replaced by debt service as the second largest budget item. This cut is causing some controversy, however. Many defense dollars are spent in local communities: support services for military bases, orders for military equipment, for example. Cutting those dollars can economically depress communities or sectors of the economy, as the 1993 fight over base closings highlighted. At the same time, the absence of an overwhelming threat has led many observers to recommend that those controllable defense dollars be redirected toward other priorities. Early indications suggest an additional reduction of about 5 percent and a reorientation of research and development monies to projects with both military and civilian applications.

In historical perspective, DOD had the paramount role in the military dimension of the Cold War and was created specifically to deal with the prospect of a World War III, in which the United States was projected to lead one coalition and the Soviet Union the other. When the threat was lively and the confrontation serious, these projections were matters of potential national life and death. Accordingly, the national security establishment had a very high priority within the government; the simple appeal to national security was enough to guarantee whatever the Defense Department wanted.

The end of the Cold War has changed that elevated position. Although both the United States and the Russian Republic maintain large nuclear arsenals with which they could still incinerate one another, the motive to employ them has vanished. In former President Bush's 1992 campaign phrase, we no longer "go to bed worried about nuclear war." The post–Cold War world offers no apparent equivalent of the Soviet menace, and, as a result, the Defense Department may lose its special status within the government.

To think of DOD as a monolith representing defense interests with a single, uniform base would do disservice to our understanding of the department. Like the government more generally, the Pentagon has instigated a series of informal checks and balances representing competing interests and perspectives and assuring the representation of differing viewpoints before decisions are made. To understand how this informal check and balance works requires a brief look at how DOD is organized and the dynamics of interaction within "the Building."

### Organization

The basic operating principle underlying the entire defense establishment is civilian control of the military. Beginning with the American Revolution, the people expressed a fear of a standing military that might pose a threat to civilian institutions. In the eighteenth century, this fear was so great and produced such tight control over the military that General George Washington, during a particularly unpleasant interchange with the Continental Congress, once decried that he could understand why the Congress opposed an army in peacetime, but that he could not understand why they opposed an army during war.

Through most of U.S. history, the peacetime military was very small. In fact, only since World War II and the onset of Cold War has the United States maintained large numbers of active-duty military personnel. The principle of civilian control means that every military person, regardless of role, reports and is accountable to a civilian official: the chairman of the Joint Chiefs of Staff to the president, the chief of staff of the Army to the secretary of the Army, and so on. This arrangement often creates some friction—specifically, military personnel feel civilians are incompetent to review and reverse sheerly military judgments, for instance—but it does assure tight civilian control over the military.

Any depiction of an organization as vast as DOD requires a simplification that is somewhat distorting, as is shown in Figure 3.1. For present purposes, we can think of that organization in four parts. At the pinnacle is the secretary of defense, the cabinet official who reports directly to the president and is responsible for the overall operation of the DOD. The second part is the Office of the Secretary of Defense, which consists of a number of subcabinet-level functions that cut across military services. The third part is made up of the services themselves, each with its separate bureaucracy and set of interests. The fourth is the Joint Chiefs of Staff, which has the presumptive role of coordinating the military activities of the various services. Each area is noted in Figure 3.1.

*Secretary of Defense* The secretary of defense, or the SECDEF, as the individual is known within the Pentagon, is the chief adviser to the president on defense matters. (The chairman of the Joint Chiefs of Staff is, by law, the chief military adviser to the president.) As such, it is his or her responsibility to advise the president on defense matters. For example, should we use force in a given situation? what kinds of weapons and levels of personnel do we need? In addition, the SECDEF is a policy implementer, being responsible both for carrying out the policies mandated by the chief executive and the Congress and for managing the department's internal affairs.

*Office of the Secretary of Defense* In carrying out his or her tasks, the SECDEF is assisted by the group of agencies known as the Office of the Secretary of Defense (OSD). Normally headed by an undersecretary or an assistant secretary, OSD agencies are broadly functional in their responsibilities, not unlike functional bureaus within the State Department.

Reorganizing OSD to conform to his idea of the post–Cold War era was an early priority of Secretary Aspin. Previously, over two dozen undersecretaries and assistant secretaries reported directly to the SECDEF. The new organization, shown in Figure 3.2, changes the pattern in two ways. First, it reduces the number of people reporting to the Secretary to four undersecretaries (USDs) and six assistant secretaries (ASDs). Second, it alters the titles and functions from previous organizations.

The pattern depicted in Figure 3.2 replaces the box in Figure 3.1 designated "Office of the Secretary of Defense." That box was purposely not specified because of the large number of offices and functions it contained. In reorganizing the pattern, Aspin has sought to accomplish three apparent goals.

The first, accomplished through the USD designations, is to pull some DOD-wide functions directly into OSD, thereby strengthening the SECDEF's hand and weakening the hands of the services. This is particularly true in the area of personnel and readiness and the area of technology and hardware, which deals with equipment and weaponry. Second, he has realigned the ASD level so that it more closely parallels the State Department, presaging an oversight and competition between the two agencies. In the process, he has created functional areas that would have been quite unthinkable during the Cold War—ASDs for economic and environmental security, regional security, and democratic security, for instance.

Third, the reorganization wipes out a number of historically important offices within OSD. Gone, for instance, are the positions of ASD for international security affairs and international security policy, two of the historically most powerful ASD positions. Also reorganized out of existence is the position of ASD for special operations and low-intensity conflict (SOLIC), a position mandated by Congress in the Cohen-Nunn Act of 1986, which is the subject of a case study in Chapter 5. This latter position may be subject to negotiation because of its statutory mandate; the others are matters of internal organization not subject to direct congressional oversight.

*Service Departments*    The third layer of agencies that help the SECDEF consists of the service departments. Each military service has its own individual department within the Pentagon that attends to the interests of and administers the individual services. At the top of each of these bureaucracies is a service secretary (the secretaries of the Army, Navy, and Air Force), who is assisted by the chief of staff of each service. The service chief (chief of staff of the Army and the Air Force, chief of naval operations) is responsible for the internal operation of his service and acts as his service's representative to the Joint Chiefs of Staff (JCS).

The Defense Department was created largely to bring all the services

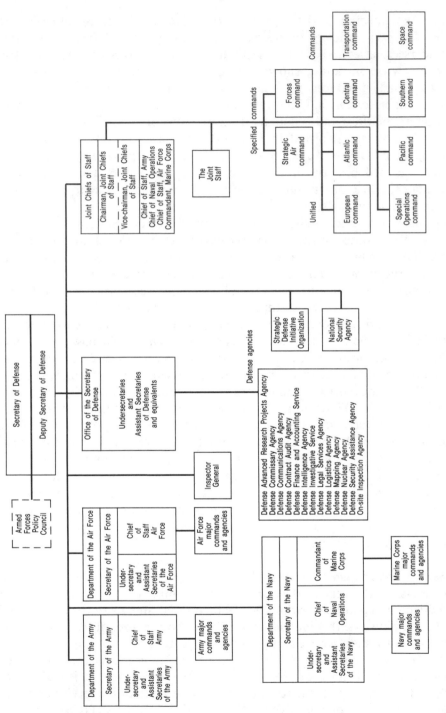

**FIGURE 3.1    Department of Defense**

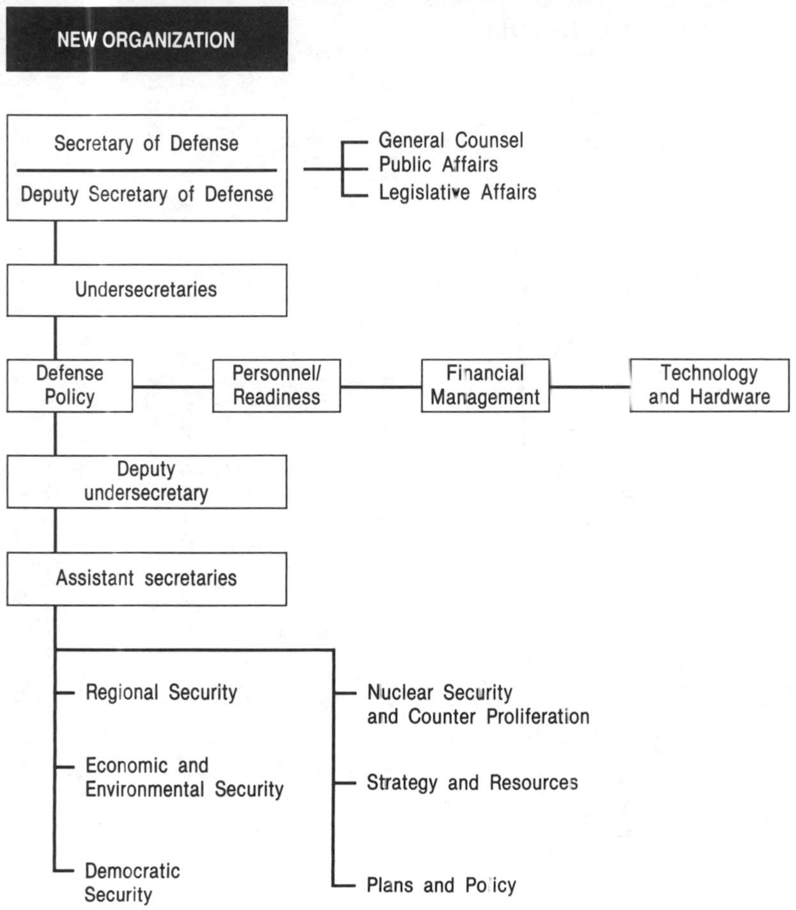

**NEW ORGANIZATION**

**WHAT HAS CHANGED**

The general counsel and officials handling public affairs and legislative affairs will function like the executive staff to the head of a large corporation.

These four officials replace more than two dozen who reported to former defense secretary Richard B. Cheney.

New titles reflect Pentagon role on some matters long the province of the State Department.

Secretary of Defense

Deputy Secretary of Defense

General Counsel
Public Affairs
Legislative Affairs

Undersecretaries

Defense Policy

Personnel/Readiness

Financial Management

Technology and Hardware

Deputy undersecretary

Assistant secretaries

Regional Security

Economic and Environmental Security

Democratic Security

Nuclear Security and Counter Proliferation

Strategy and Resources

Plans and Policy

SOURCE: Defense Department

**FIGURE 3.2** Proposed Organization of the Pentagon

under one umbrella and thereby reduce interservice bickering and rivalry over such matters as budgetary allocations. (Prior to the National Security Act of 1947, each service independently argued for its budget before Congress.) The individual services remain extremely powerful, however, and the locus of primary loyalty for their members. As a result, to outside observers of the process, service considerations often appear more important than broader national objectives.

*Joint Chiefs of Staff*   Overcoming service rivalries and facilitating interservice cooperation was a major purpose of creating the Joint Chiefs of Staff. The original idea was to provide, through the service chiefs and a modest Joint Staff, a vehicle for interchange and coordination. Because loyalties and rewards such as performance evaluations and promotions remained the province of the services, joint staff assignment has historically been considered odious duty for service members. At best, being a "purple suiter," as joint staffers are known, was considered an interruption in useful service; at worst it was considered an absolute hindrance to one's career.

In 1986 Congress passed the Goldwater-Nichols Defense Reorganization Act (for more detail, see Chapter 5) in part to strengthen the chairman of the JCS and the Joint Staff. The legislation was motivated by the belief that the absence of coordination and cooperation had hindered military efficiency in a number of recent operations (Grenada and the Desert One hostage rescue attempt in Iran in 1980, for example), that the nature of modern warfare required much closer coordination of military elements, and that strengthening the JCS and thereby weakening the power of the services was the best way to accomplish that coordination.

### Rivalries within the DOD

No one has ever accused the defense structure of excessive efficiency. This huge, complex organization houses multiple interests and rivalries that individually and cumulatively may hinder efficiency, but that at the same time promote the kinds of informal checks and balances that may ultimately contribute to the department's effectiveness.

Rivalries exist at several levels, one of the most obvious being between the civilian and military personnel who work for DOD. Career military people tend to be suspicious of the competence of their civilian counterparts (unless the civilians are retired military officers, or so-called phony civilians). This is especially true of political appointees at the middle and upper ranks of the department (e.g., deputy assistant secretaries and above), who typically arrive from outside the establishment with a new administration and return to private life when that administration leaves. This level of rivalry institutionally focuses on the services, which are more closely controlled by the uniformed personnel and OSD, which is more the preserve of the civilians.

Rivalry also exists between the services themselves and between the services and the JCS. Interservice rivalry arises primarily over mission assignments and budgetary allocations, two matters that are, of course, related. When the extremely long and complex budget cycle is being conducted (which is a full-time, year-round exercise), there are no more critical reviewers of the service budgets than the other services. An extra dollar appropriated for the Army, for instance, is a dollar unavailable to the Navy.

At the same time, the issue of control of operations and the unified and specified commands between the JCS and the services forms another layer of competition. Each of the commands, which contains military elements from all the services, is administratively assigned to an individual service. Hence, the European Command is assigned to the Army, which would have the primary operational responsibilities in a war there, the Pacific Command is commanded by a Navy admiral, and the Space Command is assigned to the Air Force. Historically, however, funding for each command came through the individual service budgets, and services tended to be more generous to those commands they controlled than to those they did not. Part of the 1986 legislation was intended to allow the individual commanders in chief (CINCs) to appeal directly for funding, bypassing, and weakening the budgetary control of the individual services.

Congressional review and oversight is particularly important in the defense area as well. The reason is simple enough: the defense budget is so large and affects so many congressional districts so intimately that members of Congress want to be apprised of anything going on in "the Building" that might affect them. This interest is often the source of considerable friction as Pentagon officials (civilian and uniformed) are dragged before Congress for what appear to be endless congressional hearings or are forced to answer detailed inquiries from congressional staffers who are often considerably junior in age and experience to those on whose time they are intruding. At its worst, this process is derisively known within the Pentagon as congressional "micromanagement."

## Effects of Change

How is the Defense Department likely to be affected by the twin impacts of the end of the Cold War and the arrival of a new Democratic administration? The question is particularly important in the context of the decade from which we have just emerged. The 1980s was a decade of considerable prosperity and growth for the Defense Department, particularly in the early part of the decade when the Reagan buildup—the largest increase in peacetime defense spending in the nation's history—was occurring.

Three obvious sources of change are evident, each of which has both substantive and organizational ramifications. The first is size, structure, and roles in a post–Cold War environment. The entire structure of the defense establishment was, of course, designed to meet the military threat posed by a military adversary that simply no longer exists, a structure Aspin has moved to change, as noted. By some accounting schemes, fully 60 percent of defense spending (personnel, equipment, weapons, planning) in the Cold War was devoted to the problem of massive ground and air war in Europe. Some of that equipment proved useful in Operation Desert Storm. Such a force structure, size, and preparation seem appropriate for few (if any) other foreseeable contingencies.

As a result, a major concern will be how much cutting and restructuring can occur. Not all possible needs and problems can be confidently predicted in advance. Who, for instance, would have predicted a major U.S. expedition to the Persian Gulf in the first half of 1990? As a result, a naturally conservative, cautious military will always be reluctant to cut back, given the uncertainties about the future. This, in essence, is the rationale for General Powell's "base force," a military capability approximately three-quarters the size of the Cold War force. Powell contends that a more drastic cut in the force would cause it to lose effectiveness and the ability to meet different problems.

The second area of concern arises from the breakdown of the old international system and the military's role in it. The Cold War, as observed earlier, possessed a symmetry and predictability that the post–Cold War world lacks. With a clearly defined adversary, it was possible to design forces, doctrines, and arrangements to meet these known problems. Unfortunately, those constructs no longer clearly apply in the much less structured, more fluid environment that developed after 1989. Since then, the military establishment has been called upon to undertake activities for which the Cold War preparation was arguably irrelevant.

As an example of this change, let us look at the active uses of American force since 1989. In December 1989, a total of 22,500 U.S. troops were dropped into Panama (Operation Just Cause) to capture and bring to justice Manuel Noriega, interrupt the rampant drug trade through the country, and reinstitute political democracy by restoring the elected president to power. In August 1990 Operation Desert Shield landed in the Saudi desert and transformed itself into Desert Storm in 1991. Desert Storm then spawned the relief effort to save the Kurds, which ultimately produced an "exclusion zone" for the Kurds in northern Iraq from which Iraqi authorities are excluded from operating by U.S. forces (Operation Provide Comfort). Also in 1991, U.S. forces flew relief supplies into flood-ravaged Bangladesh (Operation Sea Angel), followed in 1992 by expansion of the exclusion zone idea to protect Shiites in southern Iraq (Operation Southern Watch) and by mounting the massive relief effort to stop Somali starvation (Operation Restore Hope).

These are, to put it mildly, unconventional defense missions, raising the third concern: new missions and new conditions for military application. If the aforementioned list of activities has a common thread, it is the use of force within states to ameliorate internal disorder by multilateral contingents. One institution that the end of the Cold War clearly helped revive is the United Nations, which has become the legitimating body for so-called peacekeeping and peace enforcement operations. The U.S. defense establishment has never given such actions high priority, nor has it been structured to cooperate with international authorities.

How does the Defense Department respond to changing circumstances? If "humanitarian intervention" of the Somali variety is to be a staple in the future, is the U.S. Army the appropriate vehicle? How does the decision process adapt to such contingencies? Does DOD now need to create an assistant secretary-level position to deal with the Somalias and Bosnias of the world, possibly complete with a new command that augments traditional forces with peacekeepers and dispensers of humanitarian aid? Do doctrine and practice have to be modified to take part in U.N.-sponsored actions? Or can we continue to finesse the situation by mounting a U.S. operation under the guise of the United Nations and then turn it over to the United Nations when we leave, as we have done in Somalia?

These questions of role and missions will be important concerns for the Clinton administration, partly because the structure of the post–Cold War international system is still evolving, and the problems of the new order are different and less predictable than they were in the past. At the same time, the way we react to each new problem can be precedent-setting, predisposing us either to do or not to do things in the future based on our current experience. Thus, the DOD will have to deal with the changing shape of the national security architecture in creative ways that will require changes in both structure and policy.

## The Intelligence Community

Not surprisingly many of the comments that have been made about the defense establishment apply to the intelligence community as well. Like the DOD, the complex of agencies that collectively comprise the intelligence capability of the United States came into being to deal with the Cold War competition. Because the Soviet threat activated the intelligence community, it developed in a manner that would be most attuned to that problem. As a result, the evaporation of the Soviet threat leaves an intelligence structure that is not obviously functional in the new order.

The development of the U.S. intelligence community owes much to its effective competition with its Soviet counterpart, the Committee on State Security (KGB). The Soviet organization was highly clandestine, paramilitary in structure and practices (its officers have military rank), and highly protective of information in a closed, hostile society. The one organization sought to gain politically useful information from and about the other from generally secret, protected sources. The KGB attempted, through various means, to obtain secret American information; U.S. intelligence sought to prevent that, and vice versa. Inevitably, U.S. intelligence agencies came to share some unfortunate aspects of the Soviet agency, such as excessive secretiveness.

With the end of the Cold War, the appropriateness of an intelligence structure designed to counter an agency like the KGB has come into question. Certainly, clandestinely organized intelligence agencies continue to exist in other countries, and the United States still requires information about other governments that is not always publicly available. The important question is whether we need a system designed for the Cold War to carry out current and future tasks.

The current intelligence community is a large, complex set of organizations within the federal government that can be grouped into three categories by bureaucratic sponsor (see Figure 3.3): the Central Intelligence Agency, defense-related agencies, and cabinet-level agencies.

### The Central Intelligence Agency

The most visible component is the Central Intelligence Agency (CIA), which for many Americans *is* the intelligence community. Created as part of the National Security Act of 1947, the CIA was the nation's first peacetime civilian intelligence-gathering agency. It is an independent agency and is attached to no other cabinet-level agency. It is led by the director of central intelligence (DCI) who, by law, has the additional responsibility of coordinating all government intelligence activities.

### Defense-Controlled Agencies

The largest category in terms both of agencies and employees are those intelligence agencies controlled by the Department of Defense.

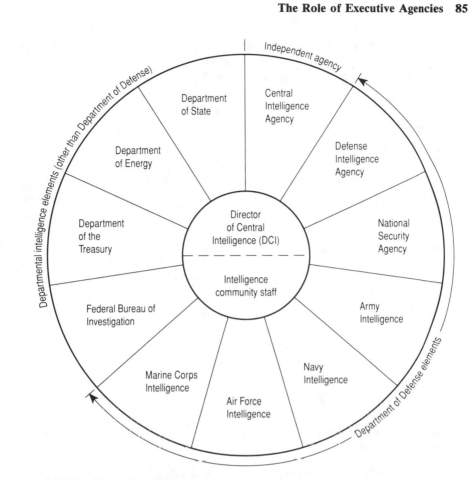

Source: *Factbook on Intelligence* (Washington, D.C.: Central Intelligence Agency, September 1987), p. 20.

**FIGURE 3.3     The Intelligence Community**

There are six such agencies, four of which are associatcd with the individual services (Army, Air Force, Navy, and Marines) and have intelligence responsibilities relevant to their individual service missions. Although some observers have suggested that "military intelligence" is oxymoronic, for instance, Air Force Intelligence has for years conducted extensive aerial satellite reconnaisance through photography of Soviet nuclear missile capabilities.

The other two defense-controlled agencies also have specified tasks. One of them, the National Security Agency (NSA), is the most clandestine and technical. It was created in 1952 by secret presidential directive, and its major responsibility is to intercept foreign electronic communications and prevent other states (notably the former Soviets) from intercepting U.S. government communications. This activity is known as signal intelligence

(SIGINT) and is highly technical and convoluted in action, earning its headquarters the nickname "puzzle palace."

The final defense-controlled agency is the Defense Intelligence Agency (DIA), a body created in 1961 to consolidate the information gathered by the various service intelligence agencies. In this way, it provides the secretary of defense with an independent source of information relevant to defense. At the time it was created, the DIA was expected eventually to absorb some of the duties of the service agencies, thereby causing them to shrink. Each service, however, has proven highly jealous and protective of its intelligence operation, a problem we will see presently in the overall intelligence community.

### Cabinet-Level Agencies

Cabinet-level agencies other than the Defense Department also have intelligence capabilities. For the most part, these are relatively small and specialized efforts. The Department of Energy, for instance, monitors nuclear weapons programs internationally, through an effort headed by an assistant secretary. The Treasury Department collects information on foreign economic activity, as well as violations of the alcohol, tobacco, and firearms laws. The Federal Bureau of Investigation is not directly involved in foreign intelligence collection, but it works with other agencies to assist in its investigation of treason and other forms of security violations by U.S. or foreign nationals. Finally, the State Department operates the Bureau of Intelligence and Research (INR). Although this agency does not engage in systematic intelligence collection (beyond analyzing routine cable traffic), it does interpret "raw" intelligence from other agencies from the bureaucratic vantage point of the State Department.

This multiplicity of agencies is supposedly coordinated by the DCI and the intelligence community staff. The DCI is essentially "dual-hatted" in that he not only runs one of the competing agencies, but he also coordinates overall community activity. This makes perfect sense in all but a bureaucratic setting: it should avoid unnecessary duplication in effort, including the prospect that two or more agencies might be competing for a given bit of intelligence. In principle, no one disagrees that coordination is desirable.

In practice, however, attaining cooperation in the intelligence field has been rather elusive. Cabinet secretaries who have their own intelligence agencies (like the Defense Department) become protective of them and their control. Since the CIA is one of the competing players, the DCI's objectivity in parsing out cooperative tasks is suspect. Moreover, the heads of the various intelligence agencies report to and are rewarded by their secretaries, not the DCI. Given contradictory instructions by the DCI and the SECDEF, it is not at all difficult for the director of the NSA to decide whose orders to carry out. These kinds of dynamics make reforms aimed at streamlining and coordinating the actions of the intelligence community bureaucratically easier said than done.

## Intelligence and Operations

The intelligence community's activities, especially those of the CIA, are also the cause of some controversy that dates back to the agency's first days. Intelligence organizations can have two basic duties, intelligence and operations, and in different countries some have both, while others have one or the other. Intelligence refers to the gathering, by public or clandestine means, and analysis of information. As such, intelligence is akin to academic research, except that some of the information is secret and is collected by "extracurricular" means. Operations, on the other hand, refers to actions taken clandestinely to affect politics in foreign countries. The most obvious form of operations is covert action, activities undertaken by the U.S. government secretly to affect foreign governments, but in such a way that the target does not recognize American action and the U.S. government can deny culpability (what is known as "plausible denial").

Operations is far more controversial than intelligence because it is done in secret and is obscured not only from the target but also from the American public, thereby stretching standards of accountability. Secrecy is often taken to its extremes. One report (naturally neither confirmed nor denied) has it that during a fire alarm at CIA headquarters (the so-called campus), a number of operations personnel actually wore bags over their heads to obscure their identities from other CIA personnel.

Many of operations' actions are also illegal, both within the United States and the target countries where they occur. Operations can involve activities such as making illegal payments to political groups or individuals, arranging sexual liaisons for foreign government officials and then bribing them by threatening to reveal the actions, and the like.

Operations thus raises some difficult moral dilemmas that have caused many people to conclude that the United States should not engage in covert actions or that at least they should be severely limited. Currently, covert actions are governed by the Intelligence Oversight Act of 1980, which requires a presidential "finding" (a written statement by the president authorizing the activity and justifying it on national security grounds) before covert action can be carried out.

When the CIA was originally formed, the prevailing sentiment was that it would be strictly an intelligence, and not an operational, agency. The vagaries of the developing Cold War quickly intruded on the CIA's purity of mission, however, so that by the end of the 1940s, the CIA was engaged both in intelligence and operations. The most important "directorates" (administrative subdivisions) of the CIA remain the Directorate of Intelligence and the Directorate of Operations. Although these are distinct administrative entities, they retain some overlap, since some intelligence is gathered by what are called extralegal, covert means.

The operations mission has come under assault because with the Cold War ended, many now question the continuing need for such a capability. A major rationale for such a capacity has always been that the other side engaged in covert action and that the United States would be figuratively competing "with one hand tied behind its back" if it lacked a similar capability. Moreover, the geopolitical importance of winning the Cold War meant acting in ways that we would not have otherwise. Effectively, it was not our fault if we violated our own moral and legal values; "the devil (the Soviet Union) made us do it."

With the Soviet threat dissipated, the geopolitical rationale has largely disappeared as well, which strengthens another argument against the operations mission: covert actions can and often do lead to some very bad policy that, if or when revealed, is very embarrassing to the U.S. government. The prime lingering example is the Iran-Contra scandal of the early 1980s.

The series of activities that became known as the Iran-Contra scandal was not so much an intelligence as a covert action disaster. The CIA was implicated in the operation to trade weapons for the release of hostages and to divert the profits from weapons sales to the Nicaraguan Contras only indirectly. There is widespread if not conclusive evidence that DCI William Casey was involved in some of the planning and encouraged Lieutenant Colonel Oliver North, around whom the operation centered. The exact nature and extent of that alleged involvement went to Casey's grave with him when he died during the investigation.

Iran-Contra was notable because it was a covert action that violated the basic rules of reporting such actions. Proper procedures were not followed in rendering a finding for the operation, and the White House activities took great liberties with congressional bans on Contra aid and obstructed congressional attempts to investigate Iran-Contra-related activities. Moreover, as the scandal unraveled, many observers judged it to have been such a hare-brained scheme that it would have been stopped instantly had it been subjected to normal and proper scrutiny.

### *Proposed Changes in the Intelligence Community*

This combination of a changed international environment and the residue of the Iran-Contra scandal would have been enough to make structural reform of the intelligence community likely under any administration in power in 1993. Indeed, legislation parallel to the Goldwater-Nichols Defense Reorganization Act was introduced in 1992 as the Intelligence Reorganization Act. The co-sponsors of that legislation were Senator David Boren (D-Okla.), chair of the Senate Select Committee on Intelligence, and Representative David McCurdy (D-Okla.).

Among its other recommendations to President Clinton, the Carnegie-IIE special report advocates a review of the entire intelligence community. Clinton's strategy of concentrating first on economic issues means that such a review will not receive the new administration's early attention. Since Chairman Boren helped formulate the reform legislation, it will be an active effort.

Although the details of likely structural and policy change were not available at the time of writing, a few modifications are fairly predictable. Structurally, three changes are likely. First, almost certainly a move will be made toward consolidation, in an effort to end duplication and reduce the overall size of the community. Within DOD, for instance, both the size of service and DOD-wide agencies will automatically shrink as they absorb their parts of general defense budget cuts. If a battle line is drawn, it will be between the services, seeking to protect their individual intelligence services, and OSD, attempting to absorb those functions into agencies such as DIA.

The second and third changes relate to rationalizing the system. In order to facilitate a consolidation and assault on duplication, a more hierarchical system must come into existence in fact as well as on paper. Thus, elevation of the DCI and the intelligence community staff to the supervisory role originally envisaged for the DCI is a second likely reform. To accomplish this change, however, the DCI needs to be divorced from day-to-day operation of one of the competing agencies. Removing that hat from the DCI so that he can be an honest broker between agencies and make recommendations for change free of the accusation of parochial self-interest is a third likely change. In the process, a Directorship for the CIA inferior to the DCI will have to be created.

As a matter of policy, the Directorate of Operations within the CIA will likely be greatly reduced in size and mission, if it is not dismantled altogether. President Carter and his DCI, retired Admiral Stansfield Turner, attempted such a program in 1977, but it was roundly criticized because of the supposed need to have a covert, action-oriented capability to combat the Soviets' similar capacity.

The need for such a capability evaporated with the end of the Cold War. Moreover, the Democrats in office tend to be somewhat more liberal and idealistic than the Republicans, which means that it will be more difficult for them to solve some of the moral problems that involvement in operations often creates. The one part of operations that is not likely to be affected, however, is the so-called covert collection of intelligence — the gathering of information from extralegal channels and sources. In addition, it would not be surprising to see a movement toward much greater Third World expertise within CIA. If undertaken, such a reorientation would have great personnel consequences for an agency dominated by Soviet experts.

## The State Department

It is one of Washington's most predictable rituals: an incoming president proclaims that he will look to the State Department to play the lead role in his administration's foreign policy-making and execution, followed, usually in a matter of mere months, by expressions of presidential disillusionment with State's weak leadership of the foreign affairs machinery. The proud institution first headed by Thomas Jefferson has been scorned by recent presidents as being both insufficiently responsive to presidential perspectives (Jimmy Carter thought it too conservative, while Richard Nixon and Ronald Reagan felt it was much too liberal) and simply not sufficiently aggressive in interagency tussles to take the lead role (John Kennedy dismissed the State Department bureaucracy as "a bowl of jelly"). Virtually every recent president has shared the conclusion that State is too sluggish, unimaginative, and bureaucratically timid to truly "take charge" of U.S. foreign policy-making, but none has described it as colorfully as did Franklin Roosevelt. "Dealing with the State Department," he once said, "is like watching an elephant become pregnant; everything is done on a very high level, there's a lot of commotion, and it takes twenty-two months for anything to happen."

It was not always so. Prior to the United States' emergence as a world power, the State Department was at the center of both determining and carrying out the nation's limited international role. Even during the first half of the twentieth century, when the United States had attained the rank of major power, but prior to the protracted struggle of the Cold War, State retained its pride of place as the preeminent cabinet agency and the hub of foreign policy-making. The post–World War II erosion of its influence, at least in relative terms, and the State-bashing that routinely occurs among students and practitioners of U.S. foreign policy reflect important changes in the nation's policy-making process. However, since much of State's diminished stature is due to the way the institution conducts itself, first we need to explore some fundamental matters of organizational structure, behavior, and institutional culture. Then we will attempt the more ambitious task of accounting for the diminished role of today's State Department in the foreign policy-making process.

## Organization

Like the rest of the federal government, the State Department has grown exponentially over the years. The first secretary of state presided over a "bureaucracy" consisting of five clerks, one translator, two messengers, and two overseas diplomatic missions, then called legations. In contrast, today's State Department is housed in a ponderous eight-story building that sprawls across 12 acres in northwest Washington's "Foggy Bottom," named for the area's once-swampy topography. Whether measured by budget (in excess of $1.5 billion), employees (over 24,000), or overseas embassies, consulates, and missions (nearly 300), the State Department of the 1990s bears no resemblance to the department that Jefferson presided over in the 1790s. In some ways, however, these numbers are misleading. Today's State Department may spend more money hiring more people to do more things than ever before, but it remains the *smallest* of all the cabinet-level agencies. Its budget amounts to only 6 percent of the Pentagon's, and its employees number fewer than 1 percent of the Pentagon's.

*Secretary of State* Organizationally, the State Department is a conventional hierarchy built atop an array of geographic and functional bureaus. At the head of the organizational pyramid is, of course, the secretary of state. As a presidential appointee, the secretary often finds himself caught between the competing pressures of his loyalty to the president and of his role as an advocate of the department's institutional perspective within administration councils. Although the two roles are not always mutually exclusive, they frequently are. Secretaries who become too closely identified with their agency's outlook run the risk of becoming suspect as a member of the president's inner circle. This is a particular danger to secretaries who serve in administrations committed to the collegial style of decision-making, as was the case with Kennedy, Carter, and now Clinton. Alternatively, secretaries who are seen as too closely identified with White House perspectives run the risk of eroding the morale and authority of the

State Department's career professionals, thus weakening the very organization they were appointed to lead.

Alexander Haig, Ronald Reagan's first secretary of state, exemplifies the pitfalls of the first approach. Despite his gruff public demeanor, Haig was a strong advocate within the administration for the moderate, pragmatic policies typically favored by career diplomats on issues such as how to deal with the Soviets and how to respond to leftist pressures in Central America. He developed working relationships with State's career professionals and served as a vigorous protagonist of his agency's perspectives. His relative moderation put him at odds with the more devoutly conservative ideologues surrounding Reagan, however. This stance, coupled with Haig's insistence on his own and his department's position as first among equals in the policy-making process, assured the briefness of his tenure as secretary of state: it lasted a mere 18 months.

The second approach, stressing the secretary's personal role as a member of the presidential team to the detriment of his leadership of the department's bureaucracy, was exemplified by John Foster Dulles in the Eisenhower years, Dean Rusk during the Kennedy-Johnson years, and Henry Kissinger in Nixon's aborted second term and Ford's brief presidency. In each instance, the secretary of state, as an individual, exerted considerable influence in molding presidential decision-making on international matters. However, each also remained aloof from the professional corps of career diplomats who comprise the State Department's greatest resource. Instead, they preferred to rely on a small circle of aides whose careers revolved around their personal loyalty to the secretary rather than to the institutional perspective of the State Department. A strong secretary of state, then, does not necessarily mean a strengthened role for the Department of State. As often as not, it leads to precisely the opposite: a leaderless, ignored, and demoralized institution.

Immediately below the secretary is the deputy secretary, who ordinarily functions as the department's principal day-to-day manager. The two most recent secretaries of state — Laurence Eagleburger in the waning months of the Bush administration and Warren Christopher in the Clinton administration — previously served as deputy secretary and thus assumed the top job with an intimate familiarity of the State Department machinery. At the third tier are four undersecretaries of state: one each for political affairs, economic and agricultural affairs, international security affairs, and management. At a comparable rank is the counselor, who serves as the department's principal legal adviser.

Next in rank are the assistant secretaries, and they numbered 24 in the Bush administration. Sometimes wielding considerable influence in the policy process, each assistant secretary directs the department's principal administrative units: its bureaus.

*The Bureaus*  Of the 24 bureaus, 18 are referred to as functional; that is, they concentrate on a particular function rather than a specific part of the world. Among the more prominent functional bureaus in the policy process are the Bureau of Human Rights and Humanitarian Affairs, which prepares an influential annual report to Congress assessing human rights practices around the world; the Bureau of Intelligence and Research (INR), which analyzes intelligence collected by other agencies, thus giving State some in-house capacity for independent intelligence analysis; the Bureau of Legislative Affairs, which is State's liaison with a Congress that is more involved in foreign policy-making than ever before; and the Bureau of Public Affairs, which reflects the department's belated recognition that as foreign policy has become increasingly politicized and democratized, the State Department must maintain a constant public relations effort to help its views receive public attention comparable to that given more aggressive bureaucratic rivals and private interest groups.

Of greater influence in policy-making, however, are the geographic bureaus (Europe and Canada, East Asia and the Pacific, South Asia, the Near East, the Americas, and Africa). The regional assistant secretaries frequently attain public visibility rivaling that of the secretary himself and often exert considerable influence in formulating U.S. foreign policy toward their area. During the Reagan administration, for example, two assistant secretaries virtually dominated executive branch policy-making in their regions of expertise: Elliot Abrams, who was the principal architect of a new hard-line policy against leftist movements in Central America and the Caribbean, and Chester Crocker, assistant secretary for African affairs, who was responsible for the controversial policy of "constructive engagement" with the white-minority regime of South Africa.

Within the geographic bureaus are the true custodians of State Department expertise: the numerous desk officers and country directors who both manage the day-to-day relations between the United States and their nation of specialty and possess the specialized knowledge and analytical insights on which sound policy-making depends. While the assistant secretaries and the officers above them are presidential appointees, and hence are drawn from a variety of professions as well as from the ranks of State's career professionals, the desk officers within the regional bureaus are nearly always Foreign Service officers (FSOs), the nation's much-criticized and underutilized corps of professional diplomats. Shortly, we will look at the problematic character of the distinct

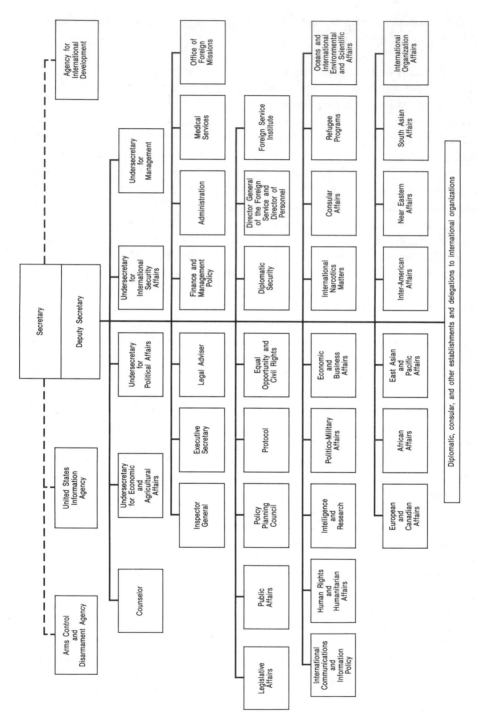

**FIGURE 3.4    Department of State**

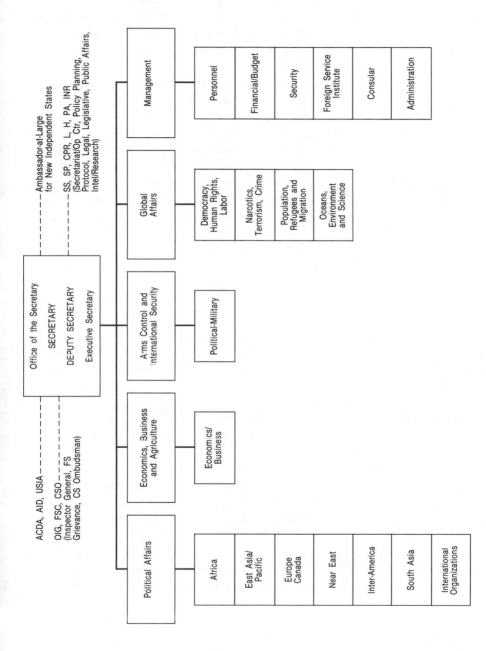

**FIGURE 3.5    Proposed Organization of the State Department**

95

Foreign Service culture, which has been routinely denounced in a steady stream of academic and government studies. Here, however, we simply note that the talented men and women of the Foreign Service conduct the routine tasks of diplomacy and sometimes play a role in molding U.S. foreign policy. The State Department organization described above is shown in Figure 3.4 (see page 94).

Warren Christopher's first act as Secretary of State was to reorganize and simplify this structure, as depicted in Figure 3.5 (page 95). In an undated "Message for All State Department Employees" issued as he took his oath of office, Christopher moved to realign the department. Five Undersecretaries—for political affairs, economics, business and agriculture, arms control and international security, global affairs, and management—would become his "principal advisers." Positions would be rearranged to create "new focal points," eliminate "redundancies," and reduce "excessive layering to streamline information flow and decisionmaking."

The reorganization parallels that done by Aspin and does result in two agencies with similar structures. The major innovation is the establishment of an undersecretary for global affairs, under whose auspices a whole series of activities associated with the post–Cold War world will be housed—human rights, refugees and migration, and environment, for instance. This impressive array explains why a former U.S. senator, Tim Wirth of Colorado, would be attracted to an undersecretary-level position. Another innovation is the undersecretary for economics, business and agriculture, reflecting the Clinton administration's emphasis on global economic competitiveness.

*Embassies, Consulates, and Missions*　Before leaving the topic of organizational structure, some mention needs to be made of the nearly 300 embassies, consulates, and missions the United States maintains abroad. U.S. embassies are the principal locus of conducting U.S. foreign policy overseas. Each is headed by an ambassador named by the president. Ordinarily, about two-thirds of all ambassadors are selected from the ranks of FSOs. The rest are political appointees, who, as we have observed earlier, range in quality from the distinguished to the unqualified, who are usually—and not coincidentally—wealthy campaign donors. In July 1990 President Bush strengthened the authority of ambassadors overseas, so that today they are, in theory, at least, in charge of all executive branch U.S. offices and personnel in the country to which they are accredited, except for military personnel. The rise of instantaneous communications and jet travel may have diminished the significance of ambassadors, but they remain important both as symbolic representatives abroad and as head of the U.S. "country team." Their information-gathering, analysis, and reporting of local trends and thinking are indispensable inputs into Washington's policy-making process.

### Foreign Policy Role

The much-noted erosion of the State Department's role in the foreign policy-making process is a phenomenon that some applaud and others lament, but one that few deny. Like an ailing patient, the State Department is constantly probed and examined by a legion of scholars and journalists, all hoping to uncover the malaise that has allegedly drained the grand old institution of its vigor and left it a limp and fragile player in the rough-and-tumble game of Washington policy-making. Three factors may explain State's loss of primacy in foreign policy-making: (1) the rise of security, economic, humanitarian, and environmental issues that have joined State's traditional preoccupation with diplomacy as central components of foreign policy, and the related rise of institutional players with special expertise in these policy domains; (2) the trend toward personal presidential dominance of foreign policy-making and conduct, and the related centralization of policy-making in the White House-based National Security Council (NSC) staff; and (3) some deeply ingrained features of the Foreign Service's culture which tend to isolate FSOs from other bureaucratic players and limit their influence in interagency dealings.

First, as we saw in Chapter 1, our concept of foreign policy has been stretched beyond its traditional preoccupation with state-to-state diplomacy. A host of issues that used to be regarded as purely domestic in character are now properly understood to include an international dimension. The drug problem, for example, requires both domestic efforts to reduce demand and international efforts to reduce supply. Similarly, environmental protection is increasingly recognized as a problem that transcends national boundaries and demands international coordination. Furthermore, it is now a commonplace to note that the United States' economic well-being is closely bound up with international factors such as reducing trade barriers, coordinating monetary policies among the leading industrial nations, and providing a measure of hope and stability to the peoples of the Third World where much of the planet's natural resources are located.

As these and other "intermestic" issues have joined the traditional diplomatic concerns of the State Department, they have brought in their wake a proliferating roster of executive agencies with special expertise and institutional stakes in the shaping of policy affecting "their" policy domains. The Commerce Department, for example, is now much more involved in promoting the United States' economic interests than was the case when the United States was less dependent on international trade and capital flows. Similarly, agencies as diverse as the Energy Department, the Department of Agriculture, the Treasury, the Drug Enforcement Agency, and the Environmental Protection Agency insist that they be included in the foreign policy-making process whenever their policy domains are under discussion. Clearly, the biggest institutional challenger to State Department primacy in foreign policy-making is the Department of Defense. As noted earlier in the chapter, the rise of the protracted Cold War struggle brought to the fore a new emphasis on national security policy, which in turn opened the door for aggressive Pentagon planners to quickly catch up to — and in some ways surpass — the influence of the State Department.

Despite the vast changes we will hardly return to a simpler world that permits a tidy distinction between domestic and international issues. Therefore, it follows that the State Department seems destined to accept a policy-making climate in which it is just one of many bureaucratic players. Many of these players have demonstrated an aggressiveness and political adroitness that leaves Foggy Bottom traditionalists nostalgic for the good old days when everyone just knew that *real* foreign policy was the province of the State Department.

Second, as discussed in detail in Chapter 2, with the rise of the United States as a world power, presidents have increasingly sought to establish their personal dominance of foreign policy-making. The reasons for this trend range from the personal and petty (international statecraft is dramatic and exciting in a way that, say, determining price support levels for agricultural commodities is not) to the high-minded. (In the atomic age, the stakes of international politics are so great that presidents feel a heightened sense of responsibility to assume greater personal direction of the nation's foreign policy.) The creation of the National Security Council (NSC) in 1947 greatly strengthened White House dominance of the overall policy-making process, permitting presidents to integrate more coherently the views and expertise of the various agencies and, in the course of doing so, supplant State's traditional role as the chief foreign policy-making institution in the executive branch.

Third, a peculiar culture permeates the world of the Foreign Service. Without doubt, the 9,000 men and women who comprise the Foreign Service are a remarkably talented elite. Since the passage of the Rogers Act in 1924, the State Department has developed a world-class corps of professional diplomats who are hired and promoted on the basis of merit. Entry into the Foreign Service is gained through an intensely competitive process. (In a recent year, 17,000 people took the rigorous written examination, of whom only 2,500 passed. Through a grueling day-long series of oral examinations and participation in group simulations, the pool of candidates was winnowed down to 600, of whom 200 were granted entry into the exclusive ranks of the Foreign Service.) In addition, the department's "up or out" personnel system requires that FSOs earn promotion to successively higher ranks within a limited period of time or be "selected out" of the Service. As we can attest, individual FSOs are among the most intelligent, articulate, and analytically sophisticated members of the foreign policy community. Collectively, however, they manage the remarkable feat of adding up to less than the sum of their parts. As a group, their influence in formulating policy is typically well below what one would expect in light of their individual excellence. To understand why this is so, we need to delve into the much-studied phenomenon of the FSO culture.

*The Foreign Service*  Once admitted to the elite circle of the Foreign Service, its members are surrounded and conditioned by an ingrained set of institutional values and attitudes. These values and attitudes strengthen the internal cohesion within the Foreign Service, but, at the same time, they also erect a psychic distance between FSOs and other participants in the policy-making process. The very elitism of the Foreign Service gives rise to an unusually high degree of resistance—even disdain—toward the views of outsiders. Foreign affairs specialists who are not members of the FSO's exclusive club (academics would be an example) often find that not only are their insights not welcomed by FSOs but also that their very presence in State Department circles (for example, as members of the Policy Planning Staff) is opposed. While many professions inculcate a strong sense of identification with the group and a heightened sense of separateness from those outside the group, this tendency appears to be especially pronounced in the insular and exclusionary culture of the Foreign Service.

Foreign Service Officers have also been long noted for their tendency to remain generalists. Similarly, they are disinclined to embrace the more rigorous and formal methods of social science analysis that have been widely adopted within the intelligence community and the DOD. Fully aware of their unusually high intellectual capabilities, FSOs retain an exaggerated confidence that a broadly educated generalist can do just about any foreign affairs job. This institutional resistance to subject-matter specialization and the more advanced forms of social science analysis account for the broad perception that, despite the impressive gifts of individual FSOs, the State Department's analyses of world affairs are typically less sophisticated and rigorous than those of rival agencies, especially the Pentagon and the CIA.

The FSO culture stresses caution, an aversion to confrontation, and the appearance, at least, of undue timidity in advancing controversial policy proposals. Playing down differences, seeking common ground, and avoiding open confrontation are simply inherent in the diplomatic enterprise. The kind of personal subtlety and tendency to compromise that often facilitate international conciliation can prove to be a liability in the elbows-out world of interagency Washington struggles to define U.S. foreign policy. Moreover, the State Department is one of the few cabinet-level agencies that lacks a domestic political constituency. Thus, it is an easy target for the scapegoating bullying of demagogues such as the late Senator Joseph McCarthy (R-Wis.), who in the early 1950s ruined the careers of numerous loyal FSOs and intimidated countless others through his sensational and utterly unfounded accusations of procommunist treason within the Foreign Service. Long after McCarthy's death, his legacy remained in the form of an extraordinary degree of caution and a tangled system of cross-clearances. As a result, new ideas from the Foreign Service rank-and-file emerge at a glacial pace. Finally, the intensely competitive nature of advancement within the Service leaves many FSOs exceedingly cautious about making waves or advocating unorthodox views for fear that doing so will harm their all-important performance evaluations. Conformity, caution, and a disinclination to speak out on behalf of new or unpopular ideas are thus innate characteristics of the FSO culture.

Another factor that holds the FSOs back is the perception that they are haughty and arrogant. Not all, and probably not even most, FSOs could fairly be described this way, but the tendency to project a sense of social and intellectual superiority is sufficiently ingrained among them that many of the more down-to-earth participants in foreign policy simply dislike them.

Taken together, these four traits—resistance to outsiders, preference for generalists and for intuitive analysis, inordinate caution, and too-frequent imagery of snobbery—define much of the institutional culture that influences the thinking and behavior of FSOs. Most outside observers agree that these norms and values are simply self-defeating. But while organizational change can be effected through simple edict, cultural change occurs slowly. Until the Foreign Service takes independent steps to cast off its outdated and self-defeating culture, it will remain a remarkably talented corps of men and women with diminished actual influence on policy-making. As noted in Chapter 2, President Clinton's national security adviser, Anthony Lake, is an ex-FSO who has long argued that the views and expertise of the Foreign Service should play a greater role in shaping policy than it has in the post–World War II era. While influential friends like Lake can help the State Department recapture its former pride of place as the central institution in the United States' dealings with the world, State's career diplomats can still best help themselves by aggressively reforming their own peculiar institutional culture.

# The Economic Agencies

Improving the U.S. economy was the core of the Clinton presidential campaign. Indeed, in the transition period between the election and his inauguration, economic matters dominated the visible aspects of Clinton's actions. The "cluster" of economic appointments, centering around the new Economic Council, were his first appointments, and the two-day December 1992 economic summit in Little Rock was likened to a graduate seminar in economics.

While Clinton's primary concern is the domestic economy, international economic matters will no doubt form the cornerstone of his overall foreign policy because, first, economic issues are among the most intermestic of all foreign policy areas. It is hard to imagine a major domestic economic decision that does not have international ramifications, and vice versa.

Second, the health of the American economy depends largely on the state of the world economy. The recession that created the conditions that helped elect Clinton was global, and the U.S. recession was just one case of that global slump. Any recovery of the U.S. economy requires recovery among the Group of Seven (G7) nations. This leads to a third reason: for the recovery to be complete, these countries (the United States, Canada, Japan, Great Britain, France, Germany, and Italy) must become primary markets for U.S. goods and services.

## The Little Rock Seminar: New Economic Themes

The themes sounded at the Little Rock seminar also suggest a heavy emphasis on economic themes that have an acknowledged heavily intermestic content. The group assembled, which was hardly representative of the spectrum of economic policy opinion, sounded several themes that are often elucidated by those who favor a more active U.S., including federal, intrusion into international economic affairs. The bellwether of these themes is Secretary of Labor Robert Reich, who has been a prominent spokesman for these themes in the past. Three of the most important themes — competitiveness, emphasis on high technology, and industrial policy — are interrelated and all lead toward the global economy.

*Economic Competitiveness* Economic competitiveness is an inherently international economic concept. Underlying this theme is the notion that U.S. prosperity requires greater competitiveness against other national economies. Advocates point out that the United States has systematically lost the competitive edge in a number of productive areas, from consumer electronics to automobiles and conceivably to aeronautics, biotechnical products, and mainframe computers in the future.

The issues surrounding competitiveness are complex and contentious. They also combine domestic and international policy responses if the United States is to reestablish its competitive edge. Among domestic policy priorities is a revival of U.S. education, especially in the areas of science, mathematics, and engineering. In these subject areas, among the student populations of the most developed countries, American students now rank among the lowest in standardized tests. Another domestic policy area, which is also part of industrial policy, involves tax breaks (subsidies, deductions) provided for engaging in research and development or for collaboration between industry and education.

Internationally, it is necessary to protect U.S. "intellectual capital." Specifically, care must be taken that scientific discoveries and the like do not find their way into foreign manufacture before they are commercialized in the United States. This capital has sometimes been lost because of the absence of restrictions on the international transportation of ideas. In other situations, the United States has simply given away technologies. For instance, the Sony Walkman was originally designed by a U.S. firm which discarded the idea because it did not believe Americans would buy small radios with tinny sound systems. Sony reasoned differently; the rest is history.

*Emphasis on High Technology*   This theme is largely the product of the last decade and a half. The so-called high-technology or Third Industrial Revolution is the result of remarkable progress in three related areas: knowledge generation, knowledge dissemination, and derivative technologies, as noted in Chapter 1. Progress in knowledge generation is the product of advances in computing which allows greater and greater amounts of information to be processed with increasing speed, thereby accelerating exponentially the amount of knowledge that can be generated.

Progress in dissemination is the result of the telecommunications revolution in areas such as satellite transmission and fiber optics, which allow enormous amounts of data to be shared worldwide, thereby increasing communications and commercial and scientific interactions. Finally, the first two areas have helped spin off and accelerate a number of derivative technologies in areas as diverse as fiber optics, materials science, biotechnology, avionics, and computer-aided design/computer-aided manufacturing (CAD/CAM).

Moreover, all three of these areas, as we have said, are interactive. Advances in computing facilitate better designs of satellites and progress in materials that are incorporated into the next generation of computers.

Advances in telecommunications promote the interchange of scientific information between scientists and engineers at remote locations, thereby speeding up scientific progress. Fiber optics, a major derivative technology, speeds the transmission of accurate information, including such things as the use of fiber optics networks transmitting multiple television programs (making the telephone company a competitor of cable television systems).

High technological proficiency (or its absence) is crucial to international economic competitiveness. The key aspect is commercialization of high technology. In other words, in order to maximize its position in the world economy, the United States must not only lead in the high technological areas tied to basic research and science, but it must also be at the forefront of realizing the market potential of discovery and getting those technologies to market. This has become an area of American disadvantage that has caused invidious comparisons between the United States and Japan: the United States leads in scientific breakthroughs, but the Japanese are first at discovering and exploiting the commercial potentials of those technologies.

Restoring the commercial edge in areas of American scientific advantage is crucial to U.S. competitiveness, at least partially because high technological advantage and its commercial applications mark the cutting edge of knowledge and production in the future. The Clinton administration, through apostles such as Reich, seems to recognize this fact; their vehicle for doing so is industrial policy, another theme enunciated at Little Rock.

*Industrial Policy*   Industrial policy calls for the government, through incentives and disincentives, to create public policy that will move private entrepreneurial activity in directions that will maximize competitiveness and profitability. The idea is controversial. Republicans (especially the conservatives) oppose government involvement in the private sector, arguing that such intervention is harmful because private entrepreneurs will make better business decisions than government functionaries. As a result, there was no industrial policy during the Reagan and Bush presidencies. Industrial policy advocates (once again led by Reich) retaliate that the United States is the only major industrialized country without such a policy.

The Clinton administration will attack this area through two strategies, one primarily domestic, and the other more international. The first strategy is to urge collaboration in areas specified for emphasis. Part of this collaboration will be among firms operating in the same areas, relaxing antitrust regulations and encouraging a pooling of resources, in areas such as electronics. Another part of this collaboration is to encourage more advanced cooperation between corporations and research scientists largely located in colleges and universities. Here the government's role is to serve as facilitating agent through stratagems such as tax incentives and funding for research in designated areas where commercial applications seem promising and where U.S. preeminence can be established.

This leads to the second strategy, the targeting of specific areas where U.S. commercial advantage can be extrapolated from basic scientific advantage. In its earliest statements, the Clinton-Gore administration promoted environmental engineering, which would prepare U.S. firms to be at the forefront in producing and operating systems designed for environmental cleanup. To this end, it announced its intention to share research findings sponsored by the Department of Energy and Environmental Protection Agency with firms designing commercial cleanup systems and to create tax incentives for firms entering the field.

As noted earlier, another announced application is in the area of defense-related research, whereby systems with both military and commercial applications would be favored over those with only military outcomes. Funding aerospace and nautical research that can lead to better airlift and sealift capability (a Clinton defense priority) and commercial airplanes and ships is an example.

In order to implement these changes, Clinton promised institutional change. Having campaigned on the promise of forming an "economic security council" to parallel the National Security Council, he moved quickly during the transition to form an Economic Council and to create the position of economic adviser, which he filled with Robert Rubin. The idea of the Economic Council was endorsed by the Carnegie-IIE study, which also supported the idea of a third Domestic Council to deal with strictly internal concerns.

The purpose of the Economic Council is clear: to bring order and coherence to economic policy in both its domestic and international dimensions. One might well ask why the council has become necessary, given the obvious importance of economic matters to the national well-being. Several overlapping reasons appear to have contributed.

First and foremost, for most of the Cold War period, the problem did not seem pressing. The United States' position was preeminent until the mid-1970s, and deterioration was so gradual that it was not widely recognized until the mid-1980s, when the competitiveness issue began to appear widely in professional economic discussions. Second, administrations tended to be more fixated on national security concerns phrased in military and geopolitical terms. When the Soviet threat was present, this approach was appropriate. As the Soviets began to falter, however, definitions of national security began to expand to include economic issues as well.

Third, the bureaucratic nature of the problem stunted coordination. The primary cabinet-level actors, the Departments of Treasury, Commerce, and Agriculture, were all more clearly focused on the domestic aspects of their responsibilities. International economic matters were relegated to subcabinet officials within each. Until the Omnibus Trade and Competitiveness Act of 1988 specified the United States trade representative (USTR) as the official responsible for trade policy formulation and implementation, there was no clear symbol within the government. Moreover, the USTR did not have cabinet rank; rather, she or he served as the equivalent of an ambassador with a relatively small staff.

Fourth, during their 12-year ascendancy, the Republican administrations were reluctant to enter this field forcefully. This attitude was, of course, an extension of the general conservative reluctance to involve the government in the economy. President Reagan did propose a Department of International Trade and Industry (DITI) in 1983, but this clone of the Japanese Ministry of International Trade and Industry (MITI) proved to be stillborn in Republican circles and was quietly dropped.

The Clinton administration is more focused on economic policy in all its aspects. The great symbol of this commitment—the campaign office reminder "The economy, stupid"—reflects these priorities. They will likely come together and be focused on the Economic Council.

The Council is in its formative stages; both its composition and role are likely to evolve with time. At its core certainly will be the new economic adviser, who will serve as convener along with the president. The traditional foreign economic policy actors—the secretaries of treasury, commerce, and agriculture (historically in that order of importance) and the USTR—will clearly play important roles. If the Carnegie-IIE study is any guide, additional actors will include the vice president, the director of the Office of Management and Budget (OMB), the secretary of state, the secretary of labor, the chair of the Council of Economic Advisers (CEA), the secretary of energy, and the head of the Environmental Protection Agency.

This is a much larger and hence potentially more unwieldy body than the National Security Council, and its evolution is not clear. If convened as a whole, it may serve as a continuation of the Little Rock meeting; President Clinton clearly relishes the role of seminar leader. For formulating concrete policy, it may well break down into functional clusters that add and subtract members; the secretary of education would be relevant to some domestic policy areas but not trade, for instance. Moreover, a subcabinet working-level group made up of deputies of the major actors will come into being. Such a structure would parallel the Reagan-Bush National Security Council organization (discussed in Chapter 5) and is also part of the Carnegie-IIE recommendations.

International economic policy will likely be the focal point of policy and structural innovation during the Clinton presidency. Clinton brings a level of interest, enthusiasm, and expertise to the economic area that is unique among recent presidents. His direction and success are not entirely within his grasp, however. As an integral part of the international economy, the United States' progress cannot be achieved unilaterally. Therefore, his success in his dealings with the G7 will be pivotal. At the same time, structural economic problems such as the deficit, health care, and the nation's infrastructure are long-term, intractable problems that cannot be dismissed easily, a point he has made repeatedly. Finally, the philosophy he brings to economic matters is not universally accepted. If the economy does not respond to his medicine, conservative opponents of areas such as industrial policy will be quick to attack his policy and structural innovations.

## SUGGESTED READINGS

Carnegie Endowment for International Peace-Institute for International Economics. *Special Report: Policymaking for a New Era*. Washington: Carnegie Endowment, 1992.

Clark, Duncan. *American Defense and Foreign Policy Institutions: Toward a Solid Foundation*. New York: Harper & Row, 1989.

Cohen, Stephen D. *The Making of United States International Economic Policy*. 3rd ed. New York: Praeger Publishers, 1988.

Gilpin, Robert. *The Political Economy of International Relations*. Princeton, N.J.: Princeton University Press, 1987.

Johnson, Loch K. *America's Secret Power: The CIA in a Democratic Society*. New York: Oxford University Press, 1989.

Lairson, Thomas D., and David Skidmore. *International Political Economy: The Struggle for Power and Wealth*. New York: Harcourt, Brace, Jovanovich, 1993.

Richelson, Jeffrey T. *The U.S. Intelligence Community*. 2nd ed. Cambridge, Mass.: Ballinger Books, 1989.

Rosati, Jerel A. *The Politics of United States Foreign Policy*. New York: Harcourt, Brace, Jovanovich, 1993.

Rosecrance, Richard. *The Rise of the Trading State: Commerce and Conquest in the Modern World*. New York: Basic Books, 1986.

Rubin, Barry. *Secrets of State: The State Department and the Struggle over U.S. Foreign Policy*. New York: Oxford University Press, 1985.

Smith, Hedrick. *The Power Game: How Washington Works*. New York: Ballantine Books, 1988.

Turner, Stansfield. *Secrecy and Diplomacy: The CIA in Transition*. Boston: Houghton Mifflin, 1985.

# CHAPTER 4

# The Legislative Branch

The second branch of the federal government with major foreign and defense responsibilities, the U.S. Congress is unique among the world's legislative bodies. Congress has broad policy-making powers and a constantly changing relationship with the executive branch.

## The Uniqueness of the American Congress

No other legislative assembly on earth quite compares with the United States Congress. Nearly all other democracies have opted for the British-style parliamentary model, under which executive leaders are chosen by the legislature and are accountable to it. Though theoretically enjoying legislative supremacy, parliaments in fact are typically dominated by the strong executives who arise within their ranks.

In contrast, the United States is one of the few democracies to have adopted a separation of powers system. Under this system, the powers of government are first split apart and then constitutionally distributed among the three branches of the federal government. Originally conceived as a means of warding off the potential tyranny that could result if any one leader or group of leaders consolidated the coercive capabilities available to modern governments, the separation of powers system has two principal consequences for U.S. foreign policy-making in our time.

First, it creates a legislature with an extraordinary amount of independent policy-making authority. No other legislature plays such a crucial role in determining foreign policy. Some constitutional scholars believe that the Founding Fathers actually intended Congress to be the dominant policy-making organ. Congress, after all, was the first branch treated in the Constitution (in Article I), and considerably more detail is given to enumerating its powers than is given to the executive branch (in Article II). Other scholars doubt that the Founding Fathers necessarily intended to elevate the legislature above the executive. However, no one doubts that they set about to establish a vigorous legislative body that would enjoy comparable status to the president in determining the nation's international stance.

Second, that fragmentation of authority between the two elected branches can produce the phenomenon known as *gridlock*, which is the result of policy disagreements between Congress and the president. When the two branches are unable to achieve a working agreement on the nation's proper international role and interests, the separation of powers system makes governmental stalemate and policy paralysis an ever-present possibility. Gridlock is especially likely to occur when partisan divisions intensify the institutional rivalry inherent in a separation of powers structure. This problem has been acute in recent decades, which have seen the White House in Republican hands for the past quarter-century (except for Jimmy Carter's single term), while the Democrats have controlled the House of Representatives continually since 1954 and, with exceptions such as a six-year stint in the early 1980s, have dominated the Senate as well. The election of Bill Clinton, a Democrat, in 1992 augurs well for a sharp diminution of interbranch gridlock and for a new era of executive-legislative cooperation. In addition, the extraordinarily high number of new members elected to Congress in 1992 (110 representatives and 12 new senators) means that fewer legislators were personally conditioned by the sometimes bitter interbranch "blame game" between Congress and the executive of the Reagan-Bush years.

Although Congress is constitutionally empowered to wield vigorous authority in making foreign policy, it has not always done so. As noted in Chapter 2, American history has witnessed repeated oscillations between periods of executive and congressional dominance of the policy process. As a broad generalization, from the 1930s to the 1970s, Congress often deferred to presidential leadership in dealing with the crises of the Great Depression, World War II, and the Cold War. During the first quarter-century of the Cold War, Congress was generally content to follow the foreign policy course set by the president in the belief that the nation could not afford to appear divided and irresolute in the face of a protracted global crisis. Indeed, it was a member of Congress, Senator J. William Fulbright (D-Ark.), who in 1961 wrote:

> I wonder whether the time has not arrived, or indeed already has passed, when we must give the Executive a measure of power in the conduct of world affairs that we have hitherto jealously withheld. . . . It is my contention that for the existing requirements of American foreign policy we have hoppled the President by too niggardly a grant of power.

Just 13 years later, however, the same Senator Fulbright was voicing a vastly different message:

I believe that the Presidency has become a dangerously powerful office, more urgently in need of reform than any other institution in American government. . . . Whatever may be said against Congress—that it is slow, obstreperous, inefficient or behind the times—there is one thing to be said for it: It poses no threat to the liberties of the American people. (Quoted in Brown, 1985.)

Fulbright's pronounced change of heart captures in microcosm the sea change of opinion that had washed over Congress in the late 1960s and early 1970s. What caused this sudden congressional reassertion of its place in the constitutional order? We have already seen the principal reason in Chapter 2. As noted, the decade bounded by Lyndon Johnson's escalation of the war in Vietnam in 1965 and Richard Nixon's resignation in disgrace in 1974 was a time of torment and bitterness for the American people. The protracted agony of Vietnam coupled with the White House criminality of Watergate gave the nation back-to-back disasters that eroded the moral legitimacy of the presidency. Long after Johnson and Nixon had left Washington, their legacy of presidential failure lingered, puncturing the myth of superior presidential wisdom. From that bitter decade came a broadly renewed rediscovery of and respect for the constitutional design of policy codetermination by the two coequal elected branches.

Added to the diminished luster of the presidency were other developments which, taken together, produced a much more assertive Congress in the foreign policy-making process. These developments included a large infusion of young congressmen and senators in the mid-1970s, the weakening of party discipline, the erosion of the seniority system, the proliferation and expanded authority of subcommittees, and the growth in congressional staff. All these changes culminated in the reality we confront today: a Congress unwilling to submit meekly to the president's lead in defining U.S. foreign policy. It is a reality that some applaud and many curse, but it is a reality not likely to change anytime soon.

## Congressional Procedures and Committees

Although we speak of Congress in the singular, it is, of course, a bicameral body consisting of a House of Representatives, comprising 435 members who represent comparably sized districts and serve two-year terms, and a Senate, consisting of two senators from each state serving six-year terms. As a result of their size as well as the wave of internal democratization that swept Congress in the mid-1970s, both chambers are highly decentralized bodies. While most students of U.S. policy-making are familiar with the decentralization of congressional authority over the past two decades, it should be noted that the House of Representatives has recently adopted new rules that greatly strengthen the speaker's authority over committee chairpersons. The first public demonstration of the speaker's enhanced position occurred early in 1993, when Speaker Tom Foley (D-Wash.) removed Congressman Dave McCurdy (D-Okla.) as chairman of the House Intelligence Committee because of McCurdy's unseemly efforts to undercut his fellow Democratic congressmen in a futile attempt to be named President Clinton's secretary of defense. But the McCurdy case is the exception that underscores the general rule of congressional decentralization.

The fragmentation of authority in Congress expands the opportunities for individual legislators to affect foreign policy issues and opens the body to a wide spectrum of opinion, but it also creates additional obstacles in forging coalitions large enough to pass legislation. Whereas 20 years ago, power in Congress was concentrated in the hands of a small number of powerful committee chairpersons chosen through seniority, today's chairs are less able to crack the whip and demand compliance by their more junior colleagues. The resulting opening up of the legislative process means that all views will be heard, but it also indicates that majorities may be even harder to forge. When we add to that the fact that, in order to enact a law, both the House and the Senate must adopt identical measures, the legislative process can seem distressingly unwieldy.

Despite their caricature as corrupt and out of touch, most members of Congress are intelligent, hard-working, honest, and well informed of the views of their constitutents. The very diversity of those constituent views, however, can make legislative agreement elusive. Unsurprisingly, a congressman from Pittsburgh will be more likely to seek protectionist relief for the nation's (and his district's) troubled steel industry, whereas a congressman from rural Iowa will argue against trade protectionism, in part because his district depends heavily on export markets for its agricultural products. The constant turbulence of competing outlooks is the essence of legislative life. It is not neat, it sometimes leads to deadlock, but it captures the inherent tugging and hauling among diverse points of view that is the essence of democratic life.

### Organizing Mechanisms

A measure of order and coherence is imposed on these inherently fractious bodies through the organizing mechanisms of political parties and legislative committees. The Democratic majority in each chamber chooses its majority leader and an array of lieutenants to oversee the flow of legislation and attempt to unite party members behind major bills. The

Republican minority does the same. Although the formal discipline of the United States' political parties has eroded over the years, each party has become more internally homogeneous and readily identified with certain policies. Twenty years ago both parties were divided between their own liberal and more conservative wings. Today, the Democratic party is more consistently the home of political liberals and moderates, while the Republicans are overwhelmingly conservative to moderate. This growth in programmatic coherence within each party gives form and substance to an otherwise fragmented Congress.

Another organizing mechanism in the House and Senate is the system of committees that are organized by subject matter and ordinarily have the most important influence in determining the fate of legislative proposals. About 10,000 bills and resolutions are submitted to Congress each year. Of these, fewer than 10 percent clear all the legislative hurdles to become law. The committee system makes Congress's workload possible. By dividing the vast number of proposals among its standing committees (21 in the House and 16 in the Senate), bills are given closer attention and members are able to develop a degree of policy expertise that comes with specialization. Since the early 1970s the work once performed by full committees is increasingly being done by the proliferating number of subcommittees. This development was necessitated by the growing complexity of policy proposals and the demand of junior members to expand the policy-making opportunities within Congress. Today, about 90 percent of legislative hearings occur before subcommittees. Similarly, it is subcommittees who, by developing expertise on the proposals before them, very nearly hold life and death power over bills. An unfavorable vote in subcommittee makes it unlikely that the bill will even be considered by the full committee, let alone the full House or Senate.

In the Senate, the most important foreign policy committees are Foreign Relations, Armed Services, Appropriations, and the Select Committee on Intelligence. Given the Senate's special prerogatives in approving presidential appointments and ratifying treaties, its Foreign Relations Committee has long been among the most august in Congress. Reaching the modern peak of its influence under the long-running chairmanship of J. William Fulbright, the committee has seen a gradual erosion of its authority owing both to the diminished status of committees in general and the succession of less influential leaders who succeeded Fulbright as committee chair.

In the House, the key foreign policy committees are Foreign Affairs, Armed Services, Appropriations, and the Select Committee on Intelligence. Traditionally considered the poor cousin of its prestigious Senate counterpart, the House Foreign Affairs Committee has recently acquired a new stature, as a result of a growing interest in foreign policy issues in the House and the aggressive role in policy-making played by younger committee members such as Congressman Lee Hamilton (D-Ind.), the committee's chairman since 1993.

## Congressional Powers

Determined to prevent too much power from being concentrated in the hands of the executive, the Founding Fathers bestowed generous grants of constitutional authority on the Congress. Constitutionally, the Congress is able to affect American foreign policy through its (1) lawmaking power, (2) power of the purse, (3) confirmation power, (4) oversight power, (5) war power, and (6) treaty power. All six of these formal powers are either specifically enumerated in the Constitution or are logical derivatives of explicit constitutional grants.

### Lawmaking Power

In a sense the preeminent power in any government, the lawmaking power is the capacity to create legal authority for certain actions and to forbid others altogether. The person or agency that possesses the law-making power is thus a matter of fundamental importance. The Founding Fathers settled this crucial issue in the very first section of the first article of the Constitution, which reads in its entirety: "All legislative Powers herein granted shall be vested in a Congress of the United States, which shall consist of a Senate and House of Representatives." While ordinary legislative enactments are subject to presidential veto, vetoes can be overridden by two-thirds of the House and Senate, thus giving Congress the last word on defining what is legal and what is illegal.

In the field of international affairs, Congress uses its lawmaking power to shape policy in several ways. It can adopt legislation that directly defines U.S. policy. For example, whether or not China continues to be granted Most Favored Nation (MFN) trading status is subject to the lawmaking authority of Congress. Through its lawmaking power Congress can also delegate certain tasks and powers to the president. For example, in 1974 Congress initiated the so-called fast-track authority on trade matters which President Bush used to enter into negotiations with Canada and Mexico over creation of a North American Free Trade Area (NAFTA). Under fast-track procedures, presidents submit trade agreements to a prompt up or down vote with no floor amendments allowed. Congress can also influence foreign policy indirectly by structuring the executive branch and stipulating its budgetary resources and legal authority. Examples would be charging the Commerce Department with supervising exports of sensitive products or establishing a trade representative with cabinet-level status.

The 1986 South Africa sanctions bill illustrates the congressional use of lawmaking authority to shape foreign policy. Since its independence in 1910, South Africa has been ruled by its white minority. That rule became especially odious in 1948 when the right-wing National party instituted a thoroughgoing policy of apartheid, or racial separation. The nation's black majority was systematically oppressed through forced segregation, inferior education and jobs, and the denial of basic liberties. By the 1980s South Africa's 25 million blacks increasingly challenged a system that denied them any political voice, while the country's 5 million whites dominated a three-chambered Parliament that included segregated chambers for the nation's 3 million people of mixed race and 1 million Indians.

The Reagan administration agreed with Congress that the United States had a moral obligation to help end apartheid but insisted that its policy of constructive engagement offered the best hope of a political solution. The brainchild of Assistant Secretary of State for African Affairs Chester A. Crocker, constructive engagement assumed that through quiet diplomacy the United States could encourage the South African regime to dismantle apartheid and achieve regional settlements in Southern Africa. Thus, the Reagan administration strongly opposed stringent economic sanctions against the white supremacist regime. In 1985, in an effort to head off mounting congressional sentiment for tough sanctions, Reagan issued an executive order that imposed on Pretoria some of the milder penalties then being discussed on Capitol Hill.

By the summer of 1986, however, it was apparent that Reagan was out of step with many of his fellow Republicans on this issue as momentum built in Congress for a tough sanctions bill. In June of that year the Republican-controlled Senate passed a strong measure that barred new U.S. investments in South Africa (though existing investments were left untouched) and also prohibited imports of crucial South African commodities such as coal, uranium, steel, iron, agricultural products, and textiles. The measure cleared the Senate by a wide margin of 84 to 14. In September, the House adopted the bill by a similarly lopsided vote of 308 to 77.

On September 26, 1986, President Reagan vetoed the measure, calling economic sanctions "the wrong course to follow." His veto pitted him not only against congressional Democrats, but also against some of the leading Republicans in Congress. Indiana Republican Richard Lugar, then chairman of the Senate Foreign Relations Committee, announced that he would lead Senate efforts to override Reagan's veto. On September 29, the

Democratic-controlled House voted 313 to 83 to override the veto, well over the two-thirds majority required. In the floor debate on the issue, Representative William Gray, a Pennsylvania Democrat, declared that "this bill will send a moral and diplomatic wake-up call to a President who doesn't understand the issue." Two days later the Senate, by a comfortable margin of 78 to 21, dealt Reagan a decisive defeat by re-passing the sanctions bill, thus enacting the measure over determined executive opposition.

The stringent U.S. economic sanctions proved to be instrumental in the decision of South African President de Klerk to begin dismantling apartheid in 1990. One by one, the symbols and instruments of South Africa's racial oppression have fallen: the state of emergency that gave Pretoria extraordinary police powers was lifted; the notorious Population Registration Act and Group Areas Act were repealed; democratic political parties were legalized; and negotiations were begun with black leaders to establish a democratic system. South Africa still has a great deal to do to accomplish the difficult transition from autocratic minority rule to democratic multiracial governance, but, once set in motion, democratization now seems inevitable.

As vice president in 1986, George Bush had opposed the sanctions bill, but in 1991 President Bush tacitly acknowledged the bill's role by proclaiming apartheid's end "irreversible." He announced that sufficient progress had been made in South Africa that he was lifting some of the most severe sanctions, as the bill permitted him to do. Hence the Congress, in following its own judgment, set U.S. foreign policy on a course that led to the dismantling of one of the world's most loathsome political systems. This example shows the kind of influence Congress can wield through its power to decide what is legal and what is illegal for American citizens and their government.

### Power of the Purse

This power is really two powers in one: legislative control over revenue raised by the federal government and congressional control over how that money is spent. On this point the Constitution is crystal-clear: Article II, Section 9, states that "no money shall be drawn from the Treasury, but in Consequences of Appropriations made by Law." Since the lawmaking power belongs to Congress, it follows that the all-important power to determine "Appropriations made by Law" is also a congressional prerogative.

If, as some have argued, *policy is what gets funded*, then the power to decide what gets funded is a very great power indeed. The power to resolve perennial issues such as the size and composition of the defense budget and the U.S. contribution to the U.N. budget indicate the kind of policy influence Congress has through its control of the nation's purse strings.

The annual debate over foreign aid offers a useful look at how Congress wields its financial authority to shape U.S. foreign policy. Beginning with the hugely successful Marshall Plan which helped rebuild Europe after World War II, the United States has utilized economic assistance as one of its foreign policy tools. In 1961 Congress passed the landmark Foreign Aid Authorization Act, which created the Agency for International Development (AID) to administer general development assistance and established the policy framework that has guided American aid efforts ever since. Although foreign aid always had its critics on Capitol Hill, working majorities in support of annual aid appropriations could reliably be forged from an unlikely alliance of Cold War "hawks" and liberal "do-gooders," each of whom saw foreign economic assistance as advancing its objectives. Despite its mixed political motives, the United States has served as an inspirational example of generosity to other nations. Recent foreign aid budgets have been about $16 billion annually, a figure that includes activities as diverse as direct bilateral economic development grants, food donations, military assistance, contributions to multilateral agencies such as the World Bank, and international environmental projects. Wielding its constitutional prerogatives, Congress has regularly earmarked foreign aid monies for a few favored nations. Nearly two-thirds of recent U.S. aid has gone to four countries: Israel, Egypt, Greece, and Turkey. Today the United States remains the largest foreign aid donor in the world, although as a percentage of gross national product its contributions rank it only seventeenth among the aid-giving industrial nations.

In recent years, congressional support of foreign aid has declined sharply. A primary reason is the end of the Cold War, which left much of the program without an overarching strategic rationale. Propping up anticommunist clients in remote locales is no longer a politically saleable rationale for giving away American taxpayers' money. Moreover, the combination of unmet social needs here at home, together with the enormous federal budget deficits, means that many lawmakers no longer see the United States as a nation with an abundance of money to give away to foreigners. Finally, empirical evidence shows a great gap between the idealistic aspirations of the early foreign aid programs and the actual results in Third World nations. In Africa, for example, a disproportionate share of U.S. assistance has gone to five nations which, at various times, figured prominently in Washington's strategic objectives. Those five nations — Zaire, Sudan, Ethiopia, Liberia, and Somalia — actually posted *lower* economic growth rates than the rest of Africa from the 1960s to the 1980s. Similar disappointments in the outcomes of American assistance serve to undermine the persuasiveness of members of Congress who continue to advocate generous foreign aid programs. The prospects for the United States' historic foreign aid program are frankly rather bleak. By fiscal year 1994 budget agreements that forbid shifting money from foreign to domestic programs will have expired. That will leave foreign aid exceptionally vulnerable in a congressional environment that has become increasingly dominated by concerns about the nation's own eroded economic base.

Sometimes congressional authority over how federal dollars are spent is undermined by the way executive officials carry out — or fail to carry out — appropriations decisions. A telling illustration is the case of the transport ships that the Pentagon refused to buy. For some time defense-oriented legislators had worried about the military's ability to deploy rapidly large numbers of troops and their equipment in the event of a serious regional crisis. (The Middle East was widely considered to be the most likely occurrence.) Transporting a single mechanized division from the United States to the Middle East requires eight fast sealift ships and entails a two-week voyage from east coast ports. (Regular freighters need twice that time.)

Since the Defense Department had only eight of those fast sealift ships, in 1989 Congress appropriated $600 million to be used to purchase four more such vessels. The Navy, however, has traditionally had little interest in transport ships, which it tends to view as unglamourous utility craft of use principally to the Army. Navy leaders are much more interested in warships such as aircraft carriers, destroyers, and submarines.

Deferring to the Navy, Defense Secretary Cheney approved the diversion of some of the $600 million appropriation for other programs of interest to the Pentagon and simply refused to spend the rest. In other words, the Pentagon effectively overrode the express will of Congress, believing that its judgment was superior to that of Congress and arrogating to itself the right to ignore a clear congressional mandate.

After Saddam Hussein invaded Kuwait in August 1990, however, the Pentagon was confronted with the extraordinary logistical challenge of moving huge quantities of troops and equipment 12,000 sea-miles (8,000 miles by air) from the continental United States to Saudi Arabia. The Navy was so lacking in rapid sealift capability that it was forced to activate older and slower freighters from its ready-reserve fleet to transport heavy armored equipment such as tanks and personnel carriers.

It was sheer good fortune for the United States that Saddam Hussein failed to continue his military drive into Saudi Arabia as had been widely feared. Instead, Iraqi forces held their lines of conquest at the Kuwait-Saudi border, thus allowing U.S. forces the fortuitous luxury of time to carry out their enormous deployment of troops and equipment to the Persian Gulf. The next time a similar crisis occurs, however, the Pentagon might not be so lucky. Unglamourous though it may be, adequate military transportation is essential to ensure the nation's rapid response to sudden regional contingencies.

Congress was clearly right in this case. Had its 1989 appropriations been carried out by the Defense Department as Congress intended, the United States would today be better prepared for the kind of sudden regional contingency encountered in the Persian Gulf in 1990–1991.

### Confirmation Power

Unlike the previous two powers, the confirmation power is exercised only by the Senate. Its constitutional basis is found in Article II, Section 2, which stipulates that the president "shall appoint Ambassadors, other public Ministers and Consuls, . . . and all other Officers of the United States" *subject to* "the Advice and Consent of the Senate." Thus, foreign policy-makers such as the secretary of state and secretary of defense must win Senate approval before they can take up their duties. In the normal course of events, presidential nominees ordinarily win Senate approval; indeed, failure to confirm the president's choice is regarded as a major setback for the White House. Rather than risk the embarrassment of Senate rejection, presidents sometimes choose to withdraw their more problematic nominees.

Early in his term, for example, George Bush nominated a number of his more generous campaign contributors for senior executive positions, including ambassadorships. Among the most egregious cases was his selection of Joy A. Silverman to be U.S. ambassador to Barbados. Mrs. Silverman had no discernible foreign policy credentials and, for that matter, had had virtually no paid employment in her life. In explaining why she felt she was qualified for the rank of ambassador, Mrs. Silverman wrote that she had "assisted husband . . . by planning and hosting corporate functions." Apparently her real credential, in the Bush administration's eyes, was the nearly $300,000 she had donated to the Republican party between 1987 and 1989. However, faced with a determined Senate opposition led by Maryland Democrat Paul Sarbanes, the Bush administration quietly withdrew the nomination in favor of a qualified diplomat.

The confirmation power permits the Senate to influence the policy process. Specifically, confirmation hearings are sometimes used as highly public forums for airing substantive policy controversies and, in the course of doing so, altering executive positions on important issues. This was the case in 1989, for example, when a number of senators developed serious doubts about the agreement already negotiated with Japan for joint U.S.-Japanese codevelopment of an advanced jet fighter, the so-called FSX. (For a full account, see Chapter 8.) The senators seized the opportunity afforded by Secretary of State–designate James Baker's confirmation hearings to get Baker to agree to an interagency review of the deal.

Baker was confirmed in due course, but the subsequent review of the FSX agreement opened up an interagency brawl between the project's defenders (centered principally in the Departments of State and Defense) and its critics (mostly found in the Department of Commerce, Office of the Trade Representative, and Department of Labor). The review led to new negotiations with Japan, which thought it had a final agreement with the United States and deeply resented what it regarded as high-handed treatment at the hands of the Americans.

A more dramatic way the Senate can use its confirmation power to affect the policy process is through outright rejection of presidential appointees to high office. An illustration was the bitter battle over President Bush's first choice to be secretary of defense, former Senator John Tower of Texas. A 24-year Senate veteran and former chairman of the Armed Services Committee, Tower was by all accounts well versed in the substance of defense policy. His nomination by President-elect Bush in December 1988 to head the Department of Defense, however, quickly ran into trouble among his former colleagues on Capitol Hill.

Opposition to Tower came from three fronts. First, some conservative activists, including the lobbying group Americans for the High Frontier, which was ardently committed to space-based missile defenses, opposed Tower because he did not fully support the Star Wars missile shield envisioned by Ronald Reagan. Second, although few would say so publicly, most senators had little regard for Tower personally. His four terms in their midst had won him few friends but had left instead a reputation for aloofness and arrogance in an institution that prizes smooth collegiality. Finally, and most importantly, the twice-divorced Tower was dogged by persistent rumors of hard drinking and womanizing. Although the Senate's eventual vote against confirming Tower closely followed party lines, the first public allegations of the diminutive Texan's drunkenness and philandering were made by a conservative Republican activist, Paul M. Weyrich. Despite a thorough FBI investigation of the charges surrounding Tower, the issue of his character remained inconclusive. But it is no doubt true that the deluge of rumors, including a particularly colorful account of an alleged drunken dalliance with a Russian woman, created a political climate of doubt that simply could not be dispelled.

Although President Bush's Republican supporters argued that the Senate should not block his choices for cabinet heads, most Senate Democrats, including the respected chairman of the Armed Services Committee, Sam Nunn, asserted that the Senate had a constitutional responsibility to decline a nominee whose character and judgment were so surrounded by doubt. After Tower's defeat in March 1989, President Bush nominated in his place former Congressman Dick Cheney of Wyoming. Cheney's affable relations with the Hill and unblemished personal record won him easy confirmation as secretary of defense.

### Oversight Power

Though not specifically enumerated in the Constitution, the power to review how the laws it passes are being implemented by the executive branch and the actual effects of the policies it creates follows logically from the constitutional grant of lawmaking authority. In the course of exercising its oversight prerogatives and responsibilities, Congress engages in an ongoing round of studies, hearings, and investigations. Those activities, in turn, require a substantial amount of time and effort from executive branch officials, who are called on to prepare reports ordered by Congress and provide testimony to congressional committees engaged in oversight activities.

It is useful to distinguish routine congressional oversight from the more dramatic investigations it sometimes undertakes. A good example of routine oversight is congressional monitoring of CIA activities. Until its burst of institutional reassertiveness in the mid-1970s, Congress often had little awareness of U.S. intelligence operations and lacked a systematic means of acquiring information about them. In 1975, however, the Senate established a select committee to investigate allegations of CIA involvement in covert activities such as destabilizing the leftist regime of Chilean President Allende, orchestrating a secret war in Laos, and intervening in factional warfare in Angola. Chaired by then Senator Frank Church of Idaho, the committee uncovered evidence of covert intelligence operations that bore the imprint of U.S. policy but about which the Congress had virtually no knowledge. Determined to routinize its oversight of intelligence activities, Congress established new intelligence committees in both houses and adopted legislation that required the president to both authorize any covert operations and report those operations to the House and Senate Intelligence committees. The purpose of the legislation was to strengthen democratic accountability over secret CIA operations. By requiring both presidential clearance and congressional notification, the two elected branches of government are now more firmly in control of—and responsible for—covert operations.

A much more dramatic form of congressional oversight occurs when Congress conducts special investigations into especially troubling policy issues. In a number of instances, especially during the Vietnam years, the nation's foreign policy climate was altered by congressional hearings. Throughout the 1960s, as the war in Southeast Asia escalated in scope, costs, and casualties, so too did doubts about its wisdom begin to grow. Those doubts were given a prominent and respectable showcase in a series of highly publicized Senate hearings presided over by the chairman of the Foreign Relations Committee, Senator J. William Fulbright. A former Rhodes scholar and university president, the bookish Fulbright was an articulate internationalist who had been an early supporter of the Kennedy-Johnson escalation of American commitment. By 1965, however, Fulbright was having second thoughts, and in early 1966, well in advance of most of his contemporaries, he reversed course and broke with his long-time friend Lyndon Johnson over the wisdom of the United States' Vietnam policy.

Fulbright then exercised his prerogative as committee chairman by conducting a series of televised hearings on the war. The first, held in January and February 1966, created a national sensation. Lavish media coverage served to focus the nation's attention on a wide-ranging discussion of U.S. interests in Vietnam, the nature of the threats to those interests, and the best means of countering those threats. Viewers around the country were exposed to the reasoned, articulate criticism of U.S. policy from such men as the diplomat-scholar George F. Kennan and Lieutenant General James Gavin. Their stature, in turn, helped dispel the notion that foreign policy dissent was merely the unpatriotic chanting of a few student radicals. Their cogent analysis and critique of the Johnson administration's policies served to crystallize doubts that many Americans had begun to feel.

More recently, the nation's foreign policy climate was influenced by televised congressional hearings on the Iran-Contra scandal. During the summer of 1987 the nation's television viewers were alternately fascinated and appalled by gripping insider testimony provided by dozens of witnesses, including, most famously, Marine Lieutenant Colonel Oliver North, the National Security Council staffer who orchestrated much of the ill-conceived policy. By the time the joint House-Senate investigating committee concluded its public inquiry, the American people had received a memorable lesson in the perils of secret and sometimes illegal covert actions carried out by amateurs acting in the name of an intellectually disengaged president. The hearings made it clear for all to see that federal laws had been broken by executive officers, democratic accountability was undermined, and the nation suffered a needless international embarrassment.

As its hyphenated name suggests, the scandal was really two separate misadventures. The "Iran" half of the scandal arose from a series of arms sales to the Muslim fundamentalist regime that had seized power in Iran in 1979 and had supported terrorist violence against the United States and its citizens ever since. During the summer and fall of 1985 President Reagan, reacting emotionally to pleas by the families of American hostages held in Lebanon by Iranian-backed groups, authorized the sale to Iran of 504 TOW antitank missiles and 120 HAWK antiaircraft missiles. Reagan was apparently convinced that selling advanced weaponry to a terrorist-sponsoring, anti-American regime would be a good way both to get the hostages back and improve U.S. relations with Iran.

Secretary of State George Shultz and Secretary of Defense Caspar Weinberger advised Reagan against the weapons sales, arguing that the policy was both politically misguided and of dubious legality. Reagan, however, was determined to proceed with the missile sale and so turned to an odd assortment of private citizens and National Security Council (NSC) staffers to carry out the operation.

The "Contra" half of the scandal's name refers to White House efforts to engage in secret fundraising for the rebels in Nicaragua (the Contras) who were attempting to overthrow a leftist regime that had come to power in 1979. Congress had ordered a cutoff of U.S. aid to the Contras in fiscal year 1983 and again in 1985 (the so-called Boland amendments). Thus thwarted, Reagan's operatives on the NSC staff sought to evade the law through an elaborate covert program of Contra assistance funded by contributions from private sources and foreign governments. The two operations became linked when profits from the arms sales to Iran were diverted to the secret Contra fund.

When this clandestine White House foreign policy was exposed in late 1986, leaders of the House and Senate agreed to conduct a joint inquiry through a special House-Senate investigating committee. The sheer scope of its investigation was remarkable: 311 subpoenas were issued, over 200,000 documents were examined, and witnesses presented about 250 hours of public testimony during forty days of open hearings.

Television viewers were treated to memorable testimony, such as Fawn Hall, Colonel North's secretary, setting out her novel legal theory that "sometimes you have to go above the written law." Similar confusion emanated from Admiral John Poindexter, former national security adviser to the president, who asserted that "the buck stops here with me." Observers were quick to point out that, as Harry Truman never forgot, the buck of responsibility rightly stops with the president, not his underlings. Some administration witnesses detailed their strong objections to the secret misadventure. Secretary of Defense Weinberger, for example, believed that there were no "moderates" in Iran and that the regime then in power could not be made more pro–U.S. by selling it arms. Other officials made clear their willful ignorance of the operation's more sordid aspects. Assistant Secretary of State Elliot Abrams admitted that "I was careful not to ask Colonel North questions I did not need to know the answers to."

Through the 1987 hearings, Congress informed both itself and the public of foreign policy activities that were illegal, counterproductive, and undemocratic. The pattern of *illegal* action included (1) deliberate violation of the statutory requirement that Congress be notified of all covert actions in a "timely fashion" (Poindexter said he kept Congress in the dark because he didn't want "outside interference" in the foreign policy process); (2) North's admission that he and other officials repeatedly lied to Congress about the two covert actions and that he had destroyed or altered official documents; and (3) the illegal diversion of U.S. government proceeds from the Iran arms sale to the Nicaraguan Contras in clear violation of the Boland Amendment prohibiting U.S. assistance to the Contras.

The policies were *counterproductive* because they undermined U.S. credibility with allies by secretly selling arms to Iran while publicly urging other nations to refrain from just such sales. The number of American hostages was not reduced, nor was a better relationship achieved with the hostile regime in Teheran. Hence, the Iran-Contra shenanigans dealt a serious blow to the United States' international reputation for prudent diplomacy.

Finally, the episode revealed much that was *undemocratic* in the worldview and behavior of key Reagan administration officials. Numerous officials, including North, Poindexter, and Abrams, lied to, misled, or withheld information from Congress. The hearings reflected a profound hostility toward Congress as an institution and a contempt for the constitutional design of separation of powers and checks and balances. From Poindexter's belief that Congress should be kept in the dark regarding covert action on behalf of the Contras because "I simply did not want any outside interference" to North's admission that "I didn't want to tell Congress anything" about his covert activities, a deep strain of executive branch disdain for both the Constitution and the Congress was evident.

In addition, within the executive branch, certain important officials were often shut out of critical decisions, thus lessening accountability. President Reagan himself has said that he knew nothing of North's covert actions to help the Contras and was not told of the diversion of arms sale funds for that adventure. The secretary of state, who deals with foreign governments, was not told of North's solicitation of millions of dollars from those governments to funnel to the Contras.

What the Iran-Contra hearings of 1987 revealed was disturbing. In the end, however, the system of checks and balances was vindicated. Vigorous congressional efforts to get at the truth of what had happened and to educate the public on what had gone wrong reflected the Founding Fathers' intent when they created a separate legislative branch and endowed it with a robust array of independent powers.

### War Power

In Article I, Section 8, of the Constitution, the Founding Fathers established that "The Congress shall have Power . . . to declare War." Records of the Constitutional Convention show broad agreement that the executive must not be enabled to commit the nation to a course of war on his own authority. While bestowing on the president the role of commander in chief of the armed forces and acknowledging that he would have inherent authority to use force to repel sudden attacks, the Constitution's framers were nonetheless clear in their insistence that the fateful decision to initiate war must await formal declaration by Congress.

The practice of the past two centuries, however, has borne little resemblance to the Founding Fathers' carefully constructed design. As the United States rose from isolation to the leading rank of the world's nations and as the technology of modern aircraft and intercontinental missiles created the requirement for rapid response to international crises, the actual power to initiate and carry out wars tilted from the interbranch balance of the Constitution to a pronounced strengthening of the president's role. Of the more than 200 instances in which U.S. armed forces have been used abroad, only five have been sanctioned by formal declarations of war.

By the middle of this century, some authorities believed that the whole concept of declaring war was obsolete. So too, some argued, was the constitutional concept of joint war-making by the president and the Congress. The trauma of the protracted, failed, and undeclared war in Vietnam stimulated Congress to set out to recapture its war powers which had gradually atrophied through disuse. The resulting War Powers Act of 1973 represents an historic and controversial effort by Congress to restore the interbranch balance to something more closely approximating the codetermination envisioned by the writers of the Constitution. In Chapter 5, we will examine the whole question of war powers and the effects of the 1973 legislation in detail.

## Treaty Power

The treaty power is spelled out in Article II, Section 2, of the Constitution, which states that presidents may make treaties with foreign governments "by and with the Advice and Consent of the Senate . . . provided two thirds of the Senators present concur." Here it should be noted that, like the confirmation power, the congressional treaty power is assigned to the Senate alone. Its possession of these two constitutional prerogatives gives the Senate greater stature than the House of Representatives in the foreign policy process.

We should also note the requirement for an extraordinary majority. Simple majorities are difficult enough to attain in fractious legislative assemblies; getting two-thirds of the Senate's members to agree on anything presents a formidable challenge. Why, then, would the Founding Fathers have designed a process that made treaties so difficult to attain? The question nearly answers itself. Deeply isolationist and profoundly suspicious of the monarchies then ruling Europe, the framers of the Constitution deliberately made it quite difficult for the new nation's leaders to enter into formal "entanglements" with foreign governments. Recall that George Washington's famous Farewell Address warned against the pernicious lure of "entangling alliances." Washington faithfully mirrored the American outlook of his day.

Occasionally, Congress and the president become so deeply opposed on fundamental issues that they are unable to work out their differences and find a compromise formula for a treaty. This difficulty was classically illustrated in the aftermath of World War I when President Woodrow Wilson was unable to secure Senate approval of the Treaty of Versailles in the form in which he had negotiated it. U.S. membership in the newly created League of Nations was one of the treaty's chief provisions. The fact that the United States did not join the League seriously weakened it as a credible international body, and it was an emasculated League of Nations that was shortly confronted with armed aggression by the fascist regimes of Germany, Italy, and Japan. Many textbooks blame World War II on the League of Nations' failure to stop the Axis powers' aggression at an early stage. It was unable to do so, they argue, because the United States failed to join it. That failure, in turn, is often laid at the feet of Congress, which allegedly was a hotbed of isolationist sentiment.

Critics of congressional influence in foreign affairs often point to this episode as a cautionary tale against the alleged isolationism and parochialism of Congress in contrast with the progressive internationalism of the executive. In actual fact, however, the U.S. failure to join the League of Nations was at least as much the fault of President Wilson as it was the

Senate. Wilson, a rigid idealist, had refused to include congressional representatives in the U.S. delegation at the Versailles Peace Conference and later presented the Treaty of Versailles to the Senate with the demand that it ratify *his* treaty as is. When the Senate leader, Henry Cabot Lodge (R-Mass.), persuaded the Senate to adopt a series of rather innocuous reservations to the treaty, Wilson stiffly refused to compromise. In a titanic struggle of wills, Wilson would not budge an inch. In the end, he had so thoroughly alienated enough senators by his rigidity that the Senate dealt him a defeat and rejected the treaty that Wilson regarded as his crowning achievement. Solid majorities of the "isolationist" Senate favored the Treaty and with it U.S. participation in the League.

Mindful of Wilson's historic miscalculation, modern presidents ordinarily attempt to ensure congressional involvement in the treaty-making process in hopes of improving the chances that the negotiated document will be ratified. Sometimes, however, even this strategy is not enough. In the recent history of strategic arms control agreements, for example, President Jimmy Carter went to great lengths to keep legislators fully apprised of the progress of negotiations on the second strategic arms limitation talks (SALT II). But by the time the draft treaty was ready for Senate consideration in 1980, the political climate between the United States and the then Soviet Union had markedly worsened. The Soviet invasion of Afghanistan in December 1979 was the final straw. Aware that he did not have the votes to ratify the SALT II Treaty and moving towards a more hard-line position himself, Carter withdrew the treaty from Senate consideration.

This section should dispel the myth that the Founding Fathers intended the Congress to play second fiddle to the president in charting the nation's international course. Its impressive array of constitutional powers – to pass laws, fund programs, confirm executive appointments, oversee executive conduct, declare war, and ratify treaties – give it a strong repertoire of formal authority to share coequally with presidents in the foreign policy-making process. We now turn to an examination of how Congress wields its considerable policy-making powers in a previously neglected policy domain that promises to be a national issue throughout the 1990s: the politics of trade.

## Congress and the Politics of Trade

Just as the Cold War dominated American life from the late 1940s to the fall of the Soviet Union in 1991, so too will the struggle to reinvigorate its economy likely be the nation's greatest preoccupation in the 1990s. The

United States' Cold War primacy was undergirded by its unquestioned economic supremacy. In the aftermath of World War II the United States accounted for nearly half of the world's economic productivity. As expected, the nation's position has gradually eroded in relative terms. We now account for about one-fifth of global productivity, a decline due in large part to the very success of postwar U.S. efforts to rebuild Europe and Japan and stimulate international economic activity. More alarmingly, however, it has by some measures declined in absolute terms as well, as evidenced in particular by the fourfold growth of the national debt since 1980.

The prospect of handing the next generation a less abundant society than the one they inherited has aroused ordinary Americans in the same way that the specter of communism galvanized public opinion in the 1950s. Voters in the 1992 presidential election were more concerned about the nation's future economic health than about any other issue, foreign or domestic. Their selection of Bill Clinton, whose campaign focused on the theme of economic renewal, was widely seen as mandate to the nation's elites to pay more attention to the economic well-being of the ordinary American citizen who had borne the burdens of defeating international totalitarianism for the past half-century. While the nation's economists and political leaders remain deeply divided over how best to attain the shared goal of economic renewal, they all agree that the United States' economic well-being is inseparably linked to the increasingly interdependent global economy.

This was not always the case. Blessed with a large domestic market and abundant resources, the United States has traditionally been less intertwined with economic forces beyond its borders than have most industrial nations. As recently as 1960, trade accounted for only about one-tenth of the nation's gross national product (GNP).

Today, however, the U.S. economy and the global economy are irreparably joined at the hip. The United States is as heavily dependent on trade as are Japan and the European Community (EC). About one-fourth of U.S. GNP comes from imports and exports of goods and services. The proportion of the economy accounted for by trade has increased by two and one-half times since 1960. Most people know that the United States is the world's largest importer, but fewer noticed that in 1991 it passed Germany to become the world's largest exporter as well. About half of its economic growth during the early 1990s was due to its strength in exports.

Members of Congress, acutely sensitive to issues affecting jobs and prosperity in their home states and districts, have responded to the nation's growing economic interdependence by elevating trade policy to the top of the political agenda. The increasing politicization of trade issues both reflects growing interest among political leaders and, in turn, serves to stimulate further political attention to the domestic consequences of trade policy. As Congressman Dan Rostenkowski (D-Ill.) put it, "Trade is becoming very, very parochial. It's employment, it's our jobs." As Congress devotes more time and attention to a multitude of trade issues, its approach will be shaped by the fragmentation of authority within Congress; the nation's philosophical division between free traders and protectionists; and the influence of partisan and constituent interests.

### Fragmentation of Authority

Neither chamber of Congress has a standing committee devoted principally to trade policy. The result is a balkanization of committee jurisdictions that results in delays and duplication of hearings and deliberation, multiplies the access points for interest group lobbying, and greatly complicates the inherent task of forging coherent legislation.

In the Senate, the Finance Committee — and within it, the International Trade Subcommittee — exercises primary authority over trade legislation, but at least a half-dozen other committees typically view some aspects of trade issues as falling within their sphere of authority. They include the Agriculture Committee (through its Domestic and Foreign Marketing and Product Promotion Subcommittee), the Commerce, Science, and Transportation Committee (Subcommittee on Foreign Commerce and Tourism), Committee on Foreign Relations (Subcommittee on International Economic Policy, Trade, Oceans, and Environment), Judiciary Committee (Subcommittee on Patents, Copyrights, and Trademarks), and the Small Business Committee (Subcommittee on Export Expansion).

In the House there is a similar lack of clarity of committee jurisdiction. As a result, the new attention to trade issues invites a swarm of committees and subcommittees, each jostling with the other in attempting to put its stamp on legislative proposals. A partial listing of the most important House committees (and their pertinent subcommittees noted in parentheses) involved in trade matters would include: Agriculture (Subcommittee on Department Operations, Research, and Foreign Agriculture), Banking, Finance, and Urban Affairs (Subcommittee on International Development, Finance, Trade, and Monetary Policy), Foreign Affairs (Subcommittee on International Economic Policy and Trade), Small Business (Subcommittee on Exports, Tax Policy, and Special Problems), and Ways and Means (Subcommittee on Trade).

Trade issues inherently touch on both international and domestic matters. As mentioned earlier, some writers use the term *intermestic* to refer to this blurring of traditional distinctions between internal and external affairs. For Congress to be able to deal coherently with all the diverse aspects of trade matters, then, it should establish new committees in each chamber to deal specifically with trade legislation.

## Free Traders versus Protectionists

Today's advocates of free trade are the doctrinal heirs of Adam Smith and David Ricardo. Smith, an eighteenth-century Scottish writer, codified the principles of free market economics in his classic work, *The Wealth of Nations*, published in 1776. Essentially the bible of modern capitalism, Smith's tract set out to show the advantages of minimal governmental control of economic activities. According to Smith, the free market, driven by the laws of supply and demand, will stimulate productivity, enhance individual freedom, raise living standards, reward effort and talent, and ensure an abundant flow of desired products at optimal prices. The force of competition, Smith believed, would act as a sort of "hidden hand," assuring fairness, quality, and responsiveness to consumer tastes — all without the heavy hand of governmental control.

Smith's principles were extended into the realm of international economics by the theorist David Ricardo, who argued in 1817 that nations should concentrate their capital and labor on those things they do best and depend on other nations to provide them with the things they cannot do themselves. Nations with lower labor costs, for example, can produce labor-intensive goods at lower cost, thus benefiting consumers in high-wage societies. Nations with large numbers of highly educated (and expensive) workers could be expected to focus on high-technology manufacturing, thus spurring the pace of technological advance and product development. The concept of *comparative advantage*, Ricardo argued, points in the direction of free trade, whereby all nations stand to gain by doing what they do best and receiving the benefits of what other nations do best. According to free trade theory, restraints on trade such as tariffs (which make foreign products less competitive by raising their cost) or quotas (which limit the amount of foreign goods that can be imported) reduce the beneficial effects of competition among producers and diminish incentives for manufacturers to lower costs and improve quality.

The free trade doctrine has been dominant in U.S. policy-making circles since the 1930s. There has been a broad consensus that the anti-free trade protectionism manifested in the notorious Smoot-Hawley Tariff Act of 1930 served to contract the volume of world trade and make the Great Depression even more devastating to the nation's workers and business-people. The United States used its towering dominance of the international system in the years after World War II to set in place multilateral treaties and institutions that would encourage free trade and global economic liberalization. The most important treaty regarding trade was the 1947 General Agreement on Tariffs and Trade (GATT). Originally a "club" of the industrialized nations, GATT today has 100 signatories who work to harmonize their trading practices and promote open markets.

Although it remains a more open market than most major traders, including the Japanese and the Europeans, the United States is by no means the wide-open trading mecca that many Americans seem to believe it is. The United States maintains quotas on 3,600 products ranging from wool suits to peanuts, and tariffs on nearly every imported good from coffee to computers. The sugar industry provides a classic case of domestic producers banding together to persuade legislators to enact steep tariffs and quotas on imported sugar. The result is that American consumers pay the difference between the 8.5 cents per pound that sugar costs on the world market and the 21.5 cents a pound in tariffs on imported sugar. On balance, however, the U.S. economy is still among the most free and open to international trade of the world's major economies.

While free trade doctrine has generally prevailed among U.S. economists, recently a school of thought has emerged which challenges the nation's attachment to classical laissez-faire ideals. Although most analysts would resist the label "protectionist" as pejorative, their calls for a national industrial policy and emphasis on preserving certain key industries lends them a broadly protectionist quality. One of their most prominent spokesmen is Clyde Prestowitz, now president of the Economic Strategy Institute in Washington, D.C. Prestowitz is a former Commerce Department official with long experience in U.S.-Japan trade issues. His observations of the deep differences between U.S. free trade practices and Japan's government-orchestrated export strategy led him to conclude that free trade works only when all the major players are playing by the same rules. In Japan's case, he concluded, the rules were to relentlessly expand its global market share by undermining foreign producers while systematically denying them equal access to Japan's home market.

To Prestowitz and other advocates of so-called managed trade, the United States must take necessary steps to ensure the survival of critical manufacturing industries. As Prestowitz is fond of pointing out, the ability to make potato chips is quite different from the ability to make computer chips. Simply leaving the fate of critical industries to the laws of the market risks making the United States dangerously dependent on foreign firms whose governments have refused to permit the decline of their industrial base in the name of comparative advantage.

### Partisan and Constituent Influence

This debate among economists is repeated on a daily basis among members of Congress, but congressional debate is seldom a pure exercise in academic theorizing, because of partisan and constituent influence. Since any trade policy will produce winners and losers, it is not surprising that members of Congress are heavily influenced by the economic characteristics of the districts and states they represent and the extent to which their constituents are helped or harmed by trade. Among the winners of liberalized trade policies are most sectors of agriculture, aircraft manufacturers, machine tools, pharmaceuticals, telecommunications, and mainframe computers. Sectors that have fared less well amid global competition include textiles, steel, and automobiles.

Members of Congress who represent these less competitive, high-wage manufacturing industries will naturally be less inclined to support free trade policy than members who represent, say, export-dependent wheat-growing areas. As a broad generalization, the heavily unionized, traditional manufacturing areas of the Rust Belt—an area that extends across the Great Lakes states from Michigan to New York—tend to be strongholds of the Democratic party, while the agricultural west and service-oriented Sun Belt have become more heavily Republican. Thus, as one would expect, a Democratic congressman from Michigan who represents a large number of autoworkers is more likely to be a protectionist on trade issues than would be a Republican congressman from Kansas who represents corn growers dependent on foreign markets for their produce.

Let us now turn to three recent and current disputes involving trade policy to which Congress has devoted a great deal of time and attention. They are (1) the issue of Japan and the battle over a policy tool known as Super 301, (2) the debate over how best to influence China's human rights practices and the conflict over Most Favored Nation (MFN) trading status, and (3) controversy over the North America Free Trade Agreement (NAFTA) and the related issue of so-called fast-track negotiating authority.

### Japan's "Unfair Trade" and the Battle over Super 301

Japan is the United States' greatest trading rival. The extraordinary Japanese economic renaissance since World War II can be ascribed to a combination of admirable qualities at home—including a strong work ethic, an emphasis on high educational achievement for all students, a high savings rate, cooperative labor-management relations, and a commitment to quality goods — and fortuitous external circumstances, especially the liberalized international economic order created largely by the United States. During most of its postwar history, the Japanese government (particularly its Ministry of International Trade and Industry, known as MITI) has pursued an aggressive industrial policy, bringing financiers and industrialists together, identifying emerging manufacturing opportunities, targeting likely export markets, and erecting protectionist barriers against imports. The United States, with its traditional free market laissez-faire philosophy, typically left economic outcomes to the play of market forces and, compared to Japan, allowed much greater import access to foreign producers.

By the mid-1980s it was becoming apparent that the two economies were not interacting as classical market economics would suggest. Instead, Japan's single-minded drive for exports, coupled with its broadly protectionist policies against manufactured imports, was producing extraordinarily high trading imbalances in Japan's favor. In 1987 the U.S. trade deficit with Japan reached a stunning $56 billion out of a worldwide U.S. deficit of $160 billion. Clearly, such an extraordinary outflow of the nation's wealth, and with it the loss of U.S. manufacturing jobs, was politically untenable.

In 1988 Congress, frustrated by Japanese foot-dragging on trade talks and aroused by constituent anger over perceived Japanese "unfairness," adopted the so-called Super 301 provision contained in that year's trade bill. Super 301, named for Section 301 of the 1974 trade act, was an unusually strong effort by Congress to direct the executive branch's handling of trade disputes. Opposed by the Reagan and Bush administrations, Super 301 was assailed by free traders and by foreign governments for its unilateralism and as a possible violation of GATT rules. Under its provisions, the U.S. trade representative was required to identify countries whose trade practices were systematically unfair to U.S. exporters, attempt to alter those practices through negotiations, and, as a last resort, impose retaliatory penalties on the offending nations. It was readily apparent that the law was written with Japan foremost in the legislators' minds.

Implementation of Super 301 was, of course, in the hands of the executive branch. As proof of its seriousness, however, Congress kept a close eye on the Bush administration's approach to determining which nations to list as trade offenders. In May 1989, when it appeared that the administration might elect not to list Japan for fear of undermining the overall political and strategic relationship, a number of influential senators — among them Lloyd Bentsen of Texas (now Clinton's secretary of the treasury), John Danforth of Missouri, and Robert Byrd of West Virginia —

met with Trade Representative Carla Hills to warn of the certain eruption of congressional anger the administration would confront if it did not cite Japan. In order to placate Congress, the administration in late May 1989 cited Japan for discriminatory trade practices in communication satellites, supercomputers, and wood products. Partly to avoid the impression that Japan was being singled out, Brazil and India were also listed as unfair trading partners.

Japan escaped the stiff retaliatory penalties provided for in Super 301, largely by agreeing to enter into comprehensive discussions over how to harmonize economic relations with the United States—the so-called Structural Impediments Initiative (SII) talks. To a number of legislators, however, the SII talks looked like an elaborate evasion of Congress's clear intention for the United States to get tough with Japan, once and for all. Senator Lloyd Bentsen (D-Tex.), who at the time was chairman of the Senate Finance Committee, was speaking for many of his colleagues when he said, "I've never had a lot of faith in the idea of those talks." Meanwhile, Super 301 expired in 1990.

The next congressional round with Japan would be the comprehensive debate scheduled for 1992. Anticipating that debate, House Majority Leader Richard Gephardt (D-Mo.), a leading congressional advocate of protectionism and trade retaliation, unveiled his own tough proposal late in 1991. Assailing the Bush administration for a "failed" trade policy, Gephardt proposed not only reauthorizing Super 301 but also rewriting it to require the administration to (1) target any country that accounted for 15 percent of the U.S. trade deficit and (2) take action against all nations so targeted.

Gephardt's plan was too protectionist even for his Democratic House colleagues. Instead, they closed ranks behind a bill crafted by Dan Rostenkowski (D-Ill.), the influential chairman of the Ways and Means Committee and ordinarily a voice for free trade among House Democrats. In an effort to paper over differences among Democrats, the Rostenkowski plan, endorsed by Gephardt, dropped Gephardt's earlier insistence that any country that maintains a substantial trade surplus with the United States would be subject to retaliation. It captured the essential concerns of the Gephardt-led "trade hawks," however, by reauthorizing for five years the controversial Super 301 provision. In an effort to ward off even more protectionist amendments from other House Democrats, Rostenkowski's bill also included tough language on limiting Japanese automobile imports. Thus, there was little doubt that the main target of the bill was Japan. As Congressman Sander Levin (D-Mich.) put it, "When you've got this persistent trade deficit on the part of the Japanese, you just can't keep going the way we're going."

The Rostenkowski bill passed the House Ways and Means Committee in June 1992 and was adopted by the entire House on July 8. In order to become law, however, it would have to overcome three formidable obstacles. First, the U.S. surge in exports in the early 1990s seriously undercut the political appeal of trade legislation that risked provoking retaliatory action from other nations. The unilateral character of the Super 301 procedure was widely criticized by other nations, who threatened similar national action against what they regarded as the United States' own protectionist practices. Second, the Senate is a less protectionist-oriented chamber than the House and was unwilling to go along with the Rostenkowski plan. In the end, the Senate simply failed to act on the House-passed measure. Finally, the Bush administration threatened to veto the House bill if it were adopted by Congress. The arithmetic was plain to all: the House had adopted the Rostenkowski bill on a 280 to 145 vote, not nearly large enough to override a veto. Taken together, these three obstacles proved too great for the House's trade hawks to overcome.

The failure of Congress to renew Super 301 means that the executive branch retains more latitude in conducting ongoing trade talks with Japan and other trading partners than it would otherwise have had. For the time being the political appeal of trade protectionism has waned and, with it, congressional support for tough retaliatory policies such as Super 301. Should the encouraging surge in American exports falter, however, and the U.S. trade deficit once again begin to climb to the extraordinarily high levels of the late 1980s, Congress's trade hawks will most certainly renew their drive for tough legislation that will require the Clinton administration to take retaliatory steps against the Japanese and other nations seen on Capitol Hill as unfair trade partners.

### China and the Battle over MFN

One of the most emotionally charged trade issues of the 1990s is, in fact, only secondarily concerned with trade per se. More fundamentally, it reflects a deep split between Democrats and Republicans over the United States' stance toward China. Given the fact that the Democrats controlled Congress while, prior to Clinton's 1992 triumph, the Republicans have dominated recent presidential elections, the issue has also reflected an interbranch rivalry. The immediate issue is under what conditions the United States should extend Most Favored Nation (MFN) trading status to the communist-controlled government of China. The United States grants MFN status to virtually every nation in the world. The concept simply means that imports from nations enjoying MFN status will be permitted to enter U.S. markets at the lowest tariff rates, those imposed on our "most favored nation." The 100 members of GATT routinely grant MFN status to one another's exports.

The Jackson-Vanik amendment to the 1974 Trade Act sharply curbed the president's ability to extend MFN to communist countries, however. To do so, the president must (1) negotiate a commercial trade agreement, which would be subject to congressional approval, and (2) either certify that the country was allowing free emigration or waive this requirement on the grounds that the country was improving its emigration policies. If he opted for the waiver, he would have to renew it annually.

In 1980 China first received MFN status from the United States as part of a commercial trade agreement that is renewable every three years. Since then, presidents have annually renewed the waiver to the Jackson-Vanik emigration provision.

Following Beijing's brutal crackdown on student protesters in the Tiananmen Square slaughter of June 3-4, 1989, a deep policy split developed between congressional Democrats and Republican presidents and legislators over how to deal with the Chinese regime. Broadly speaking, Republicans—including, most notably, President Bush—have argued that the United States can encourage the progressive, modernizing elements in China by retaining active trade ties. In 1990 Bush argued that "The people in China who trade with us are the engine of reform, an opening to the outside world." A year later, in a May 1991 address at Yale, he returned to the same theme: "If we withdraw MFN or imposed conditions that would make trade impossible, we would punish South China . . . the very region where free-market reforms and the challenge to central authority are the strongest."

Congressional Democrats, on the other hand, have sought to use trade as an instrument to influence the hard-line rulers of China. As Congressman Don Pease (D-Ohio) argued in 1990, "Our aim as a nation should not be to cut off MFN but to use the leverage of annual renewal to make progress." Similarly, Senator George Mitchell (D-Me.), the Senate's majority leader, argued in 1991 that "Clearly, the Bush administration's China policy has failed. It hasn't produced improved human rights conditions in China."

The result has been a continuing effort by congressional Democrats to enact legislation that would make China's continued eligibility for MFN status dependent on a number of conditions that the Beijing regime would have to meet. Their reasoning is that trade is an ideal vehicle for U.S. policy because (1) it is a peaceful, noncoercive policy instrument, (2) China's growing trade surplus with the United States—second only to Japan's—makes continued access to U.S. markets a major interest to China's rulers, and (3) the fact that loss of MFN would raise U.S. tariffs on Chinese imports from an average of about 8 percent to nearly 48 percent means that China's sales in the lucrative U.S. market would plummet. To many congressional Democrats, then, legislating MFN conditionality seemed an ideal way of influencing the repressive regime in China. As in the case of the effort to enact tough trade legislation aimed at Japan, the House of Representatives has been in the vanguard of attempts to legislate MFN conditionality for China. The Senate has been slower to act, and, when it has acted, it has adopted milder measures than the House.

The first round in the ongoing skirmish between Congress and the president occurred in 1990. In October of that year the House adopted, by an overwhelming 384 to 30 margin, HR 4939. Sponsored by Ohio's Congressman Don Pease, the bill required the Chinese government to take a number of steps to correct human rights abuses in order to be eligible for MFN renewal in 1991. Among the required steps would be releasing political prisoners, lifting martial law, accounting for all those arrested since the 1989 Tiananmen Square massacre, and ending restrictions on the news media. The Bush administration strongly opposed the measure, but even a number of House Republicans departed from their president to join their Democratic colleagues when the measure came to a vote. The Senate, however, neither took up the House-passed bill nor adopted a measure of its own. For 1990, therefore, the president would have no congressional mandate regarding trade policy with China.

In 1991 and early 1992, however, both houses of Congress adopted tough legislation tying China's continued eligibility for MFN not only to progress on human rights practices, but also to changes in its trade policy (especially its protectionism and violation of U.S. copyright and patent protections) and limits on its sales of nuclear, biological, and chemical weapons. Although both chambers adopted the measure (HR 2212) by solid margins (409 to 21 in the House's November 26, 1991, vote and 59 to 39 in the Senate vote of February 25, 1992), Senate support was not sufficient to withstand President Bush's veto on March 2, 1992. The House voted to override Bush's veto by an overwhelming 357 to 61, but the Senate's March 18 vote of 60 to 38 fell six votes short of the two-thirds necessary to override.

In 1992 the commercial trade agreement with China was up for another three-year renewal. The year found congressional Democrats more determined than ever to punish China for its gross violations of human rights, which were seen most vividly in the 1989 massacre of student protesters. President Bush continued to insist that Congress should not attach conditions to China's continued MFN status, arguing that the result would be a more sullenly isolated China, not a more reform-minded one. His arguments failed to persuade House and Senate Democrats, however, who once again attempted to craft a legislative vehicle that could win solid enough majorities in both chambers to render it veto-proof.

Once again, the principal push came from the House, whose bill was co-sponsored by Representatives Don Pease (D-Ohio) and Nancy Pelosi (D-Calif.). Whereas previous bills threatened MFN status for all Chinese exports, the Pease-Pelosi bill (HR 5318) targeted only China's state-owned industries. This bill was an attempt to win additional backing by undercutting the Bush administration's argument that threatening China's MFN status was tantamount to threatening the emergence of China's growing ranks of reform-minded entrepreneurs. The Pease-Pelosi bill would authorize renewal of MFN for 1993, provided China made "overall significant progress" in human rights, trade practices, and weapons proliferation. If it failed to do so, the measure would obligate the administration to impose steep tariffs on imports from Chinese state-owned industries. Passed by the Ways and Means Committee on July 2 and adopted by the entire House by an overwhelming 339 to 62 vote later that month, the Pease-Pelosi measure once again identified the House of Representatives as the more activist and aggressive chamber within Congress. As in past years, the Senate was in a largely reactive mode, moving slowly and allowing House activists to define the parameters of its own deliberations. While the Senate did pass the House measure by voice vote in September 1992, unlike the House of Representatives, it was unable to muster the requisite two-thirds needed to override President Bush's September 28, 1992, veto of the bill.

Bill Clinton's campaign rhetoric suggested that he would take a drastically different approach than Bush toward China's aging dictators. In October 1992 he charged that Bush was too eager to befriend "potentates and dictators," and he said that if elected he would be more willing than Bush to use trade sanctions to promote human rights. Less than three weeks after his election, however, Clinton struck a sharply different tone, publicly praising China's "progress" on human rights and trade violations under Bush's policies. While Clinton must consider the views of his fellow Democrats in Congress, including Senate Majority Leader George Mitchell (D-Me.) who has described the Bush policy toward China as "immoral" and has called for a revocation of MFN status to compel China to relax its human rights policies, it seems unlikely that Clinton will lead the charge for such legislation. Without a clear summons from a fellow Democrat, it is unlikely that Congress will undercut Clinton by adopting a revocation of China's MFN status over Clinton's objection.

## NAFTA and the Fast-Track Negotiating Authority

Our final case study of congressional efforts to mold U.S. trade policy concerns the historic effort to create a North America Free Trade Area (NAFTA). If fully implemented, a preliminary agreement announced on August 12, 1992, will — over a 15-year period — join the United States, Canada, and Mexico in the world's largest free trade zone. The eventual elimination of tariffs and other trade barriers among the three nations would permit goods produced anywhere in North America to be traded freely throughout the continent. With a population of 360 million and a combined economic production exceeding $6 trillion per year, NAFTA would represent a greater duty-free market than the European Community (EC), which served as its model.

The United States and Canada had previously established a free trade agreement that went into effect on January 1, 1989. When President Bush and Mexico's President Carlos Salinas agreed in June 1990 to negotiate a U.S.-Mexican free trade agreement, Canada joined the talks in the shared hope that a true continental customs union would result.

The accord announced in August 1992 is subject to the ratifying procedures of the three signatory nations. In the case of the United States, congressional influence is wielded in two ways: (1) in legislating the procedures under which the trade agreement negotiated by the executive is treated in Congress, and (2) in exercising its authority to accept, modify, or reject the NAFTA agreement altogether. Let's look at each of these congressional controversies in turn.

Congress alone determines the rules that will govern its own handling of trade issues. Acutely aware that trade bills, with their intricate domestic implications, can all too easily become "Christmas trees" on which all sorts of specialized amendments are hung, Congress in 1974 first established what is known as fast-track legislative procedures for trade measures. Under fast track, Congress gives itself 60 days from the time a trade agreement is presented to it to vote the measure cleanly up or down; no amendments are permitted under fast track. In many ways a statesmanlike move by Congress, the adoption of fast-track procedures involved a frank acknowledgment of its vulnerability to special pleading by constituents and organized interests. Its achievement was to make clear Congress's determination to overcome the morass of conflicting parochial interests and vote directly and expeditiously on major trade matters. Specifically, fast track requires that (1) committees cannot amend trade bills and must approve or disapprove them within 45 days, (2) both the House and the Senate have to vote on the bill within 15 days after committee action, and

(3) floor debate in each chamber is limited to 20 hours and no amendments are permitted.

In 1988 Congress reauthorized the fast-track procedure until 1991. Included in the reauthorization was provision for an additional two-year extension to 1993 *unless* either chamber objected. This short "window" was specified in hopes that it would encourage successful completion of the so-called Uruguay Round of GATT talks, which deals heavily with agricultural matters. By 1991, however, the politics of permitting fast track to extend until 1993 were inseparably bound up with the free trade talks then underway with Mexico.

Hence, 1991 saw efforts by the more protectionist wing of the Democratic party to block the two-year extension of fast-track authority as a surrogate way of expressing disapproval of the forthcoming trade agreement with Mexico. Hoping to head off legislative attempts to terminate fast track — which would surely spell trouble for the NAFTA agreement then being negotiated — the Bush administration issued an action plan on May 1, 1991. Contained in the document were administration pledges to address the principal concerns voiced relative to the proposed free trade agreement with Mexico, including promises regarding environmental protection, retraining of workers adversely affected by the agreement, and help for affected industries in the form of protracted transition periods. With its action plan in place, the Bush administration hoped to be able to paint congressional opponents of free trade — and of its 1991 surrogate, fast track — as retrograde protectionists who were working against the nation's long-term economic interests.

Most congressional Democratic leaders gave lukewarm support to Bush's plans for NAFTA and, with it, extending fast track through 1993. House Speaker Tom Foley expressed cautious support, as did the then chairman of the Senate Finance Committee, Lloyd Bentsen, and the chairman of the House Ways and Means Committee, Dan Rostenkowski. But all of these key Democratic leaders voiced concern that the final NAFTA agreement might prove too costly to American workers and might not contain adequate environmental safeguards. As Congressman Rostenkowski put it, "My inclination is to be supportive, but I see the storm brewing out there."

Powerful interest groups lobbied hard to defeat fast-track extension and, with it, to make ratification of a NAFTA agreement extremely unlikely. The AFL-CIO argued that free trade with Mexico would come at the price of lost American jobs, while environmental groups such as Friends of the Earth argued that Mexico's lax pollution standards would generate pressure to relax U.S. air quality standards in order to keep manufacturers from relocating to Mexico. Both groups made defeat of fast track a top lobbying priority for 1991.

Although Chairman Rostenkowski favored extending fast track through 1993, he agreed to bring a bill to terminate it, sponsored by Congressman Byron Dorgan (D-N. Dak.) to a vote in his Ways and Means Committee and then before the whole House. The committee voted against Dorgan's bill by a vote of 9 to 27 on May 14, and on May 23 the House similarly defeated the Dorgan measure by 192 to 231. As a sop to the Democrats' more protectionist wing, however, Rostenkowski and Richard Gephardt co-sponsored a nonbinding resolution pledging that Congress would terminate fast track if the administration failed to keep its promise to protect the environment and U.S. workers in the forthcoming agreement with Mexico. On the same day that it defeated Dorgan's bill to suspend fast track, the House also adopted the nonbinding Rostenkowski–Gephardt resolution by an overwhelming 329 to 85 vote.

Meanwhile, the Senate was presented with a similar measure to kill fast track, sponsored by Ernest Hollings (D-S.C.). Senator Bentsen's Finance Committee voted against the measure 15 to 3 on May 14, and 10 days later the Senate as a whole also rejected Hollings's proposal on a 36 to 59 vote.

On June 1, 1991, therefore, the two-year extension of fast track went into effect. This meant that the new Clinton administration would have until June 1993 to insure expeditious handling of the NAFTA agreement. Moving swiftly prior to his inauguration in January 1993, Clinton emerged from a meeting with Mexican President Salinas to proclaim that his administration would press for speedy congressional approval of the North American Free Trade Agreement *providing* Mexico agreed to specific understandings protecting U.S. workers and the environment. As a Democratic president, and hence the leader of a political party more beholden to powerful domestic labor and environmental interests, it was an act of considerable courage on Clinton's part to embrace NAFTA — and attempt to ensure its approval in Congress during the remaining five-month window of assured fast-track processes — in the face of considerable opposition to the treaty within his own party.

As these three cases show, Congress is increasingly involved in the intermestic details of contemporary trade issues. As we have seen, Congress is not optimally organized to deal with trade matters, with numerous committees claiming jurisdiction over various facets of trade matters. The House and Senate are also split philosophically between devotees of free trade doctrine and advocates of a more retaliatory and protectionist stance. Further divisions grounded in partisan and constituent interests are also evident in congressional proceedings. Yet, as in the case of its adoption of fast-track procedures, Congress has shown both a desire and a willingness to rise above these limiting divisions and to treat complex trade matters as serious issues affecting the nation's future. Whether we agree or disagree with the positions Congress adopted in the cases we have examined, clearly the congressional approach to trade issues has been governed by a seriousness and concern for the nation's economic future. Not for the first time has Congress shown itself to be a more admirably high-minded body than its legion of critics would care to admit.

## Congressional Activism in Foreign Policy-Making

The contemporary pattern of congressional assertiveness in U.S. foreign policy is nothing if not controversial. Here we will look at three arguments often leveled against congressional activism and assess the merits of those arguments.

### Need to Present a United Front

Some observers argue that, if Congress does not willingly accept second billing to the president, the United States will present an inconsistent face to the outside world. Without clearly accepted presidential leadership, it is stated, other governments will be confused as to who is speaking for the United States and what the nation's policy actually is. Whereas the executive branch is headed by a single chief executive and thus can speak with one voice, the decentralized Congress sometimes threatens to act like "535 secretaries of state," the critics say.

This is indeed sometimes a problem, particularly if individual legislators overstep the bounds of shaping foreign policy and begin to involve themselves in its actual conduct. In 1987, for example, then Speaker of the House Jim Wright (D-Tex.) injected himself in the struggle between Nicaragua's leftist Sandinista regime and the Contra rebels seeking to overthrow it. President Reagan had refused to meet with the Sandinista leader, Daniel Ortega, but Congressman Wright held his own talks with Ortega. Understandably, some foreign observers did not know whether official U.S. policy was to back the Contras' effort to bring down the Sandinistas or to act as a conciliator between them. Similarly, former Congressman George Hansen (R-Id.) set out for Iran in 1980 on his own (unsuccessful) effort to secure the release of U.S. hostages.

These and similar actions can indeed distort the U.S. position on international issues, and it is reasonable to expect responsible legislators to refrain from grandstanding acts that might undermine U.S. foreign policy. At the same time, however, it is also true that rival factions and agencies within the executive branch frequently pursue different and incompatible foreign policy agendas. Their incessant maneuvering to prevail within the executive branch and win support in Congress and with the public sometimes sends contradictory signals abroad and undercuts the coherence of U.S. policy. In the increasingly important bilateral relationship with Japan, for example, the Pentagon and State Department often appear to have a de facto bureaucratic alliance based on their shared institutional perspective. That perspective stresses the strategic and political sides of the relationship and takes pains to play down "secondary" economic frictions that could destroy a pivotal link in the architecture of world order. Other agencies, including most notably the Office of the U.S. Trade Representative, Department of Commerce, and Department of Labor, pay much more attention to the economic aspects of the U.S.-Japan connection and are not at all comfortable with what they see. These agencies often press for a more aggressive U.S. stance toward Japan's challenge to U.S. economic interests and believe that the Pentagon and State Department needlessly coddle the Japanese.

Thus, although an activist Congress adds to the inherent challenge of defining and implementing a clear and consistent foreign policy, congressional passivity would not thereby produce it. Interbranch politics would merely be replaced by intrabranch politics.

### Lack of Foreign Policy Expertise

Many observers contend that few members of Congress are true foreign policy experts. Therefore, the argument goes, a policy shaped by Congress is bound to be a policy of amateurism, hardly the kind of thoughtful approach that befits a great power. It is indeed a fact of legislative life that members of Congress must deal with the whole spectrum of policy issues confronting the nation. In any given legislative session, members will have to make more or less informed voting choices on issues ranging from farm price support subsidies to Alaskan wildlife preservation to school voucher programs to the problems of urban decay. For most members, the pressures to be reasonably adept generalists make it difficult, if not impossible, for them to attain the depth of knowledge they need to become true foreign affairs specialists. It is thus unrealistic to expect all of them to be fully informed on the nuances of the dozens of foreign policy issues.

It does not follow, however, that Congress is inherently incapable of acting unwisely on foreign affairs. Presidents, no less than legislators, are faced with similar demands to be more or less conversant with the whole spectrum of policy issues facing the nation, no matter how much they might wish to focus on foreign affairs. Yet no one argues that as a consequence, the president is unable to handle the foreign affairs aspects of his job.

To the extent that Congress is able to act knowledgeably on foreign policy issues, this ability is attributed mainly to the growth in congressional staff and the expertise of the Congressional Research Service and the Office of Technology Assessment. Through the much-noted explosion in congressional staff over the past two decades, legislators now have the support of subject-matter experts who do not owe their livelihood to the executive branch and so are not beholden to its policies. The same critics who want Congress to submit meekly to presidential leadership also berate it for hiring more staffers, but it is that very strengthening of its own institutional capability that helps Congress discharge the independent policy-making role envisioned by the Constitution. In addition, the less noted but no less important repository of policy expertise found in the Congressional Research Service and the Office of Technology Assessment gives Congress additional "bench strength" in analyzing international currents and evaluating the pros and cons of alternative foreign policy proposals.

Today Capitol Hill is well populated by foreign policy congressional staffers with impressive credentials. Many hold advanced degrees in the field, some are former Foreign Service officers, and most bring to their jobs considerable intelligence and solid analytical abilities. Those skills are being used in researching issues and developing legislative initiatives for individual members or for the committees employing them.

A good example of the calibre of congressional staffers is Larry K. Smith. A defense intellectual who has taught at Dartmouth College and Harvard's John F. Kennedy School of Government, Smith is well respected in academia, the think-tank community, and the government. He was hired by then House Armed Services Committee Chairman Les Aspin (D-Wis.) to help reformulate the nation's defense policy for the post–Cold War era. Smith's mastery of security policy issues combined with his pragmatic political skills have won him praise from both sides of the political aisle. As Alton Frye of the prestigious Council on Foreign Relations said of Smith, "Linking national security issues with the practical politics of getting things done: That's where his brilliance lies." Smith is not the only such expert on Capitol Hill. Equally impressive foreign policy experts arc found on the staffs of individual members as well as the appropriate House and Senate committees. Therefore, while not all members of Congress are able to immerse themselves thoroughly in the intricacies of international issues, they have available to them the considerable talents of their staff assistants to aid them in staying abreast of world events.

Also strengthening Congress's overall sophistication on foreign policy matters is the fact that some of its members do manage to develop genuine expertise on world affairs. Former Congressman Stephen Solarz (D-N.Y.), who lost his House seat primarily because of the 1992 reapportionment, offers a good example. During his distinguished congressional career, Solarz immersed himself in the complexities of Asian politics, a diligence that served him and his colleagues well during his tenure on the House Foreign Affairs Subcommittee on Asian and Pacific Affairs. Formerly a graduate student of Zbigniew Brzezinski at Columbia University, Solarz was a highly intelligent, articulate, and pragmatic policy-maker who defied easy categorization. He became personally involved in the Philippines transition to democracy in the 1980s, but more recently he won wide notice for his hawkish support of President Bush during Operation Desert Storm.

An equally impressive member of Solarz's former subcommittee is Iowa Republican Jim Leach. With degrees from Princeton, Johns Hopkins, and the London School of Economics, as well as his experience as a Foreign Service officer, Leach brings to his work a keen intellect and an exceptional command of international issues, and has won the respect of his House colleagues for his quiet, pragmatic, problem-solving approach.

Still another long-time House member worth noting is Les Aspin, a former Chairman of the House Armed Services Committee. Aspin possesses a brilliant mind (B.A., Yale University; M.A., Oxford University; Ph.D., Massachusetts Institute of Technology) and a masterful command of the intricacies of defense issues. Essentially a policy centrist on defense matters, Aspin was skilled at walking a fine line between the broadly hawkish sentiments of his committee and the overwhelmingly dovish outlook of the House Democratic Caucus. His skill in doing so testified to his political astuteness, penetrating intellect, and relentless workaholism.

Similar stories abound in the Senate. Claiborne Pell (D-R.I.), chairman of the Senate Foreign Relations Committee, was educated at Princeton and Columbia universities and spent seven years as a Foreign Service officer. Though low key in his direction of the Foreign Relations Committee, Pell is a well-respected authority on the foreign policy questions that come before the committee. Pell's predecessor as committee chairman was Richard Lugar (R-Ind.). A former Rhodes Scholar, Lugar is a quick study on international matters and much admired for his role in forging a bipartisan consensus to promote democracy in South Africa and in the Philippines. A final example of policy expertise in the Senate is Sam Nunn (D-Ga.), chairman of the Senate Armed Services Committee. Though less flashy than some of his colleagues, Nunn has emerged as a genuine expert on defense policy and as a respected coalition builder in support of a strong national defense. Nunn's essential trademarks are his exceptionally strong work ethic, his insistence on mastering the most minute details of defense issues, his determinedly nonabrasive manner, and his political moderation. Through these traits, Nunn has become an unusually respected and influential leader on defense matters. As these and numerous other legislative profiles show, Congress contains a number of members with impressive expertise on foreign policy issues.

### The Politicization of Congress

A third charge often leveled against congressional activism in foreign policy-making is that Congress is so deeply politicized, split by partisan and ideological divisions, and vulnerable to the special pleadings of powerful interest groups that it is incapable of transcending political parochialism and acting on an elevated conception of the long-term national interest. Of course, Congress is an inherently political institution, and politics in the negative sense of the term does sometimes intrude on the policy-making process. However, it is generally unfair to conclude that members of Congress are unable to think and act in terms of the higher national good. It was Congress, after all, that transcended the instinctive isolationism of its constituents and courageously enacted the critical legislation establishing our early Cold War policy. The Marshall Plan, aid to Greece and Turkey, and U.S. participation in NATO were all made possible by congressional action. More recently, as we have seen, it was Congress who insisted on a policy of strong U.S. economic sanctions to help bring down South African apartheid. Finally, Congress itself took the unusual step of tacitly acknowledging the dangers of politicized parochialism when it adopted the fast-track procedure for handling complex trade legislation.

For all its very real shortcomings, then, Congress remains essentially what the Founding Fathers intended it to be: a constitutionally independent, coequal, and democratically rooted voice in shaping U.S. foreign policy. While there is every reason to believe that Congress-bashing will remain a national pastime rivaling baseball in its mass appeal, a better reading of the evidence suggests that the U.S. Congress faithfully mirrors, more often than not, both the ideals and the anxieties of the American people.

## SUGGESTED READINGS

Barnhart, Michael, ed. *Congress and United States Foreign Policy*. Albany, N.Y.: State University of New York Press, 1987.

Blechman, Barry M. *The Politics of National Security: Congress and U.S. Defense Policy*. New York: Oxford University Press, 1990.

Brown, Eugene. *J. William Fulbright: Advice and Dissent*. Iowa City: University of Iowa Press, 1985.

Dahl, Robert A. *Congress and Foreign Policy*. New York: Harcourt, Brace, 1950.

Feld, Werner J. *Congress and National Defense: The Politics of the Unthinkable*. New York: Praeger, 1985.

Franck, Thomas M., and Edward Weisband. *Foreign Policy by Congress*. New York: Oxford University Press, 1979.

Grassmuck, George. *Sectional Biases in Congress on Foreign Policy*. Baltimore: Johns Hopkins University Press, 1951.

Lindsay, James M. *Congress and Nuclear Weapons*. Baltimore: Johns Hopkins University Press, 1991.

Pastor, Robert A. *Congress and the Politics of U.S. Foreign Economic Policy, 1929–1976*. Berkeley: University of California Press, 1980.

Robinson, James Arthur. *Congress and Foreign Policy-Making: A Study in Legislative Influence and Initiative*. Homewood, Ill.: Dorsey Press, 1967.

Rourke, John. *Congress and the Presidency in U.S. Foreign Policymaking: A Study of Interaction and Influence*. Boulder, Colo.: Westview Press, 1983.

Stennis, John Cornelius. *The Role of Congress in Foreign Policy*. Washington, D.C.: American Enterprise Institute for Public Policy Research, 1971.

Whalen, Charles W. *The House and Foreign Policy: The Irony of Congressional Reform*. Chapel Hill: University of North Carolina Press, 1982.

# CHAPTER 5

# Coordinating the Players

Before the United States became a major actor on the world stage, Americans widely believed that foreign policy, unlike domestic policy, was essentially apolitical. The United States was hardly threatened by anyone physically, foreign and security matters were relatively infrequent and tangential to most people, and the few dealings people had with foreign affairs were tainted by association with what many viewed as a corrupt European-based international system. According to this mind-set, foreign relations was minimal and consisted mostly of diplomatic relations conducted by a small corps of professional diplomats.

This depiction fairly accurately reflected the American circumstance until the Second World War forced a permanent participation in global affairs. In the Cold War system that evolved, almost anything that happened anywhere came to be viewed as consequential to some Americans and some interests. Foreign and defense policy, in a word, mattered.

## The Politicization of U.S. Foreign Policy

As foreign and defense concerns occupied a growing part of the national agenda, they would inevitably become political. First, as the agenda broadened, so also would disagreement about the United States' place in the world. At the philosophical level some disagreement occurred as to the degree to which America should be engaged; in more specific areas, the U.S. position and role with individual countries and in different situations became contentious. Since opposing policy preferences cannot simultaneously be official policy, political processes had to be engaged to decide what the U.S. policy toward the world would be.

Foreign and defense policy and its implementation became an increasing part of the competition for scarce governmental resources. In 1955, for instance, the Department of Defense budget accounted for fully half the overall federal budget; it still makes up nearly one-quarter of federal expenditures, although that proportion is declining. At the same time, any dollars spent on foreign economic assistance (as in proposals to help underwrite economic reform in Russia) compete with domestic priorities, from the development of infrastructure to education. Policy is what gets funded. In a condition of scarce resources where there is not enough money to fulfill all needs, the policy process must find ways to decide who gets what.

The relative priority of foreign and defense matters, as well as policy options in general and specific situations, cover the spectrum of opinion, and there are politicians, interest groups, and think tanks to articulate them all. As the political election season progressed in the summer of 1992, for instance, a great public debate began over the continuing intransigence of Saddam Hussein. The Iraqi leader clearly took great delight in enraging world, and especially U.S., opinion by systematically defying the U.N. restrictions he had agreed to as part of the peace agreement ending the Persian Gulf War. What should we do about this reprehensible behavior, Americans asked. The alternatives ranged from tightening economic sanctions to limited military strikes to large-scale military actions to doing nothing. Clearly, the United States — with or without the assistance of its allies from the war — could not simultaneously bomb and not bomb Iraq, nor could it assassinate and not assassinate Saddam. Policy choices were clearly necessary, in which some options would be chosen and others rejected. Complicating the process, of course, was the effect of any chosen option on the presidential election.

Policy toward Iraq, of course, represents an extreme because of the Persian Gulf War and the ongoing controversy over Iraqi-U.S. relations that heavily politicize the issue area (for more detail, see Chapter 8). With the increasing prevalence of foreign policy influences on the daily lives of Americans, inevitably the political aspects of foreign policy will increasingly be a part of, and even dominate, the political process. The content may decreasingly be military/national security, as it was in the Cold War, but economic issues will certainly come to the fore, especially in the Clinton administration.

Deciding on policies is what the policy process is for and about. In the U.S. system as described in previous chapters, the foreign and defense policy process consists of (1) interaction within the executive branch of government and (2) the lawmaking power.

## Policy-Making within the Executive Branch

The various agencies that propose and execute policy interact to choose among policy alternatives that the executive branch will implement or, if necessary, submit to the legislative branch for its approval. Generally, administrations have sought to involve Congress in foreign policy matters as little as possible. Presidents and their advisers often come to think of foreign and security policy as their own preserves, matters that they should be allowed to handle with minimum interference, especially when sensitive or classified information is involved. At times in U.S. history, Congress acceded to this attitude, but in recent decades that has clearly been less the case. When presidents ignore Congress, fail to consult it adequately (as defined by Congress), or engage in foreign policy misdeeds or misguided policies, the battle is joined.

During the 1980s the executive branch's approach to resolving policy questions came to be known as the *interagency process*. Fashioned as it was during the Cold War, the centerpiece of this system was the National Security Council. Presidents have relied on this mechanism to varying degrees across time. President Eisenhower hardly ever used it at all, whereas it was very important to President Kennedy. During the Reagan-Bush years, however, it came to involve an elaborate set of multilevel deliberative bodies that debated policy from various institutional perspectives. Although the new Democratic administration will almost certainly modify this process to some extent to fit its style, it will not do away with it entirely. A mechanism of this nature is necessary so that all interests are represented within the executive branch. More important, the process is likely to be the model for forming the mechanisms of Clinton's Economic Council.

### Executive-Legislative Interaction

Interaction between the branches is constitutionally mandated. Congress, as observed in Chapter 4, is responsible for enacting laws, and most foreign dealings have legal implications within the United States. In addition, the power of the purse means that when foreign policies require the expenditure of governmental funds—and they nearly always do—then the Congress must be involved.

The dominant theme of executive-legislative interaction has been the rise of congressional activism. When Congress feels it has either been excluded or that the executive branch has acted wrongly or unwisely, Congress reacts. It may cut off funding for foreign and defense policies. The Church amendment to the appropriations bill of 1973 cut off U.S. government support for the Republic of Vietnam, for instance, and the various Boland amendments between 1982 and 1986 (named after Representative Edward Boland, D-Mass.) sought to prevent federal funds from being provided to the Contras in Nicaragua.

When the president, in the absence of legal restriction, acts in ways that Congress disapproves of, it may pass legislation that restricts or guides the executive's actions. Three such acts, the War Powers Resolution, the Goldwater-Nichols Defense Reorganization Act, and the Nunn-Cohen Act, will be examined later in this chapter to demonstrate this form of congressional activism.

## The Interagency Process

Even the relatively like-minded people who surround the president will disagree on different policy options. Therefore, a need has arisen for a set of mechanisms whereby the options can be debated and, hopefully, resolved. Moreover, since the executive branch is the repository of most government expertise within the bureaucracies of the executive agencies, there is a need to bring that information and expertise to bear on policy problems.

Within the Reagan and Bush administrations, the mechanism for dealing with foreign policy problems became known as the interagency process. It was centered around the National Security Council, thereby bringing it fully under the control of the White House and the chief executive's closest advisers. An examination of the structure will reveal both how it was designed to deal with foreign policy problems and what areas of change the new Clinton administration may envision.

### Structure of the Interagency Process

*The National Security Council*  At the top of the hierarchy of working groups responsible for resolving policy divisions within the executive branch is the National Security Council itself. The role of the NSC is to advise and assist the president in integrating all aspects of national security policy as it affects the United States, including domestic, foreign, military, intelligence, and economic considerations. The Bush administration, in one of its first actions upon coming to office, stipulated in National Security Directive (NSD)-1 that the NSC was the principal forum for considering national security policy issues that require presidential determination. President Clinton is continuing this practice.

As stated earlier, the NSC has four statutory members (the president, vice president, secretary of state, and secretary of defense), two statutory advisers (the director of central intelligence, or DCI, and the chairman of the Joint Chiefs of Staff, or CJCS), two special advisers (the director of the Arms Control and Disarmament Agency or ACDA and the director of the United States Information Agency or USIA), and anyone else the president may dictate, always including the national security adviser (NSA) and the White House chief of staff. When convened, their role is to offer advice to the president but not to take binding votes on policy issue outcomes.

The Bush administration probably made more use of this group than any previous administration in history. One reason may be that Bush himself was part of this process in two previous positions he held: as vice president and as director of central intelligence. Another reason may be the close, symbiotic relationship that existed between Bush and those he appointed to formal positions in the process. In addition to his closest friend, Secretary of State James Baker, his relationship to Secretary of Defense Richard Cheney, NSA's Brent Scowcroft, and CJCS's Colin Powell goes back to their mutual service in the Gerald Ford administration in 1975. The result was an extremely homogeneous working (and some have argued too congenial) group. The Clinton team—SECDEF Les Aspin, Secretary of State Warren Christopher, DCI James Woolsey, NSA Anthony Lake, and Powell—is more diverse in background and was not previously close on a personal level. Whether this difference will mean they work less well together or will air more different points of view remains to be seen. Clinton has maintained that the criteria for selecting these officials included the ability to work as a "team."

*The Principals Committee*  Below the NSC itself are three layers of organization. The first layer, the Principals Committee (NSC/PC), is chaired by the national security adviser and is composed of the secretaries of state and defense, DCI, CJCS, the White House chief of staff, and any other officials who may be deemed helpful in a given policy matter. As the senior interagency forum for considering policy issues affecting national security, the Principals Committee's function is to review, coordinate, monitor, and implement basic national security policies that do not require direct and personal presidential involvement. The committee is convened when the president cannot or feels he does not need to be present.

Although it was not called the PC at the time, President Kennedy made use of the NSC in this manner during the Cuban missile crisis. He ordered that the NSC meet without him (which is essentially the composition of the PC) to discuss options during the crisis. His rationale was that the members would have franker discussions if he were absent and would not have to worry about what he might think of their ideas.

The NSC and the Principals Committee are assisted by two working-level groups, the Deputies Committee and the Policy Coordinating Committees. These bodies are responsible for doing much of the staff work necessary to flesh out decisions made at the top levels as well as to lay out policy options.

*The Deputies Committee*   The Deputies Committee (NSC/DC) is directly beneath the Principals Committee. As the name suggests, this committee is composed of the chief assistants of the members of the Principals Committee. Chaired by the deputy NSA, its members are the undersecretary of state for political affairs, the undersecretary of defense for policy, the deputy DCI, and the vice chairman of the JCS. Equivalent-level officials from other agencies meet with the deputies when necessary.

The Deputies Committee is intended as a prime working group. Officially, it serves as the senior subcabinet forum for considering policy issues affecting national security, by reviewing and monitoring the work of higher levels of the process, and as a forum to propose and consider recommendations concerning ways to develop and implement policy. For example, one function of the deputies is to formulate a complete set of contingency plans for U.S. responses to conceivable crises worldwide.

*The Policy Coordinating Committees*   These committees (NSC/PCC) are a series of working groups that draw from the major geographic and functional areas of foreign and defense policy. Geographically, Policy Coordinating Committees (PCCs) have been established for Europe, East Asia, the former Soviet Union, Africa, Latin America, and the Near East and South Asia. The job of these groups, at yet a more detailed level of specificity than the higher groups, is both to monitor and propose policies regarding national security policies in their respective areas. Functionally, PCCs have been set up for defense, intelligence, arms control, and international economics. (This is the highest level at which economic concerns are a formal part of the interagency process.)

The PCCs are made up of officials at the assistant secretary level. Chairs are appointed by different individual executive agencies depending on the area of concern. All the regional chairs are appointed by the secretary of state. Thus, the chairs are the assistant secretaries of state for each region. The defense PCC is appointed by the secretary of defense, the international economics PCC by the secretary of the treasury, the intelligence PCC by the DCI, and the Arms Control PCC by the NSA.

PCCs are the level at which detailed positions are reached and where things such as staff position papers are devised and debated for transmission to higher levels in the process. The PCC for Near East and South Asia, for instance, is the appropriate venue for discussing and devising policy positions to deal with Saddam Hussein. This is presumably where the original options were worked out for defining U.S. political objectives in Operation Desert Storm.

The agencies represented at each level in this process are the same — State, Defense, Central Intelligence — and can be considered the core actors within the executive branch. Organized as they are within the context of the

NSC system, the PCCs were clearly devised to deal with foreign and national security policy within the context of the Cold War where foreign and national security policy, as argued in Chapter 1, were viewed as essentially synonymous. Hence, the highest ranking official representing concerns about international economic policy is an assistant secretary of the treasury in the PCC. Nowhere is there a permanent representative of environmental issues or other nontraditional concerns (population or narcotics, for instance). With the parallel Economic Council and a much heightened concern for environmental issues symbolized by Vice President Gore, both areas are being elevated in importance in the Clinton administration.

### Concerns about the Interagency Process

As the Clinton administration took office, one question that it was almost immediately forced to confront was the continuing adequacy and relevance of the interagency process that it inherited. Because of the new president's relative inexperience in the foreign and defense areas, the quantity and quality of advice he receives from this process, probably filtered through the comparatively more experienced eye of the vice president, will be vital to his success or failure in this area.

The following four legacies of the Bush interagency process will undoubtedly come under scrutiny in the future as different variations of it are fashioned.

*Utilization of the Entire Process*   During the Bush administration, decision-making tended to be concentrated at the top, among the president and that group of advisers who formed the NSC and the Principals Committee, with relatively little influence from the Deputies and Policy Coordination Committee levels. The decision-making style, in terms of organization theory, appeared to be top down (instructions flowing from the top echelons downward for implementation, with little input on framing decisions rising through the ranks), as opposed to bottom up, where options and opinions are sought from lower levels in the actual formulating stages. Two examples of this style are the now familiar case of Desert Storm and Yugoslavia.

With regard to Desert Storm, many observers (including the authors here) presumed that once the invasion occurred, formulations of various possible outcomes, including the enumeration of costs, as well as benefits and second- and third-order effects of different courses of action, would be consigned to the Deputies Committee. It was thought that their counsel, in the form of staff reports and recommendations, would define the debate within the White House and how the options would be presented to the public. If sources such as Bob Woodward's book *The Commanders* are reasonably accurate, this approach was not adopted. Decision-making was so tightly controlled that CJCS Powell relates that he learned of the decision to go to war only as he watched the presidential news conference at which Mr. Bush said of the occupation of Kuwait, "This shall not stand."

With regard to the Bush administration's handling of the unraveling of Yugoslavia, including the brutalization of Bosnia and Herzegovina, the breakup of Yugoslavia came as no surprise to the expert community. It had been predicted since the 1970s, when the consequences of the death of President Josip Broz Tito (the overarching symbol of the Yugoslav state) began to be discussed in academic and governmental circles. Examining that situation, its likely directions, and possible U.S. responses was the kind of task for which the PCC is ideally suited, with the DC acting to sharpen options as events progressed. Tragically enough, most of the experts' predictions have come true. Yet, in the face of contingencies that its open process should have made it aware of in advance, the administration seemed paralyzed and indecisive during the summer of 1992.

*Like-mindedness*  When the president first assembled his group of closest advisers (Baker, Scowcroft, Cheney, Powell, Quayle), many analysts heralded the assemblage because the men involved knew one another so well and shared such similar views that the system could be much more decisive than would have been the case if a less compatible team was assembled. The negative side of this grouping was that their similarities in background and worldview were so great that the principle of informal checks and balances could not operate.

This like-mindedness was reinforced by the top-down style of the administration and the dominant role Bush assigned to members of the NSC staff throughout the process. All members of the NSC staff are personal appointees of the president, unconfirmed by the Senate, and thus serve as the president's highly personal staff. Each of the 30 or so professional members of the staff serves strictly at the president's pleasure and can be removed when he sees fit. Among these members are professionals borrowed from other agencies who bring with them their agency perspectives. Most of the staff recruited is likely to be ideologically very compatible with the president and much more sensitive to carrying out the president's wishes than, say, a Foreign Service officer working in the State Department who is protected from dismissal by Civil Service protections. That sensitivity is also likely to produce less dissent and to inject fewer ideas presumed to be heretical by the chief executive.

*Structural Inclusiveness*   Because it was set up within the confines of the National Security Act, the Bush interagency process reflected a national security structural bias, as noted. International economic concerns were not directly represented above the PCC, and other concerns, such as the environment, were not directly represented at all on a permanent basis.

That this structure may act perversely on occasion was apparently the case at the so-called Earth Summit in Rio de Janeiro in 1992. That meeting was called to try to devise global solutions to the problem of environmental degradation. This tricky agenda became quickly enmeshed in side issues such as Third World development. (Third World countries in essence demanded developmental assistance in return for ending environmentally destructive but economically productive practices such as cutting down rainforests.)

The U.S. position at the event was confused and ultimately highly criticized. The chief U.S. delegate was the director of the Environmental Protection Agency (EPA), who generally supported the goals and resolutions being proposed. At the core was a proposal for a convention protecting life species that was universally supported — except by the Bush administration, which argued that its provisions would be economically deflating by restricting scientific investigation on some species that may yield natural products that have pharmaceutical applications. When President Bush announced this extremely unpopular position in his speech before the Summit, it was widely condemned both domestically and abroad. The condemnation was all the harsher because the president's speech contradicted parts of the positions being advocated by the American delegation. With Vice President Gore spearheading environmental policy, a repeat of the Earth Summit disaster, at least, is unlikely.

*Congressional Intrusion*   In light of questionable practices and policies deemed inappropriate by Congress, numerous lawmakers contend that the system needs modification — possibly through legislation. A major part of the criticism is the exclusionary, closed nature of the system, which does not always respond to policy initiatives from Congress. In this case, one reaction is congressionally mandated change. For instance, when Lieutenant Colonel North's central role in the Iran-Contra scandal of the mid-1980s was revealed, Congress voiced considerable sentiment favoring legislatively passed limits on the NSC, including congressional confirmation of the NSA. This sentiment was not, however, translated into law.

As we will see in the following section on congressional activism, historically such intrusion has not been welcomed, primarily because it intrudes on the one area of broad presidential discretion, the White House Office, of which the NSC staff is a part. How relations will evolve now that both houses of Congress and the White House are controlled by the same party remains to be seen.

## Congressional Activism

At its best, congressional interaction with the chief executive on matters of foreign and defense policy is marked by cooperation and compromise. The president consults formally or informally with congressional leaders, weighs their advice, and takes actions that reflect that consultation. In the process, interbranch dynamics create policy around which a consensus can be forged so that Congress can support the president's positions, and vice versa.

Unhappily, this is seldom the case. As foreign and defense matters have become both more complex and more consequential, positions have divided over them, and increasingly along partisan lines. Exacerbating the problem is the fact that, in 26 of the 40 years preceding the 1992 election, different parties occupied the White House and controlled the Congress. For the past 12 years, a Republican president has faced a Democratic Congress (the partial exception being Republican control of the Senate from 1985 to 1987). As a result, foreign and national security questions have been part of the partisan debate.

The partisan wrangle becomes most pronounced when Congress, acting both from philosophical differences with an incumbent president or out of perceptions of excesses by the executive branch, enacts legislation in an attempt to curb executive power and discretion. At these times, interbranch rivalry is at its greatest, and the issues that can divide the branches are at their starkest and most dramatic. For that reason, we have chosen three particularly dramatic examples to view in some depth. They are important because their outcomes have helped frame the ongoing relationships between the branches and because they illustrate in very clear terms what causes such interactions. The first of these instances, the War Powers Resolution, pitted a Republican president, Richard M. Nixon, against a Democratic Congress reacting to the Vietnam War. The other two found President Ronald W. Reagan facing a divided Congress in 1986 over the issue of defense reorganization, in light of a number of instances in which the U.S. military had performed at questionable levels.

## Key Legislation Curbing Executive Powers

The extent and nature of disagreement between the executive and legislative branches of the government has become increasingly frequent and formalized over the past 20 years or so. The watershed event, of course, was the Vietnam War and its generally corrosive effects on both public and, by reflection, congressional satisfaction with foreign policy-making. Until nearly the end of the U.S. involvement in Vietnam (U.S. withdrawal from which was ultimately mandated by Congress), Congress felt it had been effectively excluded from the important decisions that had defined our commitment there. With the public foreign policy consensus broken by the war and support for the government generally shaken by the Watergate scandal, the opportunity for congressional reassertion was ripe.

No president has been immune from congressional wrath in the foreign and national security policy arena. Although disagreement is undoubtedly more likely and more frequent when the presidency and the Congress are controlled by different parties, this has not always been the case. Democratic President Jimmy Carter, for instance, had Democratic majorities in both houses of Congress throughout his term in office, but that advantage did not automatically translate into cooperative relations between the branches. Carter faced tough bipartisan opposition before the Senate ratified the Panama Canal Treaty in 1977, and in 1980 he was forced to withdraw the second Strategic Arms Limitation Treaty (SALT II) because of opposition highlighted by the Soviet invasion of Afghanistan in December 1979.

At least three themes recur when the branches come into direct conflict in the foreign policy arena. First, when members of Congress perceive that their constituencies are directly affected by foreign or national security matters, Congress becomes active and will oppose the executive when those constituency interests are adversely affected.

This involvement is obvious in both the economic and security areas that we have been emphasizing. In the economic sphere, for instance, the status of Japanese-American trade negotiations directly affects American workers, especially farmers. The amount of citrus fruit Japan buys from the United States has a direct bearing on the prosperity of citrus growers in Florida, Texas, Arizona, and California. Not surprisingly, the congressional delegations from those states take a very proprietary interest in those negotiations. In matters of defense, the debate over national security strategy in a post–Cold War world has equally direct consequences in areas that have traditionally relied heavily on defense procurement (e.g., the aerospace industry of southern California) or in the number and size of reserve units and armories in different states.

A second theme involves executive overreach—the so-called imperial presidency. Because of his constitutional designation as the head of state, the president is most prominent in his dealings with foreign policy and foreign dignitaries. Depending on the individual and how he includes the

Congress in foreign dealings, the appearance of haughtiness, even disdain, can creep into the relationship. This was especially a problem during the Nixon presidency. Nixon considered himself and National Security Adviser Henry Kissinger so well qualified in foreign policy that they did not seek much congressional advice. The symbol of the imperial presidency was particularly caught in Nixon's directive that the White House guards be clothed in highly militaristic uniforms that appeared to be a cross between nineteenth-century Prussian uniforms and Gilbert and Sullivan operetta costumes. These uniforms engendered such ridicule that they were discarded.

Third, Congress becomes activist when it believes the executive is mishandling foreign affairs. Sometimes, the motivation is partisan and political, as, for instance, in criticism of the Bush administration's approach to the Earth Summit in 1992. At other times, the motivation can arise from a genuine belief that executive action is both wrong politically and has potentially erosive effects on the political system. The political wrongheadedness of the policy and the evasion of statutory checks and balances in the Iran-Contra affair illustrate both concerns.

The nature and tenor of these relations can be illustrated by looking at three specific pieces of legislation. We have chosen two cases that appeared over a decade apart. The first is the passage of the War Powers Resolution of 1973 over President Nixon's objection and veto. The second case occurred in 1986 and consists of two related pieces of legislation passed a month apart and possessing the common theme of reforming the defense establishment to make it more effective: the Goldwater-Nichols Defense Reorganization Act and the Cohen-Nunn Act.

### The War Powers Resolution

Of the many powers wielded by modern governments, none has as fateful consequences or is so surrounded by emotion as the power to commit the nation to war. Social, environmental, educational, and economic policies all affect, for better or worse, the quality of the nation's life. Their impact, however, pales in comparison with the grim life-and-death implications of the decision to go to war. Given the profundity of the decision for war or peace, it follows that the legal power to make that decision is among the most fundamental and enduring issues in American democracy.

***Context for Passing the War Powers Resolution*** Enactment of the War Powers Resolution in October 1973 represented a dramatic milestone in the reassertion of congressional prerogatives in international affairs. The momentum to do so had been building since the late 1960s. Contrary to what has often been written about it, the resolution was most definitely not the product of a sudden surge of legislative hormones. Rather, it was the final product of a long-brewing debate among constitutional scholars and policy-makers in the two elected branches. The question addressed by the resolution was precisely: "Whose power is the war power?"

Why did so many leaders think it was necessary to pass legislation to clarify this most fundamental issue? And why was that controversial legislation politically attainable in the early 1970s? The answers to both questions are found in four factors: inherent constitutional ambiguity, a long-term trend toward executive dominance on matters of war and peace, the bitter legacy of Vietnam, and the shifting political balance of power between a Democratic-controlled Congress and the Republican administration of Richard M. Nixon. Let's look briefly at each of these four factors.

*CONSTITUTIONAL AMBIGUITY.*    The American constitution, revered and venerable though it may be, was itself a product of the political climate and process of its time. As a political document, it represents the outcome of a great deal of persuasion and bargaining among the 55 delegates to the Philadelphia convention of 1787. It does not detract from the historic achievement of the Founding Fathers to point out that they were the leading politicians of their day and, as such, represented a microcosm of a broad array of competing views on how government should be structured, how its leaders should be selected, what powers they should wield, and the like. The fact that the Constitution has endured for over 200 years attests to the genius of the men who created it. Nonetheless, it must be stressed that a critical part of their undeniable genius was their collective knack for leaving many contentious issues lingering in constitutional ambiguity.

In their deliberations at Philadelphia, the Constitution's framers wanted to ensure that the new Republic they were creating would be free of what they regarded as the ultimate vice of the European monarchies of the day: the easy resort to war by an unaccountable and unresponsive executive. As we have seen in previous chapters, the Founding Fathers were reflexively suspicious of any concentration of unchecked executive power. This suspicion was compounded in matters involving war and peace. It is, of course, true that the extreme dilution of executive authority of the Articles of Confederation had brought them to Philadelphia in the first place. If eighteenth-century Europe embodied all that was wrong with unaccountable executive privilege, then the manifest weakness of the failed experiment under the Articles of Confederation showed the paralysis of a too-weak executive. Somewhere between these extremes lay a balance between the capacity for decisive action characteristic of strong executives and an inclination toward deliberateness and accountability characteristic of elected legislative assemblies. The Founding Fathers were attempting to strike such a balance as they set about to create the new nation's most basic legal charter.

Records of the Constitutional Convention's debates reflect surprisingly little discussion on allocating the power to commit the nation to war. This reflects a broad consensus among the convention's delegates. Nearly all agreed that the executive must not have the power unilaterally to take the nation into war. This consensus was mirrored in the Constitution's working draft, which gave Congress sole power to "make war." At the suggestion of delegates James Madison and Elbridge Gerry, however, this language was modified to create the now-famous congressional power to "declare war." As Madison's notes make clear, this slight change was intended to give presidents the ability to respond to sudden, unexpected attacks. It was most definitely not intended to alter the Founding Fathers' determination to assign to the legislative branch the supreme power to determine if and when the nation should initiate hostilities against another nation.

In light of these considerations, why do we so often speak of constitutional ambiguity with regard to the war power? There are two reasons. First, the Constitution named the president as commander in chief of the armed forces in order to establish the important principle of civilian supremacy over the nation's armed forces. But the role itself contains the seeds of ambiguity. Ambitious presidents eager to maximize their powers have advanced exceedingly expansive interpretations of what it means to be commander in chief. Some even insist that it permits the president to commit the United States' armed forces with or without explicit congressional authorization. This is, to say the least, a highly dubious assertion.

Another source of constitutional ambiguity is the later disagreement among the men who wrote the Constitution over the meaning of what they had written. By 1793 James Madison and Alexander Hamilton, both prominent delegates at Philadelphia, were promoting opposite interpretations of the Constitution's war powers provisions. To Hamilton, the war power was an inherently executive function, subject to a few legislative checks but not thereby denied to U.S. presidents. In contrast, Madison insisted that the Constitution had clearly made the war power a legislative power, leaving the execution of legislative decisions to the president in his capacity as commander in chief.

If Hamilton and Madison, two of the leading architects of the Constitution, wound up with diametrically opposite interpretations of what the document intended, it is no wonder that later generations have struggled to make sense of the ambiguous intentions of the Founding Fathers. The result is what former Supreme Court Justice Robert Jackson once spoke of as "a zone of twilight" that lay between the powers of the Congress and the president on matters of war and peace. It is in that "twilight zone" that presidents and legislators have found themselves for the past two centuries.

*EXECUTIVE DOMINANCE ON MATTERS OF WAR AND PEACE.*   The numbers alone are starkly revealing: since the founding of the Republic, U.S. armed forces have been used abroad over 200 times, as noted. How many of these instances have been accompanied by a congressional declaration of war as contemplated by the Constitution? The answer is startling. Precisely five: the War of 1812, the Mexican War, the Spanish-American War, World War I, and World War II. While other conflicts, such as Operation Desert Storm in 1991, were authorized by congressional action short of formal declarations of war, the fact remains that 98 percent of these foreign conflicts were undertaken by presidents whose interpretation of their prerogatives as commander in chief would be virtually unrecognizable to James Madison.

Those presidents' exceedingly broad view of their powers has been buttressed by a long succession of executive branch apologists of presidential supremacy. For example, President Truman dispatched U.S. troops to Korea in the summer of 1950, leading the nation into a major conflict that would drag on for three years. Truman sought neither congressional approval of his actions nor a formal declaration of war against North Korea. His conviction that he was empowered to undertake such a momentous step on his own authority was buttressed by a State Department memorandum prepared within days of the troop dispatch. The memorandum asserted that a president's power as commander in chief is virtually unlimited and that the president can order troops into combat "without congressional authorization" owing to his inherent foreign affairs powers. In a similar vein, a former State Department legal adviser, Abram Chayes, has asserted that the declaration of war is now little more than an obsolete formality!

By the late 1960s and early 1970s, this mounting record of presidentially initiated hostilities, coupled with broad dissemination of intellectual rationalizations on behalf of executive dominance, persuaded a growing number of legislators to restore the balance between the two elected branches to a level that more closely approximated our Founding Fathers' intentions.

*THE UNITED STATES' TRAUMATIC EXPERIENCE IN VIETNAM.*   The war began in the early 1960s as a limited U.S. undertaking aimed at thwarting Nikita Khrushchev's announced intention of expanding the communist orbit by fomenting so-called wars of national liberation in the Third World. U.S. policy-makers, opinion elites, and the mass public generally regarded President Kennedy's expansion of the role of U.S. advisers to South Vietnamese forces as a necessary commitment during a particularly dangerous phase of the Cold War.

When President Johnson sharply increased the level of U.S. forces in Vietnam and expanded their mission to one of offensive combat operations during 1964 and 1965, he did so with broad support from both the American public and Congress. The most vivid and controversial expression of congressional support for Johnson's war policy was the famous Gulf of Tonkin Resolution adopted in August 1964. Passed after only token debate, the measure was unanimously endorsed by the House of Representatives and met with only two dissenting votes in the Senate. (Interestingly, both opponents — Senators Wayne Morse of Oregon and Ernest Gruening of Alaska — were subsequently defeated in their bids for reelection.)

In its haste to demonstrate a unified U.S. front to the Vietnamese communists, Congress enacted exceedingly sweeping language in support of the president. The heart of the resolution declared that "the Congress approves and supports the determination of the President, as Commander in Chief, to take all necessary measures to repel any armed attack against the forces of the United States and to prevent further aggression." A bit later, in Section 2, comes the assertion that "the United States is . . . prepared as the President determines, to take all necessary steps, including the use of armed force."

The resolution was couched in strikingly permissive language. Congress announced ahead of time that it would "approve and support" "all necessary steps" that the *president* might decide to undertake in Vietnam. Years later, when it was too late, as the national consensus that spawned the Gulf of Tonkin Resolution dissolved in a monsoon of failure in Southeast Asia, members of Congress would look back on their fateful votes of August 1964 with grief and bitterness. In handing President Johnson a blank check to do as he pleased in Vietnam, Congress had clearly abdicated its legal, political, and moral responsibility.

By the early 1970s, with the magnitude of the Vietnam disaster clear for all to see, even the most passive lawmakers knew that something had to be done. Never again, they vowed, should the Congress so promiscuously hand over its constitutional prerogatives to the president. Their determination to reclaim legislative war-making powers was strengthened in 1971 when Congress repealed the Gulf of Tonkin Resolution, only to find the Nixon administration now claiming an inherent executive right to prosecute the Vietnam War, with or without explicit congressional authorization.

*The Political Character of Policy-making*　By 1973 the Democratic party had held firm majorities in both houses of Congress for nearly two decades; the White House, however, had been captured by the Democrats in only two of the last six presidential elections. The force of partisanship, then, was joined with the built-in tensions for political supremacy created by a separation-of-powers system of government. Either force can make political cooperation difficult; added together, they too often produce interbranch gridlock.

In addition to these two political forces, two others made legislative-executive relations particularly volatile in the early 1970s: the rising tide of reassertionist sentiment taking root in Congress; and the declining prestige of the presidency caused by the Vietnam fiasco and the Watergate scandal. These two factors are closely related. If during most of the Cold War Congress had frequently deferred to presidential leadership on foreign policy issues, it was due in large part to the belief that U.S. presidents were generally honest and prudent custodians of the national interest. As we have noted in an earlier chapter, the back-to-back disasters of President Johnson's Vietnam policy and the Nixon administration's dishonesty and criminality combined to rock the foundations of presidential dignity and respect. By 1973, with Nixon ever more grimly impaled on the stake of Watergate, his political opponents — mostly liberal, mostly Democrats, and mostly members of Congress — were only too eager to seize on his weakened position in order to reclaim and reassert legislative foreign policy powers that had generally atrophied during the Cold War.

Taken together, then, inherent constitutional ambiguity, a long-term trend toward presidential dominance on matters of war and peace, the bitter experience of Vietnam, and the partisan political struggles between a newly assertive Congress and a presidency weakened by scandal — all converged to set the stage for the enactment of the landmark War Powers Resolution of 1973. That the measure was passed over Nixon's veto is further evidence of the intense emotions and partisanship that surrounded it, for only 4 percent of presidential vetoes have ever been overridden by Congress.

*The War Powers Resolution*　As finally adopted, the resolution contains three principal provisions. They specify when the president must *consult* with Congress, when he must *report* to Congress, and when he must *terminate* hostilities and withdraw U.S. armed forces. A brief look at each of these provisions will clarify what the Congress intended through this legislation. It will also help us appreciate the difficulties of translating general legislative intent into precise, unambiguous statutory language.

The requirement that presidents consult with Congress before committing armed forces to hostilities is spelled out in Section 3 of the resolution. The key language of this section states that "the President in every possible instance shall consult with Congress before introducing United States Armed Forces into hostilities or into situations where imminent involvement in hostilities is clearly indicated by the circumstances." Although the general intent of Section 3 is clear enough, translating congressional intention into executive conduct presents several problems. It is not entirely clear what presidents would have to do to satisfy the requirement that they "consult with Congress." Do they need to acquire congressional approval prior to acting? Section 3 does not seem to go quite that far, but it appears to have in mind a good bit more than mere presidential notification of impending moves.

If the precise meaning of consultation is not entirely clear, neither is the precise identity of who it is that the president must consult with. It is obviously unrealistic to expect presidents to hold discussions with all 535 members of Congress before undertaking critical national security operations, but nowhere can one "look up" the answer to the question of who and how many members of Congress must be consulted in order to fulfill the spirit of Section 3.

Finally, as the resolution's language concedes (the president must consult with Congress "in every possible instance"), in some instances prior consultations are impractical. For example, at the time of the Mayaguez incident in 1975, four key congressional leaders were in Greece, four others were in China, and others were scattered in their states and districts. Clearly, presidential consultations with Congress were not feasible under these circumstances.

The resolution's second key provision is the reporting requirement contained in Section 4. This requirement obligates the president to report to Congress within 48 hours any time U.S. armed forces are dispatched (1) "into hostilities or into situations where imminent involvement in hostilities is clearly indicated by the circumstances," (2) into foreign territory while "equipped for combat," or (3) "in numbers which substantially enlarge United States Armed Forces equipped for combat already located in a foreign nation." The president's report to Congress must specify (1) the circumstances necessitating the introduction of U.S. armed forces, (2) the constitutional and legislative authority under which such an introduction took place, and (3) the estimated scope and duration of the hostilities or involvement.

The third and final key provision of the War Powers Resolution is the famous and controversial Section 5, which deals with the termination of hostilities and the withdrawal of U.S. forces. Intent on reversing the trend toward presidentially instigated wars that could drag on unless Congress took overt action to end them, the drafters of the War Powers Resolution rewrote the "ground rules" so that any protracted hostilities by U.S. forces would require explicit legislative approval. Congress, it is said, will now share the controls of foreign policy takeoffs, not just the crash landings.

How is this congressional codetermination to be achieved? Section 5 spells out two means of doing so. First, once the president has reported to Congress that U.S. forces are being introduced into hostilities or into circumstances indicating imminent hostilities as specified in Section 4, the so-called 60-day clock begins. Thus, the president will be without legal authority to continue conducting hostilities unless Congress acts within 60 days to (1) declare war, (2) adopt a specific authorization such as the Gulf of Tonkin Resolution of 1964, or (3) extend the president's war-making authority beyond 60 days. If the Congress takes no action at all, then the president is legally bound to terminate hostilities 60 days after his initial report to Congress. (An additional 30 days are authorized if needed for the safe withdrawal of troops, for a total of no more than 90 days maximum unless Congress specifically provides otherwise.)

Section 5's second congressional tool for terminating hostilities provides that the Congress can order a cessation of U.S. involvement in hostilities at any point simply by adopting a concurrent resolution. The crucial point here is that a concurrent resolution, adopted by simple majorities of the House and Senate, does not require the president's signature to take effect and thus is not subject to presidential veto. This passage is now constitutionally suspect in light of a 1983 Supreme Court ruling (*INS* v. *Chadha*) that struck down so-called legislative vetoes. Some observers contend that the Court's ruling invalidates the way concurrent resolutions are used in the War Powers Resolution. In the absence of a definitive ruling, however, Section 5, along with the rest of the Resolution, still stands as the law of the land.

*Effects of the War Powers Resolution*    An assessment of the War Powers Resolution's impact during the two decades since its adoption must begin with a statement that in some respects a substantial gap remains between the measure's intent and actual accomplishment. To some extent this situation reflects the inherent difficulties in seeking legislative solutions to fundamental philosophical, constitutional, and political matters. But the most important reason for the limited effects of the War Powers Resolution is the executive's consistent pattern of hostility to it.

The announced purpose of the War Powers Resolution was to "insure that the collective judgment of both the Congress and the President will apply to the introduction of United States Armed Forces into hostilities." We should remember, however, that it was Congress who embraced the doctrine of policy codetermination. It should surprise no one to learn that presidents have viewed the matter quite differently. The tone was set by Nixon, who tried unsuccessfully to kill the measure by vetoing it. All of his successors — Ford, Carter, Reagan, Bush, and Clinton — have consistently objected to the resolution as an unnecessary and perhaps even unconstitutional infringement on their powers. Such attitudes cannot simply be legislated away. Presidential hostility toward the resolution has clearly affected executive branch compliance with it. This has been especially evident with regard to the resolution's consultation and reporting requirements.

Set against Section 3's requirement that "the President in every possible instance shall consult with Congress before introducing United States Armed Forces into hostilities or into situations where imminent involvement in hostilities is clearly indicated by the circumstances," the record of the past two decades is one of repeated presidential conduct that violates both the letter and spirit of the law. For example, the Reagan administration's planning for the 1983 invasion of Grenada was completed and set in motion without any effort to "consult" with the Congress. Reagan issued the order for U.S. forces to commence the invasion at 6:00 P.M. EST on October 24, 1983. Only several hours later was a small group of congressional leaders brought to the White House and informed of the impending invasion. Their advice was not sought. Indeed, under the circumstances it would have amounted to little more than reaction to an executive operation already underway.

A similar circumvention of the law occurred in March 1986, when the Reagan administration launched Operation Prairie Fire. Aimed at challenging Libyan leader Muammar el-Qaddafi's claim of sovereignty over 150,000 square miles of the Gulf of Sidra, the operation involved a large U.S. naval task force of 30 ships, 25,000 troops, and armed aircraft probes across Qaddafi's proclaimed maritime boundary, nicknamed the "Line of Death." The resulting confrontation left 40 Libyan sailors killed, two of their patrol boats destroyed, and an antiaircraft missile installation crippled. Of particular interest here is the fact that the U.S. administration pointedly informed the Soviet Union of its operational plans in advance but did not see fit to similarly inform, much less consult, the U.S. Congress. As Michael Rubner has noted, "it thus appears that in the administration's curious judgment, the Kremlin could, and Congress could not be entrusted with highly sensitive details about American military moves against Libya."

A final example of presidential avoidance of the consultation requirement is the Reagan administration's handling of the April 1986 bombing of Libya in retaliation against Qaddafi's support of international terrorism. At 4:00 P.M. Washington time on Monday, April 14, 1986, a congressional delegation was brought to the White House. At that very moment, 13 F-111 fighter bombers were already four hours into a seven-hour flight from their British base to their targets in Libya. According to the legislators present, the "consultation" consisted of briefings by President Reagan (who read from typewritten notes), Secretary of State George Shultz, and National Security Adviser Admiral Poindexter. The general congressional sense of having been manipulated by executive officials was best captured by Republican Congressman Robert Michel, who wondered aloud: "if I had some serious objection, how could I make it now?"

Although the resolution's wording requiring consultation "in every possible instance" permits presidents some flexibility regarding consultation with Congress, in these and numerous other cases congressional leaders were readily available in Washington for meetings with the president and his aides. In addition, each case permitted plenty of time for those consultations to occur. In no instance was the president required to repel a sudden assault on U.S. territory or personnel.

In most instances presidents have chosen to violate both the letter and the spirit of Section 3 because they have found that little if any penalty for doing so would be incurred. The executive view has typically equated notification with the requirement of consultation. However, the House Foreign Affairs Committee emphatically rejected that view during the 1973 debate over adopting the resolution. In its report, the committee stressed that "consultation in this provision means that a decision is pending on a problem and that members of Congress are being asked by the President for their advice and opinions."

A similar presidential attitude has shaped executive compliance with the important requirement in Section 4 that Congress be notified anytime our armed forces are introduced into hostilities or where hostilities seem imminent. While presidents generally do report to Congress, they do so in a way that skirts the clear requirements of the War Powers Resolution.

Since 1973 about 25 instances have arguably required presidential reporting under Section 4. In two-thirds of those cases, presidential reports have indeed been submitted to Congress, but the pattern has been to report "consistent with" the resolution rather than "pursuant to" the resolution. Only once, in the Mayaguez incident of 1975, was the president's report specifically "pursuant to" the War Powers Resolution.

This distinction is important because Section 5 states that the use of U.S. armed forces will be terminated "within 60 days after a report is submitted . . . pursuant to Section 4 (a) (1)." Note that the famous 60-day clock is started only by a presidential report notifying Congress of the initiation of hostilities as specified in Section 4. The point may seem obscure to laypeople, but the now-common presidential practice of providing information to Congress without specifically acknowledging the obligatory character of the War Powers Resolution renders its most important legal provision effectively inoperable. The 20-year record of presidential compliance with this critical provision of the resolution thus reflects a calculated White House strategy of performing the minimum political obligation, but doing so in such a way as to neutralize the legal heart of the resolution.

Yet it would be a mistake to conclude that the War Powers Resolution has been a total failure. Its mere existence serves to remind presidents of the importance of congressional views. The need to develop a working consensus between the two branches — which was, after all, the resolution's principal objective — was one of the Bush administration's prime concerns in the months leading up to Operation Desert Storm in 1991. Clearly, a few amendments are now needed to (1) clarify who must be consulted and what would constitute adequate consultation, (2) specify more precisely the reporting requirements, and (3) define hostilities more precisely. At bottom, however, it has been the lack of congressional will that has permitted presidents to avoid full compliance with the resolution. As long as Congress is unwilling to invoke the War Powers Resolution and demand full compliance with it, presidents will continue to maximize their own prerogatives by minimizing their adherence to it.

This unwillingness is particularly likely in the dispatch of U.S. forces for nontraditional missions tangential to U.S. security. In December 1992, for example, President Bush ordered 20,000 members of the armed forces to Somalia to establish secure food distribution to the starving people in that area. Few in Congress voiced opposition to Operation Restore Hope, as it was dubbed. A few, however, including Senator Paul Wellstone (D-Minn.) — argued that Congress "should be accountable" by invoking the War Powers Resolution. Wellstone's view was a decidedly minority one, however, and Congress essentially relegated itself to the role of sideline supporter of a major — albeit humanitarian — overseas deployment of U.S. armed forces.

The two-decade-old experiment with the War Powers Resolution shows that the "twilight zone" of war-making power remains an ongoing source of controversy in the U.S. democratic system. It shows, too, that the mere passage of legislation is no substitute for what must ultimately be a continuing political requirement: that Congress find and maintain the will to preserve its constitutional role and that presidents retain a healthy respect for the necessity of forging interbranch consensus in support of the national interest.

## Context of Goldwater-Nichols and Cohen-Nunn Acts of 1986

The effort by Congress to change the structure and direction of the United States' national security policy reached a crescendo in 1986 when Congress initiated, passed, and imposed on the executive branch two laws in the space of one month. The first and more famous, the Goldwater-Nichols Defense Reorganization Act, Public Law (PL) 99-433, passed in October and dictated fundamental changes in the organizational priorities of the DOD. The Cohen-Nunn Act (PL 99-661), which passed in November, dealt more specifically with the issue of special forces and their place in defense priorities.

Both pieces of legislation were responses to perceptions that the Pentagon was simply not doing its job effectively, that it was apparently unable or unwilling to correct those policies and procedures that were impeding its efficient conduct of its job, and that only outside—namely, congressional—intervention would solve the problem. Spearheading the inclination to reform was a bipartisan group of over 100 members of Congress who had organized in the early 1980s as the Military Reform Caucus.

A number of issues and perceptions emerged from the caucus deliberations to set the agenda for change. Although the public had been galvanized by certain aspects of what was wrong, the impetus for change came from within Congress—from elected members, their staffs, and retired military personnel who were frustrated by their prior experience and who counseled the Congress. The effort was clearly bipartisan, for both acts bore the sponsorship of members of President Reagan's own party: Senator Barry Goldwater, chair of the Senate Armed Services Committee (SASC) and GOP presidential standard-bearer in 1964, Representative William Nichols of Alabama, and Senator William Cohen of Maine. The lone Democrat, Senator Sam Nunn of Georgia, shared a generally conservative, pro-defense reputation with his Republican colleagues as ranking Democrat on SASC.

Any list of factors leading to setting the agenda for reform will suffer the risk of omitting some crucial influence, but at least six interrelated reasons can be cited: a general discontent with the performance of the All-Volunteer Force (AVF) concept; a perceived negative record of U.S. forces; the military's preparation for war; organizational flaws within the

Pentagon; waste, fraud, and abuse; and defense's indifferent record despite budget increases.

*Performance of the AVF Concept*   Discontent with the AVF had been in place since the end of 1972. In reaction to the popular discontent with the Vietnam War, the Nixon administration had ended conscription at the end of 1972. In the wake of the United States' extrication from its most unpopular and unsuccessful military experience, the armed services had vast difficulty competing successfully for quality young men and women for the rest of the 1970s. Very few young people with other options chose military service for a variety of reasons, from disgust with the military to an economy that was providing better civilian job opportunities.

The Reagan presidency was supposed to solve that particular problem. Draped in patriotism and lubricated with generous amounts of new resources (money), the result was supposed to be a renaissance of military prowess that would rekindle the United States' preeminence. Many felt it had failed, at least to that point.

*The Negative Military Record*   The problem, and hence the second cause of concern, was a perceived negative record of U.S. forces since Vietnam. The perception arose from a series of incidents in which a U.S. military force was applied with uniformly negative outcomes, representing almost a caricature of the successful application of military power.

The first incident occurred in 1975, when President Ford ordered an expedition to free the crew of the *Mayaguez*, an American freighter that had been captured by Cambodian pirates in the Gulf of Thailand. Through faulty intelligence, the ensuing assault, in which 38 American servicemen perished in a helicopter crash, was directed at an island abandoned by the pirates and after the abductors had released the ship and its crew. Ford's attempt to demonstrate that the post–Vietnam United States was not a "pitiful giant" clearly backfired.

The situation did not improve materially under President Jimmy Carter. The most notorious incident of military ineptitude during his administration was the abortive attempt to rescue the 53 Americans held hostage in the U.S. Embassy in Teheran, Iran. Known as Desert One (for the designation of the landing site in the desolate Dasht-e-Kavir area of Iran), the mission ended in tragedy. Not enough of the helicopters could brave an unanticipated sandstorm to arrive at the site, and eight American servicemen died when an Army RH-53 helicopter and an Air Force EC-130 collided during takeoff as they tried to leave the scene. Because they were most prominent in the operation, Desert One particularly stained American Special Forces. In addition to adding to the perception of the military's general ineptitude, it served as an impetus to Cohen-Nunn.

This general pattern appeared to continue under President Ronald Reagan. In 1983 U.S. Marines were inserted (for a second time) into Beirut, Lebanon, with the vague mission of helping to stabilize the religious violence that had resulted in a bloody Christian militia assault on a Palestinian refugee camp and the assassination of the Christian president of Lebanon, Bashir Gemayel. The Marines, an elite assault force curiously inappropriate for the garrison duty of guarding the Beirut International Airport (the task to which they were assigned), saw their mission end tragically as a truck loaded with bombs penetrated security and exploded at a dormitory in which Marines were sleeping, killing 241.

The final major negative episode occurred later in 1983 when U.S. forces were inserted into Grenada, a tiny Caribbean island, to rescue American medical students who were under siege as a result of the internal unrest accompanying the ascendancy of a supposed Castroite to power. Although the mission accomplished its basic purpose, it was marred by logistical and communications problems that resulted in unnecessary delays and casualties. The chief culprit was interservice rivalry that made communication between the services impossible. In the most celebrated example, the lack of common frequencies between Army and Navy radios for transmission and reception of messages necessitated that an Army officer use his long-distance telephone credit card so that DOD could relay instructions to a Navy vessel off the coast.

*The U.S. Military's Preparedness*   The cumulative effect of these incidents was to raise a third concern: Was the U.S. military system adequately preparing the country to go to war? Each of the incidents described above involved the fairly minor application of force in specific, limited ways, and yet the military proved incapable of even such small tasks. That being the case, critics reasoned, what would occur if the United States had to go to war in the most serious fashion, as in an East-West confrontation in Europe which had been the focal point of planning virtually since the end of World War II?

For some, the answer was not reassuring. A common theme that seemed to run through the U.S. forces' combat experience since Vietnam was the inability of the services to cooperate with one another in military operations. As we will see, this chronic inability had structural as well as interservice rivalry underpinnings, but the common perception was that in the puzzle palace, Pogo's dictum held: "We have met the enemy, and he is us." From this perception, the emphasis on "jointness" (interservice cooperation and joint action) that is so prominent in Goldwater-Nichols was born.

*The Pentagon's Organizational Flaws*  It was generally perceived that organizational flaws within the Pentagon contributed to poor performance by the defense establishment. The most basic aspect of this concern was organizational structure. Prior to reform, the basic focus of organization was the individual services, which controlled the funding and effectively the career destinies of career military personnel. The alternative form of organization was to focus on the Joint Chiefs of Staff and the unified and specified commands, those units assigned operational responsibility for different theaters of operation (e.g., the Pacific) or missions, as discussed in Chapter 3.

In the prereform system, the services prevailed. Thus, key elements of core activities such as budgets were funneled from the operational commands through the various service bureaucracies rather than the other way around. Even though the CINPAC (commander in chief, Pacific), a Navy admiral, had as part of his operational responsibility Air Force and Army assets, his requests for funds and resources for those other service elements were funneled through the departments of the Army and Air Force, where they had to compete with other internal service priorities.

Moreover, the system tended to downplay the role and importance of the Joint Chiefs of Staff and especially the chairman of the JCS. The idea behind the JCS was to create an entity within the military chain that could coordinate interservice planning and actions. It did not work that way, for several reasons.

With power concentrated in the services, time spent on the Joint Staff was viewed as detrimental to an officer's career. During the time an officer served on the Joint Staff, for instance, his annual performance evaluations continued to be made by his individual service and not by the Joint Staff. Since the services viewed the JCS as a rival, members of the staff quickly realized that they would be rewarded for how well they protected their service's interests, not for the degree of interservice cooperation they displayed. This dynamic extended all the way up to the various service chiefs who composed the JCS. At the same time, the CJCS, who was supposed to epitomize the interservice process, was given essentially no power. He had no operational command of forces, he was only one of the president's military advisers, and he had a tiny staff of five professionals and no full-time vice chairman.

In the eyes of the reformers, this lack of interservice cooperation — known as "jointness" in the Building — hindered the U.S. military effort in an increasingly complex world where military problems more and more required the application of different kinds of force housed in the different services. This lack of coordination helped explain why the Navy and the Army operated radio equipment on different and incompatible frequencies (the telephone credit card case at Grenada). It also led to the generalized perception that U.S. military performance would not improve markedly until real jointness became part of the system.

The problem was that the DOD itself opposed change. The service bureaucracies, including both members of the uniformed services and the large civilian bureaucracies that had developed during the Cold War were comfortable with the system as it was. This opposition extended all the way to the secretary of defense, Caspar Weinberger, who viewed congressional reform initiatives as unnecessarily meddling into his business and as examples of congressional "micromanagement" of the Defense Department.

*Waste, Fraud, and Abuse*   One of the more common criticisms of Pentagon performance was in the way the Pentagon spent public monies: the issue of waste, fraud, and abuse. During the early 1980s, defense budgets escalated as a result of Ronald Reagan's drive to reverse the decline in defense spending instituted by his predecessor, Jimmy Carter. Carter, Reagan claimed, had presided over the unilateral disarmament of the United States in the 1980 campaign. As spending levels increased, however, so did well-publicized instances of apparent malfeasance: $600 toilet seats for a new Air Force plane, $500 hammers, and the like. At the forefront of this criticism was the maverick Democratic senator from Wisconsin, William Proxmire, who annually awarded his "Golden Fleece Awards" for what he viewed as especially egregious abuses of public funds.

Whether the instances of waste were aberrations or symptomatic of a general malaise within DOD was never established. In many cases, however, the defense officials' reactions only served to worsen public perceptions that something was wrong that required fixing, such as instances of stonewalling by accused contractors.

*Lackluster Performance*   The sixth and final factor, exacerbating the rest, was that performance was not improving despite large budget increases for defense in the first half of the 1980s. During the first Reagan term in particular, increases in real spending power (additions beyond adjustments for inflation) occurred regularly. Many congressmen believed that the Reagan administration thought that the role of Congress was simply to ratify the administration's request without amendment.

Secretary Weinberger epitomized this attitude. In the Nixon administration, he had been secretary of the then Department of Health, Education, and Welfare, where his money-pinching ways had earned him the nickname "Cap the Knife" (a sobriquet he had originally earned while working in California state government) for his attempts to cut his departmental budget. As secretary of defense, that changed. Annually, he would go to the Congress with ever increasing requests on which he obdurately refused to compromise, suggesting that any decreases would gravely compromise the nation's security. He became known as "Cap the Shovel" for his apparent belief that all defense problems could be solved with the application of more dollars. As greater questions of performance and fiscal abuse mounted, Congress's generosity came to be part of the problem.

All these influences came together to produce the impetus for Congress to take the lead and to force reform on the defense establishment, despite the opposition of the president and the hierarchy of DOD itself. The two pieces of legislation, Goldwater-Nichols and Cohen-Nunn, must be seen in tandem and in decreasing order of magnitude. The Goldwater-Nichols Defense Reorganization Act of 1986 was both chronologically first in terms of enactment and in scope of reform. The problem addressed by Cohen-Nunn, special operations forces, is mentioned almost as an afterthought in the larger bill. The DOD's negative reaction to Goldwater-Nichols helped goad the Congress into speedy enactment of Cohen-Nunn.

### The Goldwater-Nichols Act

Although it has several separate, important provisions, the heart of the Defense Reorganization Act was to change the effective power structure within the Pentagon. The means of doing so was by reducing the power of the individual services and transferring that power to those organs of the Pentagon with a more interservice orientation: the commanders in chief (CINC) of the unified commands, whose commands by definition contained elements from more than one service; and the JCS, particularly the CJCS. The legislation accomplishes this task through three significant changes.

The first thrust strengthened the JCS and its chairman within the military hierarchy. To clarify and elevate the CJCS, he was designated as the principal and only military adviser to the president, the National Security Council, and the secretary of defense. Depending on the administration, the service chiefs had previously had direct access to the top leadership, bypassing the chief; under Goldwater-Nichols they had to go through him.

The entire Joint Staff was also placed under the "authority, direction and control" of the CJCS rather than the JCS as a whole. Previously, it will be recalled, the CJCS had only a very small personal staff reporting to him, while the bulk of the Joint Staff reported to the JCS as a whole, which meant that officers remained the effective "property" of their parent services. To further move away from the parochialism of service loyalty, the act created a promotion review of joint officers under the supervision of the CJCS. This review applies to former as well as currently serving Joint Staff members. Finally, the position of vice chief of the JCS (VCJCS) was created, thereby adding to the flexibility of the chief.

The act also encouraged jointness by creating a specific joint officer specialty within the services. To guarantee that the designation had clout and would attract officers, the act requires that at least 50 percent of the slots at the major/lieutenant commander (0–4) level, where much of the staff resides, would have to be officers with a Joint Staff specialty. To add further clout to the "purple suiters" (this nickname given to Joint Staff officers is based on the presumed color their uniforms would be if one mixed the colors of the uniforms of the four services), it was further stipulated that no officer could be promoted to flag rank (general or equivalent) without joint service on his or her record unless an explicit exception was made.

Another provision aimed at reforming the effective power base dealt with increasing the importance of the eight commanders in chief of the unified commands. Five of these commands have geographic responsibilities (Atlantic Command, Central Command, European Command, Pacific Command, and Southern Command), and three have functional responsibilities (Space Command, Special Operations Command, and Transportation Command). By definition, all have interservice responsibilities, and units from different services are assigned to them. Earlier, the problem was that the CINCs had neither budgetary nor total operational control over forces from services other than their own. Goldwater-Nichols remedied those problems in two ways.

On the one hand, the act designates that the CINC has direct and total control over all forces under his command. This concept was first successfully applied by General Norman Schwarzkopf, CINC of Central Command, in Operation Desert Storm. On the other hand, the CINC now makes budget requests directly to the secretary of defense without having to go through the various service departments. This provision has been somewhat controversial. Proponents argue that it assures that each command has adequate supplies and the like to conduct its mission, since the CINC's focus is on operations. The other side of the coin is that the CINCs will slight long-term investment in areas such as research and development for new, advanced weapons. It has even been argued that if CINC-controlled budgeting had been in force five years earlier than it was, U.S. forces would not have had many of the high-technology weapons used to such great effect against Iraq.

The act accomplished three other noteworthy effects. First, in response to "waste, fraud, and abuse" charges in procurement, the bill created an assistant secretary of defense position, designated as the number three person in the DOD, to coordinate and approve all Pentagon buying. Instantly nicknamed the "Procurement Czar," this position has never matured with the power envisioned by the act's drafters.

Second, the act mandated that the president provide an annual national security strategy of the United States and submit it to the Congress. This requirement was necessary because the administration probably lacked a clear strategy and thus needed to develop one, and because of a belief that such a strategy should be subject to public scrutiny and debate. These convictions were widely held in the defense community but were opposed by the Reagan and Bush administrations as an unnecessary annoyance. As a result, only four of the documents had been produced as of the end of 1992, and they have all been written, in fact, by middle-level officials within the DOD.

Finally, the act called for a review of the need for "creation of a unified combatant command for special operations missions." Before that review could be undertaken, Congress had already passed the Cohen-Nunn Act.

### The Cohen-Nunn Act

As was true of the broader Defense Reorganization Act, the impetus to pass legislation creating a congressionally mandated institution to deal with special operations and the lower end of the conflict spectrum (as discussed in Chapter 1) came from executive-legislative disagreement and distrust.

The disagreement was about the relative weight that should be given within the Pentagon to special operations and low-intensity conflict (SOLIC). The executive branch, heavily influenced by the armed service bureaucracies, tended to emphasize the traditional Cold War confrontation and the forces and strategies deriving from the East-West conflict. Those in Congress who supported the bill, on the other hand, looked at the recent record and saw in special operations such as Desert One, Grenada, and Beirut the kinds of situations the U.S. military would increasingly face in the future, but for which experience had shown them to be badly underprepared.

There was the added perception that the United States had not fared very well in the past when dealing in special operations. As Senator William Cohen, the bill's co-sponsor, said in his opening remarks when the bill was introduced as an amendment to the fiscal year (FY) 1987 Defense Authorization Act (Senate Bill S2567) on August 6, 1986, "I do not believe this [negative] record is attributable to persistent bad luck or an inadequate caliber of men in the armed services. In my view, we have not been effectively organized to fight the most likely battles of the present or the future."

Distrust came from the armed services' and the Pentagon's general attitude toward SOLIC. Because the defense bureaucracy both disliked and were not very adept at SOLIC (dislike and skill are two phenomena reciprocally related to one another), they could be expected to footdrag or subvert efforts to impose this mission on them, as they had in the past. The late Representative Dan Daniels (D-Va.), who sponsored the legislation in the House of Representatives, summarized this position in the August 1985 issue of *Armed Forces Journal International*: "No amount of directive authority—budgetary or otherwise—will overcome the capacity of Service Chiefs to commit mischief should that be their bent. And, as long as special operations forces remain outside the services' philosophical core, the temptation to do so will be near irresistible."

This distrust meant that the only way to force the executive branch to take SOLIC seriously was through a law specifically requiring them to do so. Originally, Senator Cohen had considered putting forward the SOLIC case as a nonbinding "sense of the Congress" for the Pentagon to consider. Initial grumbling and objections to Goldwater-Nichols convinced the sponsors of Cohen-Nunn that the Pentagon would ignore or push a sense of Congress to the back burner. The result was a full-fledged law.

The Cohen-Nunn Act contains four major provisions. The first provision created an institutional focus by designating a unified command, the United States Special Operations Command (USSOCOM). Eventually based at McDill Air Force Base in Florida, it has the distinction of being the first unified command designated by law. (All the others were created administratively by the executive branch.) The reason was straightforward: DOD would never have created USSOCOM on its own.

Second, the act created within the DOD the position of assistant secretary of defense for special operations and low-intensity conflict (ASD/SOLIC). Secretary Weinberger bitterly opposed this provision as an intrusion on his administrative prerogatives, as did other assistant secretaries fearful they would lose those parts of their responsibilities that touched on SOLIC. Thus, DOD waited several months before it submitted a nominee to the Senate. When it did, the name it produced was Kenneth Bergquist, a gentleman most distinguished for his vocal opposition to the legislation.

An executive-legislative branch feud ensued. The Senate promptly rejected Bergquist, and the DOD replaced him on an interim basis with Larry Ropka, an assistant to the Honorable Richard Armitage, assistant secretary of defense for international security affairs (ASD/ISA) and also a vocal opponent of the bill. Convinced that the Ropka appointment was akin to "the fox guarding the hen house," a frustrated Congress responded in December 1987 by passing another law (PL 100–180), which required that the secretary of the Army, John O. Marsh, assume the duties of the ASD/SOLIC until a confirmable nominee was presented and confirmed.

That process took nine months, when DOD nominated retired Ambassador Charles Whitehead, who was confirmed nearly 18 months after the legislation was passed. He was subsequently replaced by Jim Locher who, as an aide to Senator Nunn, had primary responsibility for drafting the legislation in the first place. As noted in Chapter 3, Secretary Aspin's reorganization plan proposes to eliminate this position.

The ASD/SOLIC position was neither the only new position created by Cohen-Nunn nor the only one that spawned interbranch conflict. A third provision of the act was to mandate a deputy assistant to the president for national security affairs for low-intensity conflict. Designating this high-level staff position had a direct impact on the prerogatives of the president and thus created resistance within the more general foreign policy bureaucracy.

The problem in principle arises from the nature of the NSC staff. As mentioned earlier, those who serve on the NSC staff are considered the personal staff of the president; he decides who they are, what their individual assignments and titles are, and the size of the staff. As such, the NSC staff, up to and including the national security adviser, is subject neither to Senate confirmation nor to congressional oversight. (Members of the staff, for instance, cannot be compelled to testify before Congress.) Moreover, none of their positions (including the NSA) are specified by law.

Cohen-Nunn anticipated that the person who filled this position would have two major responsibilities: to coordinate NSC activity in the SOLIC area on a full-time and primary basis; and to convene a low-intensity conflict board within the NSC staff.

The special assistant's position has never been filled with a full-time person. Leading opposition to it in the Bush administration was Brent Scowcroft, the NSA, who felt the position was a Trojan horse that would set a precedent for broad-scale congressional specification of positions within the NSC, including his own. As a result, the duties have been assigned as a part-time responsibility to the assistant national security adviser for international programs. Congress and the administration continue to disagree about the adequacy of the arrangement.

Fourth and finally, the legislation created the so-called LIC Board within the NSC. The idea behind this provision was to create a vehicle for interagency discussion of the LIC mission and to develop a series of scenarios and American response options to various LIC contingencies that might arise in different Third World countries.

The LIC Board provision has also languished. The Reagan administration appointed a board but never convened it. The Bush administration also appointed a board, but as of December 1990 it had met precisely twice and had not yet adopted a commonly acceptable definition of a low-intensity conflict.

## SUGGESTED READINGS

Bacchus, William I. *Foreign Policy and the Bureaucratic Process.* Princeton, N.J.: Princeton University Press, 1974.

Davis, David Howard. *How the Bureaucracy Makes Foreign Policy.* Lexington, Mass.: Lexington Books, 1972.

Destler, I. M. *Presidents, Bureaucrats, and Foreign Policy: The Politics of Organizational Reform.* Princeton, N.J.: Princeton University Press, 1974.

Elder, Robert Ellsworth. *The Policy Machine: The Department of State and American Foreign Policy.* Syracuse, N.Y.: Syracuse University Press, 1960.

Franklin, Daniel Paul. "War Powers in the Modern Context," *Congress and the Presidency,* Spring 1987, pp. 77–92.

Glennon, Michael J. "The War Powers Resolution Ten Years Later: More Politics Than Law," *American Journal of International Law,* July 1984, pp. 571–581.

Halperin, Morton H. *Bureaucratic Politics and Foreign Policy.* Washington, D.C.: Brookings Institution, 1974.

Leacacos, John P. *Fires in the In-Basket: The ABC's of the State Department.* Cleveland, Ohio: World Publishing, 1968.

Lindbloom, Charles E. *The Policy Making Process.* Englewood Cliffs N.J.: Prentice-Hall, 1968.

Rubner, Michael. "The Reagan Administration, The 1973 War Powers Resolution, and the Invasion of Grenada." *Political Science Quarterly,* Winter 1985–1986, pp. 627–647.

Smyrl, Marc E. *Conflict or Codetermination? Congress, the President, and the Power to Make War.* Cambridge, Mass.: Ballinger Publishing Co., 1988.

Turner, Robert F. *The War Powers Resolution: Its Implementation in Theory and Practice.* Philadelphia: Foreign Policy Research Institute, 1983.

Warburg, Gerald F. *The Struggle Between Congress and the President over Foreign Policymaking.* New York: Harper & Row, 1989.

# CHAPTER 6

# Outside Influences I:
# Interest Groups and Think Tanks

Not everyone who has a voice in the policy process seeks to govern or formally to enact legislation. In addition to those elected and appointed officials who compose the federal government is a large and diverse, often amorphous, conglomeration of individuals and groups who are not a formal part of the governmental structure but who seek to influence government policies.

The largest concentration of these individuals and groups lives and works in the Washington, D.C., area. They are known as the "inside the beltway" group because they work and live either within or near the Interstate 95 beltway that encircles the District of Columbia. In fact, so many people are engaged in this capacity that it is regularly asserted that Washington has more people employed to influence the government than there are employees of the government itself.

Historically, most of these actors performed outside the public spotlight, lobbying individual members of Congress to adopt positions they espoused, interacting with governmental officials informally at Washington cocktail parties, or sharing with interested individuals access to the most hotly pursued status symbol in the capital, tickets to Washington Redskins football games. In addition, this "invisible government," as it is also occasionally known, provided a revolving door for individuals, coming and going into and out of government to organizations and positions seeking to influence what government does. As the Bush administration prepared to leave and the highly visible Clinton transition began, so did the shuffling of personnel into and out of government.

The result was to add opaqueness to the public's understanding of what really transpires in government, particularly with respect to foreign and defense policy. In the area of foreign policy, general public ignorance and lack of interest meant that influencing government policy was the preserve of elite groups with special expertise. Thus, an organization such as the

Council on Foreign Relations, a brahmin-like institution with elegant headquarters at the corner of 68th Street and Park Avenue in New York, had great influence over both who and what made U.S. foreign policy. In the defense area, the highly technical and usually classified nature of many defense issues meant that related organizations hired retired military officers to influence decisions in the same areas in which they had formerly labored.

The traditional roles of those who seek to influence the government have also bred orthodox ways of categorizing and looking at what they do. As we will see, some of these roles are changing and will continue to do so as the post–Cold War world progresses. In anticipation of more detailed consideration of each category, however, it is useful to review briefly how two kinds of institutions that stand at the boundary between the population and the government operate.

The first and historically most important traditional outside influencers have been the interest groups, organizations that represent some group of people or institutions with common interests that they want to see promoted and protected. These organizations have traditionally been regarded as the "gatekeepers" between the public and the formal government itself. This gatekeeping function entails funneling to government the public's feelings and positions toward public policy. Interest groups collect what their followers feel, and they represent those interests to appropriate executive and legislative constituencies via such activities as *lobbying* (seeking to convince individual members of Congress or executive agency officials to support their groups' positions), *education* (writing articles and the like, testifying before congressional committees, etc.), and *pressure* (convincing officials that they will suffer if they defy the groups' will).

In recent years, the activities of interest groups have come under some public suspicion. Those in the field like to think of themselves as engaging in "Washington representation," a value-neutral term. Many in the public, however, including many aspiring to public office and trust, view them in a less favorable light.

Suspicion of the traditional interest group role closely parallels the American people's general suspicion of the government. The term *Washington insider* has become a pejorative, encompassing those "professional Washington politicians" that candidates regularly defile and of which traditional Washington representatives are often the consummate examples.

At the same time, the aura of favoritism and gratuities traditionally surrounding many of the traditional methods of influence (e.g., throwing cocktail parties for officials who can help one's cause, contributing to campaign funds or a politician's pet charity) offend public sensibilities in an ethics-conscious era. This sensitivity was highlighted during the Clinton transition as the new president announced an executive order banning any official in his administration from lobbying the government for five years after leaving government service (a method ex-officials have traditionally used to capitalize on their government service).

In addition, interest groups often wield what some think is disproportionate power because of the resources they have at their disposal. Here a principal target has been the *political action committee* (PAC), interest group-controlled funds that funnel campaign monies to officials who support the group and also to opponents of those who oppose them.

The defense and foreign policy-making process is not immune from these kinds of activities and suspicions. One of the first and most widely publicized examples of possibly nefarious relationships between interest groups and the government was cited in President Dwight D. Eisenhower's farewell address, when he referred to the military-industrial complex and its potential erosive and corrupting influence on the American system.

The military-industrial complex is but one, if a very important, example of a common concept in the U.S. political system, the *iron triangle*. Iron triangles are formed when those agencies or programs of the federal government that administer a given area find common cause with the congressional committee overseeing that activity and the interest group promoting the area. The iron triangle as it relates to the military-industrial complex can be seen in Figure 6.1.

The iron triangle here consists of the defense industry that contracts with elements of the armed services, the armed services who write contracts for different military hardware produced by the industry, and the appropriations subcommittees of the two houses of Congress that approve expenditures for various weapons.

There is nothing unnatural or necessarily wrong about such relation-

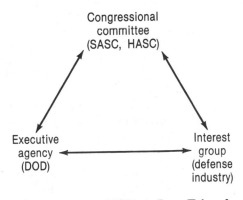

**FIGURE 6.1    Military Iron Triangle**

ships, nor are they limited to the defense area. The Air Force, for instance, wants the best possible military aircraft and shares with the manufacturer the desire to produce aircraft. At the same time, all three sides of the triangle share expertise and common interests in military aircraft. (A congressman with no personal or constituency interests in military procurement is unlikely to volunteer for those committees.)

The relationship becomes a problem when it becomes incestuous and interests become *vested*. This term refers to the revolving door phenomenon depicted by the arrows in Figure 6.1. When, for example, a prime retirement job prospect for an Air Force officer is a senior position with the aerospace company whose contracts he is monitoring, is there room for compromise? The same is true of an aerospace executive who takes a position in the civilian Air Force bureaucracy or a congressional staffer who moves to industry or the Pentagon. Abuses have spawned a number of laws intended to regulate these movements back and forth from government to industry as a means of restricting the development of vested interests.

A comparatively new group of outside influencers is exemplified by the think tanks, scholarly and research-based organizations that offer expert advice to various government organs. Sometimes, these organizations act as scholarly outlets, providing academic analyses on different problems. Much of the prestige of individual think tanks derives from their reputations for scholarly integrity and impartiality. At the same time, many of them engage in activities that are more generally associated with interest groups, and are also part of the revolving door phenomenon moving into and out of the formal governmental structure.

In the remainder of this chapter, we hope to go beyond the common analysis of these outside influences by introducing dynamics that may be changing their roles and places on the public agenda. For present purposes, we will introduce five factors that constitute potential change agents, realizing they reflect changes that, in most cases, have already been described in earlier chapters.

The first factor is the *convergence of foreign and domestic issues*. As noted in Chapter 1 and elsewhere, the old distinctions between a foreign and domestic issue have largely disappeared into the realm of intermestic policies, especially in the changing world economy. Although that confluence affects the way the government itself is organized, it also has an effect on how the public views what government does. The end of the Cold War means that the public will no longer automatically embrace defense spending, nor will the public permit government to be elusive about international economic matters. As foreign and national security policy get closer to the pocketbooks of the average citizen, the salience of those issues increases. The 1992 debate over whether public aid should be given to the new Russian Republic provides an example.

Public awareness and access is made easier by the *increased transparency of international events*. Once again, the global telecommunications revolution is at the heart of the public's greater access to foreign affairs at a time when those events are more immediate to them. Moreover, through global television outlets such as CNN, the initial information on breaking international affairs that is available to the public is precisely the same information that is available to decision-makers: the president and his advisers, as well as members of the public, see the same reportage on CNN. At a minimum, the government's treatment of the media and concern for initial public opinion must be greater than in the past. At a maximum, it may mean more detailed scrutiny of public decisions by all those outside government who seek to influence government actions.

This factor relates to a third phenomenon: the greater analytical capability that accompanies global television's ability to cover worldwide news *increasingly makes the global media an actor and influence in that process*. Global television—and CNN is clearly the leader in this regard— is the first source of information to the public and, in many cases, governmental officials. More than that, the modern news conglomerate also provides considerable interpretation of events to a public that largely lacks the knowledge and perspective to interpret those events itself. With 24 hours a day of air time to fill and not enough "hard news" to fill it, it becomes necessary to augment the bare facts with some notion of what the events may portend.

The fourth phenomenon caused by global television is *the rise of the "electronic experts,"* those people with acknowledged expertise who are used by all the networks to provide legitimacy to the interpretation of currently breaking events. These individuals, most visibly seen during the Persian Gulf War, are especially important in the defense and foreign policy arena, because much of that material is relatively technical and the public is unfamiliar with it. In the Persian Gulf War, all the networks featured both military and political experts who were drawn from outside their regular payrolls. They explained everything from the logistics of ground attack to the operation of precision-guided munitions.

These experts are generally unpaid guests and tend to come from the military, think tanks, and academia. For military analysis, many are retired military officers (mostly colonels and generals), who have experience and knowledge and contacts within the Pentagon that give them superior access to information than that available to regular reporters, who are generally distrusted by military people. Retired Air Force Lieutenant

General Perry Smith, who provided analysis of the air campaign for CNN, is an example and retired Army Colonel Harry Summers is another.

Another source for experts are the "think tanks," especially those located in and around network headquarters in New York and Washington. For instance, coverage of Operation Desert Storm gave the Washington-based Center for Strategic and International Studies (CSIS) wide exposure. Finally, experts found in academia, particularly international relations experts from around New York and Washington, frequently appear in the media. In the unraveling of the former Soviet Union, for example, Columbia University's Robert Legvold and Princeton University's Stephen Cohen were prominent analysts.

The fifth and final source of change is *growing public disaffection with the competency of the political leadership*. Running against Washington and the "insiders" first became a prominent strategy in Jimmy Carter's successful assault on the White House. It was a theme in Ronald Reagan's first campaign and became virtually an art form in the H. Ross Perot campaign of 1992. Dissatisfaction with how the system works has become broader than that evident just at the level of presidential election politics, however. Witness the number of congressmen and senators who retired in 1992 (although the reason was partly because 1992 was the last year that a member of Congress could keep excess campaign contributions beyond campaign expenses) and the number who either were defeated or almost defeated for reelection. Part of this dissatisfaction is undoubtedly fueled by the greater access to information that is a legacy of the electronic revolution. On the other side, President Clinton has used the same media to create a positive image of himself and government in forums such as the December 1992 economic meeting in Little Rock.

This discussion provides the basis for examining how interest groups and think tanks operate outside the government's formal structure and some of the forces that are changing how they operate. We will, of course, emphasize how they relate specifically to foreign and national security matters.

## Interest Groups

In political terms, an interest group can be defined simply as any organized group of people who share common interests distinct from those of others and who attempt to influence public policy in the direction of that interest. As such, interest groups share some common interest, whether it be maintenance of a strong national defense, the preservation of the environment, or the protection of the right to bear firearms. They have come together into some formal organization of like-minded individuals, and they seek to represent their common interest to the political system and to influence public policy in the direction of their interest.

### Characteristics

The characteristics of interest groups are progressive. For instance, many people have common interests, but they do not as a result organize; although organizations in fact exist, not many left-handed people belong to organizations of lefties. At the same time, not all organized groups seek to influence the political system. Left-handed people may meet to commiserate about the "tyrannies" of a right-handed world, but they do not pressure the government to provide left-handed only parking spaces at supermarkets.

Interest groups stand as gatekeepers between the public and the government. The organizations collect the interests that people share, distilling public feelings into a more manageable set of interests that they represent and can relate to the government.

The function performed by interest groups is provided for in the First Amendment to the Constitution, which guarantees the right to "petition the Government for a redress of grievances." The basic idea underlying this right was discussed in the *Federalist Papers* from which the Constitution was derived. It finds its modern expression in the idea of pluralism, the notion that all interests should be freely able to compete for influence within the government.

Theoretically, the ability to form interest groups and to compete in the arena includes the entire population and is an option available to all Americans. In fact, however, that is generally not the case. Numerous studies have shown that the upper strata of society, as measured by yardsticks such as wealth and education, are overrepresented in interest group activity. In one sense, this stands to reason, for interest group activities, like almost everything else, cost money. Hence, those who possess resources will have first access. Similarly, educational attainment and political activity are positively related.

To understand the role of interest groups, we need to examine what interest groups do in order to represent and promote their interests. We will also look at the kinds of interest groups that are active in the foreign and defense policy arena.

### What Interest Groups Do

Different observers categorize the activities of interest groups differently, and no set of categories will satisfy all of them. For our purposes, however, we can divide those activities into three categories: lobbying, education, and pressure. Each function entails distinct actions, although most interest groups use some combination of them all.

*Lobbying*   Interest groups are most closely associated with lobbying. The term itself goes back to the 1870s. Although the First Amendment to the Constitution provides for the right of petition, it prohibits the presentation of petitions on the floors of the houses of Congress. As a result, those seeking influence were forced to make their representations outside the chambers, especially in the corridors and lobbies of the Capitol Building. Hence, the term *lobbying* was born.

The purpose of lobbying, like all other interest group activity, is to persuade those with the ability to make decisions—in the Congress or the executive branch—that their interests should be reflected in public policy. Lobbying connotes the personal representations of positions to individual congressmen or executive branch agents in the effort to convince them of the virtue of their positions. Although some lobbying occurs within the executive branch, more of it occurs in the interactions between interest groups and members of Congress.

The cornerstones of lobbying are the Washington-based offices of various interest groups and lobbyists. Although precise figures are hard to obtain, it is estimated that over 40,000 people in Washington work for the Washington offices of the nearly 1,800 associations represented there. In addition, over 2,000 individuals are registered with the government as lobbyists.

Lobbyists come in several varieties. Some are amateurs, members of interest groups who are sent to Washington for the specific task of influencing a piece of legislation, for instance, by attempting to persuade their own congressional member or state delegation to vote for the bill. In the foreign and defense policy area, organizations such as the American Legion often reward rank-and-file members by sending them to Washington in this capacity.

A second kind of lobbyist is the professional. The professional lobbyist is usually someone with considerable government service who has developed expertise and extensive contacts within some policy area that he or she is willing to share with clients for a price. (Professional lobbyists typically work for several clients rather than a single one.) Many of these individuals are lawyers who have developed expertise in specific areas of the law, such as food and drug law; hence, they are attractive representatives for clients such as the pharmaceutical industry. In the foreign policy area, Henry Kissinger Associates is probably the most famous and powerful example of a professional lobbying organization.

Yet another type of lobbyist is the staff lobbyist. Unlike the professional lobbyist, the staff lobbyist works full time for the Washington office of an organization that seeks to influence the policy process. In addition to formal lobbying, staff lobbyists typically perform other administrative duties as well. All organizations with large operations in Washington employ some staff lobbyists. The aerospace industries represent an example in the defense area.

The purpose of all lobbying efforts is to gain access to decision-makers and to persuade them of the efficacy of the interest the lobbyist represents. Highly successful lobbyists will make themselves so invaluable to people within the process that they virtually become a part of it — for instance, having such great knowledge of a policy area that they are consulted on language for a piece of legislation. This quality of access is attained in part through the second form of interest group activity, education.

*Education*   Interest groups seek to influence the political system by providing expert information in an issue area that can be used to educate both those in power and the public at large of the desirability of their positions.

When educational efforts are directed at the general public, they usually take one of several forms. One obvious form is the advertising campaign, increasingly using professional television spots, to galvanize public opinion on a subject. The ad campaigns on both sides of the abortion issue are a particularly vivid example. Sometimes these campaigns are directed at the general public, and other times at specialized segments of the population. An example of the latter was a series of advertisements in the *New York Times* placed by pro-Serbian groups in June 1992 seeking to convince readers that the situation in Bosnia and Herzegovina was not a Serbian act of aggression and atrocity, but instead the continuation of Serbian resistance to Croatian fascism with roots in World War II. (Such tactics do not always work, as they did not in this case.) Another educational effort may be to provide speakers' bureaus to speak to groups or to be available for newspaper and television interviews. At the same time, groups will often provide news releases to newspapers in the hope that they will be printed in local papers.

More commonly, educational efforts are directed toward members of Congress or their staffs. Interest groups collect and make available information about their particular policy area which, while self-interested, provides a useful supplement to the member's ability to gain information through his or her staff. This information may be provided in the form of position papers, fact books, reference services to which a member has access, or even expert testimony to congressional committees and subcommittees.

Members and their staffs greatly appreciate this form of activity, if provided honestly rather than as obviously biased propaganda. Despite the great expansion of staffs described in Chapter 4, Congress is still at a disadvantage in its competition for information with the executive branch. An interest group that provides honest, valuable information thus extends Congress's capabilities. A few try to mislead Congress, but such a tactic is short-sighted and almost invariably exposed, thereby compromising the interest group in the future. When competing interest groups present conflicting information or interpretations, the member can make a comparative assessment of the various positions.

A good example of an interest group that uses educational programs as a primary tool is the Arms Control Association (ACA). It publishes its own journal, *Arms Control Today*, which it distributes to libraries and interested citizens. It features a speakers' bureau for places such as college campuses, and its leading staff members are regularly available for interviews. Congressional members receive the journal, and ACA provides both expert witnesses for testimony before congressional committees and a resource for information on weapons levels, characteristics, and the like. As a further means of endearment, *Arms Control Today* frequently publishes articles and speeches by sympathetic members of Congress.

*Pressure*   Interest groups also seek to influence the system through pressure, a form of influence-peddling that represents the most negative side of interest group activities. Pressure activities comprise actions that are designed not so much to persuade officials of the virtue of the group's position as to convince the official of the negative consequences of opposing the interest or the positive benefits of support.

In the last 20 years or so, the negative side of pressure has come to be associated with the emergence of so-called political action committees (PACs). The basic purpose and tactic of PACs is to influence elections by collecting money from their membership and using it to support candidates sympathetic to their causes and to oppose their opponents. This is sometimes done by the PAC making direct contributions to campaigns; limits on the amount that can be given to any candidate by an organization also necessitate a second tactic, which is for the PAC to encourage members of the group also to contribute.

The cost of modern campaigns, largely inflated by the expense of television advertising, makes the PACs increasingly powerful and the increasing target of regulation, as promised by candidate Clinton during the 1992 campaign in the form of election reform legislation. They are big business and growing in number and influence. The Federal Election Commission (FEC), for instance, identified 608 PACs at the end of 1974;

by the end of 1987 that number had risen to 4,165. The largest number of these — 1,775 — were PACs with corporate affiliations. The amount of money that PACs spend has also escalated. The FEC estimated PAC contributions to campaigns for 1977–1978 at just less than $78 million; by 1987–1988 that figure was over $364 million.

PAC activities are more closely associated with domestic than foreign and defense issues. Thus, two of the largest and most influential PACs are those connected with the American Medical Association and the National Rifle Association. There are, however, corporate PACs that seek to influence the size and direction of defense procurement; the aerospace industry is particularly active in this regard.

Pressure can take other forms. Lobbyists, for instance, can offer favors to sympathetic members of Congress. Historically, for instance, interest groups would offer speaking engagements, complete with speakers' fees (honoraria) and expenses; abuses of this practice have resulted in reform legislation that virtually prohibits the practice for any federal employee.

The size of the stakes involved inevitably leads to abuses and most commonly *bribery*, the offer and acceptance of illegal funds by some official from an interest group. Instances of bribery are rather infrequent, but when they do occur, they are spectacular. The most recent large-scale bribery case involved banking magnate Charles Keating and his defrauding of the federal government in the savings and loan association scandal. The corruption touched five United States senators, the so-called Keating Five (Alan Cranston of California, John Glenn of Ohio, Dennis DeConcini of Arizona, John McCain of Arizona, and Donald Reigle of Michigan).

In the foreign and defense area, one of the most famous cases involved a foreign lobbyist, Tong Sun Park of the Republic of Korea. Park, a flashly, well-liked figure, induced support for his government through lavish social occasions for governmental officials, including gifts for congressional members and spouses. These gifts ultimately got him in trouble, because the gifts exceeded allowable limits. One of the people who was forced to resign his position because of this scandal was Ronald Reagan's first national security adviser, Richard V. Allen, who accepted two watches from Park.

### Types of Interest Groups

There are as many interest groups in the country as there are interests that people hold. Most concentrate on influencing the domestic agenda. As such, their activities go beyond our scope, but we should recognize that the blurring of domestic and foreign policy means that almost all interests are affected by international events some of the time. With that rejoinder in mind, we can explore the kinds of groups that seek to influence foreign and defense policy by looking at five overlapping distinctions about kinds of interest groups.

*General and Specific*    General interest groups are those whose interests span the spectrum of policy areas, including but not specifically emphasizing foreign policy. These groups—two examples of which are the American Federation of Labor-Congress of Industrial Organizations (AFL-CIO) and the American Association of Retired Persons (AARP)—take an interest in foreign or defense policy when it may directly affect their constituents. If defense spending proposals were to impinge on retirement entitlements, for instance, AARP would become involved. These comprehensive interest groups are often large and have considerable general influence, but they frequently lack great expertise in the specific area of defense and foreign policy.

Other interest groups concentrate on foreign and defense policy or some part of it exclusively. Although it also has some of the characteristics of a think tank (see the next section for a fuller discussion), the powerful Council on Foreign Relations is an example of an organization that focuses solely on foreign affairs. Its roughly 3,000 elected members represent the Eastern establishment foreign policy elite and thus bring both great expertise and prestige to the policy process, especially because many members are also former high-ranking officials of government.

One organization that concentrates on one aspect of the foreign policy process is Amnesty International (AI). This organization, dedicated to the protection of human rights globally, investigates and publicizes instances of human rights abuses. AI often comes into direct conflict with the State Department, which has the statutory mandate to produce a list of countries that are human rights abusers. Its list, partially constructed with geopolitical considerations in mind (how important a country is to the United States regardless of its human rights record), is almost always shorter than the AI list. The AI list of abusers thus serves as a club that members of Congress can use against the State Department, a part of the system of informal checks and balances of the government.

*Permanent and Ad Hoc*    The basis of this particular distinction is the presumed longevity of a particular group. Permanent groups are those that have been in existence for an extensive period of time and expect to continue for the indefinite future. They must therefore rely on long-term, hopefully stable relationships both with their constituencies and with those inside the government they seek to influence. This in turn affects the ways they operate: they are naturally prone to more low-key activities that nurture long associations.

Examples of permanent interest groups in the foreign and defense area would include the various groups that support the services: the Association of the United States Army (AUSA), the Air Force Association (AFA), and the Navy League. In addition to providing some contact with the services for retired personnel, each of these associations seeks to influence the government toward their services and toward general veterans' issues.

Ad hoc interest groups, on the other hand, are part of the broader phenomenon of the so-called single-interest interest group, an organization that comes together to affect the outcome of a particular issue but ceases to operate when the particular issue for which it was formed is resolved. The original ad hoc groups date back to the 1960s, and a prototype of sorts revolved around a national security issue, the Vietnam War. The entire loose, sprawling anti-Vietnam War movement was spawned on American college campuses shortly after U.S. active combat involvement in the war began. (The actual genesis came before we intervened in terms of so-called teach-ins at major campuses in 1964, notably the University of California at Berkeley.) The movement widened to encompass a broad spectrum from "hippies" to the Vietnam Veterans Against the War that shared a common, but single, interest in ending the war. Once that purpose was accomplished, the movement splintered and ultimately disappeared. In the current, nonforeign policy context, the various abortion-antiabortion phenomena may provide a parallel.

*Groups with Continuous or Occasional Interests*   Interest groups with a continuous interest in foreign and defense affairs tend to be comprehensive in their approaches to what interests them and what they seek to influence. The continuity of interest helps create expertise, which makes the group's counsel more sought than would otherwise be the case. In turn, the reputation for expertise makes the group's recruitment of experts easier. Examples of this kind of group would include the Council on Foreign Relations and the Foreign Policy Association.

By definition, groups with occasional interest in foreign policy are selective in the foreign and defense issues they seek to influence. Normally with a primary focus in some other policy area, these groups intrude into the foreign policy area only when a foreign policy issue directly affects them and then only for as long as their interests are affected.

An example might be the American Farm Bureau Federation whose primary focus, of course, is on agricultural policy. But when issues such as grain sales overseas arise, they become engaged in the foreign policy process. The group might be expected, for example, to take an active position on probable legislation limiting the diversion of agricultural credits to foreign governments to other purposes (Iraq's use of credit to buy military, including nuclear, hardware). This legislation will almost certainly be one of the outgrowths of the so-called Iraqgate scandal. Similarly, the AFL-CIO has a lively interest in the North American Free Trade Agreement, and the National Association of Manufacturers has a strong concern about those parts of the Treaty of Maastricht that will exclude U.S. goods from the European Community.

*Private and Public*   The largest number of private interest groups are those that represent individual corporations that do business with the government (contractors such as the aircraft industries or defense suppliers generally) or are regulated by the government (for instance, the pharmaceutical companies regulated by the Food and Drug Administration) and associations of corporate institutions (such as the National Association of Manufacturers).

In the foreign and defense policy area, the majority of private interest groups have historically been attached to defense, especially defense procurement. As international economic issues become more important in foreign policy generally, we can expect interest groups that have historically focused on domestic politics to conduct more foreign policy efforts. The number of corporate executives attending the Clinton economic seminar testifies to this interest.

Public interest groups, on the other hand, purport to represent the body politic as a whole, especially those citizens whose interests are underrepresented otherwise. Largely a product of the 1960s, these groups typically are financed by large numbers of small donations and maintain an air of impartiality (whether deserved or not). Common Cause is the prototype of this kind of interest group.

*National and International*   We think of American interest groups seeking to influence the U.S. political system as the norm, as the kind of activity sanctioned by the First Amendment. For most purposes and most of the time this is the case; to this point the discussion has focused exclusively on this kind of interest group action.

Americans are not, however, the only people interested in influencing U.S. policy, especially its defense and foreign policy. Foreigners, notably foreign governments, also share a lively interest in trying to affect U.S. government actions toward themselves and others, and they do so in a number of ways. Sometimes they use their own citizens, such as a particularly attractive ambassador, as an informal lobbyist with the government. Prince Bandar bin Sultan, the Saudi ambassador to the United States, has been especially successful in this role, particularly when opposition to selling weapons to the Saudi kingdom have arisen and especially during the Persian Gulf War.

Foreign governments also get their interests represented by hiring Americans, quite often former government officials, to represent them. People who represent foreign governments must register as foreign agents, and quite often their value derives from their ability to gain access to officials for their foreign clients. Henry Kissinger Associates is an example. Yet another way for foreign governments to influence U.S. policy is, when possible, to nurture Americans whose origins are the same as the nation seeking the influence. "Hyphenated Americans" (Italian-Americans, Irish-Americans, etc.) can be quite effective if these organizations can plausibly be argued to represent vital segments of the American public. Probably the largest and most successful of these is the so-called Israel lobby and its action arm, the American-Israeli Political Action Committee.

Interest groups and the activities they engage in are a long-standing, integral part of the U.S. political system. In a sense, although they are outside the halls of formal government, they reflect the same kind of system of checks and balances created inside government: almost all possible interests on most subjects have an organization representing that interest. Thus, the right to petition is available. If there is a limit or shortcoming, it is the attachment between interests and money; the public interest groups notwithstanding, those who have the money can afford to hire those who represent their interests. Occasionally, the result will be some perversion or corruption of the system.

## Policy Elites and Think Tanks

A relatively new and burgeoning phenomenon is the emergence of a sizable community of individuals with expertise on public policy matters (the policy elite), which attempts to use its knowledge to affect public policy. In most cases, these individuals are aggregated in not-for-profit, nonpartisan research institutes and organizations that conduct research on policy matters and share that knowledge with policy-makers. In the jargon of Washington, these organizations have been known as think tanks since the presidency of John F. Kennedy (whose administration witnessed a proliferation of them). Before that metaphor took root, synonyms included "brain banks," "think factories," and "egghead rows." (A number of the early ones were located in a row on Massachusetts Avenue in Washington, D.C.)

Think tanks and interest groups share some commonalities, but their composition and purpose are also different enough to allow them to be considered separately. They share two apparent similarities: some of their activities coincide, and they both operate at the boundary between the government and the populace. They differ in emphasis, membership, and range of activities they undertake.

The basic purpose of both think tanks and interest groups is citizen education, though for different reasons. Interest groups view education instrumentally, as a device to cause conversion to their interest. In contrast, traditional think tanks have sought knowledge and its educational application more abstractly, as a way to improve government, although some newer think tanks are edging toward the instrumental purpose. Both types of organization also operate at the boundary between government and the public, although it is a different boundary. For interest groups, it is the line between the formal system and organized citizens with particular interests; for think tanks, it is normally the line between government and the policy active intellectual community (the policy elite).

The two entities also differ in significant ways. The emphasis of interest groups is overtly political: They generally seek to move policy in self-interested directions. Think tanks, though often ideologically identifiable, adopt a more detached, scholarly view of policy. Similarly, most of those associated with the think tanks are academics in one sense or another, or people with experience-based expertise (retired military officers, ex-government officials), whereas traditional politicians are more often associated with interest group activity.

They are also distinct in their range of activities. Because of their heritage based in academia, think tanks rarely engage in gross advocacy of particular policy issues, whereas lobbying and pressuring in favor of specific legislation is the *raison d'être* of interest groups.

The think tank phenomenon is not well understood generally. Much of it occurs inside the beltway in a low-key manner. The activities of the think tanks are particularly important in the areas of foreign and defense policy, because these issues are at least part of the agendas of most prominent think tanks. As a result, an examination of the characteristics of these organizations and their activities is important to understanding how the process works.

### Characteristics

The movement that evolved into the modern think tanks took place around the turn of the twentieth century. Its impetus came from the determination by a group of scholars, principally from the social sciences, that public policy and process could be improved by the application of social scientific means and research.

The first identifiable think tank, the Russell Sage Foundation, was chartered in 1907 and was followed fairly quickly by the Twentieth Century Fund and a handful of others. All of these early efforts viewed themselves as citadels in which disinterested research (research not associated with personal or institutional gain) could be pursued and the results applied to societal problems dispassionately. These research interests remained peripheral to the process until the activism in politics associated with the 1960s. Until then there were relatively few think tanks in existence, what they did was largely academic, and they generally did not engage in much self-promotion.

All that has changed. According to the only full-blown study of the subject, James Allen Smith's 1991 book, *The Idea Brokers* (see Suggested Readings), about two-thirds of the think tanks operating in the Washington area today have come into existence since 1970. At the same time and led by the example of the conservative Heritage Foundation, many have become more activist, openly gearing their research to promoting particular political ideas and causes.

The think tanks are important to the understanding of foreign policy, because foreign and defense policy are important to them. In the appendix to his book, Smith provides what he calls a "sampler" of 30 of the most prominent think tanks. Table 6.1 depicts those institutions in terms of the foreign and defense nature of their activities.

Of the 30 organizations listed in the table, 23 (or 77 percent) concern themselves at least part of the time with foreign and defense concerns. Among the larger institutes, it is not unusual for their research activities to be divided into three program areas: foreign and/or security affairs, economic studies, and domestic or governmental studies. This is the pattern, for instance, of the prestigious Brookings Institution. Of those with no current programmatic concern for foreign affairs, the increasing internationalization of the economy is likely to impel organizations such as the Committee for Economic Development and the Economic Policy Institute, both of which concentrate on domestic economic issues, to broaden their concerns.

The research institutes are also defined by the people who work for them. Especially among those with a foreign and defense policy emphasis, they tend to come from one of three backgrounds: academia, the military, or the government. Academics are normally individuals with doctoral degrees in political science, economics, history, or international relations who are more interested in applied research (studying and influencing concrete public policy) than in abstract, theoretical academic research.

**TABLE 6.1**
**The Foreign Policy Activity of the Leading Think Tanks**

## Exclusively Foreign Policy

Carnegie Endowment for International Peace
Center for Defense Information
Center for Strategic and International Studies
Institute for International Economics
Overseas Development Council
World Policy Institute
World Resources Institute
Worldwatch Institute
    *Total*: 8

## Partly Foreign Policy

American Enterprise Institute
Brookings Institution
Cato Institute
Center for Budget and Policy Priorities
Center for National Policy
Ethics and Public Policy Center
Heritage Foundation
Hoover Institution
Hudson Institute
Institute for Contemporary Studies
Institute for Policy Studies
Joint Center for Political and Economic Studies
Progressive Policy Institute
RAND Corporation
Twentieth Century Fund
    *Total*: 15

## No Foreign Policy

Committee for Economic Development
Economic Policy Institute
Manhattan Institute for Policy Research
Resources for the Future
Rockford Institute
Russell Sage Foundation
Urban Institute
    *Total*: 7

Some of the abstract research can be found in institutes and centers affiliated with universities, but the typification holds for most nonuniversity academics working in the think tanks.

Even a partial list of academics is impressive. It would include John Steinbrunner, Dmitri Simes, Lester Thurow, Stanley Hoffmann, Edward N. Luttwak, Walter Laqueur, Ernest Lefever, Milton Friedman, Seymour Martin Lipset, the late Herman Kahn, and Fred Bergsten, all of whom are or have been associated with research associations at one time or another. Until her appointment as U.N. ambassador by President Clinton, Madeleine K. Albright (who was president of the Center for National Policy at the time of her appointment) could have been on the list along with Robert Reich, now Secretary of Labor, and Gordon Adams, now Deputy Director of the Office of Management and Budget. Not all are household names, but a quick bibliographical check at the library, or the identifying credits when experts are voicing opinions during foreign policy crises on television, will reveal how impressive they are.

As one might expect, retired military officers tend to be concentrated in think tanks, primarily studying security rather than foreign policy problems as more broadly defined. Many who have retired below the rank of flag officer (general or admiral) are located in organizations that do contract work for the government or in institutes run in-house by the services. In addition, a number of the Ph.D.s who work in the think tanks have military backgrounds, probably reflecting a greater "action" orientation than is normally associated with academic life. Prominent examples of retired military in the research institutes include retired Rear Admiral Gene LaRoque, head of the Center for Defense Information, and retired Army Colonel William J. Taylor, an executive at the Center for Strategic and International Studies (CSIS).

Among the former governmental officials, one group includes those whose positions provided them with considerable insight and expertise that is a valuable addition to the expert and prestige base of the institutes they join. Lawrence J. Korb (Brookings Institution) and Richard N. Perle (American Enterprise Institute, or AEI), both assistant secretaries of defense in the Reagan administration, and Jeane Kirkpatrick (AEI), former ambassador to the United Nations, are examples.

Another group are high-ranking officials who, out of ideological or political conviction, lend their names to institutes by serving as chairs, members of the board, or the like. This category includes former Secretary of State Edmund Muskie, former secretaries of Defense Donald Rumsfeld and Caspar Weinberger, and former White House counsel Edwin Meese.

*Sources of Funding*    The research institutes are also defined by the sources of their funding. They vary tremendously in size of staff and extensiveness of program, and thus in the need for and size of funding base. For most organizations, however, funding comes from a combination of six sources: foundations, corporate sponsorship, bequests and large contributions, individual contributions, sales of books and periodicals, and government-sponsored research.

The first source, large foundations with considerable resources, such as the Ford or Kettering foundations, provide funds to support research, including that conducted by the think tanks. Foundation support is most likely to be associated with research institutes that do not have an activist political agenda.

With regard to corporate sponsorship, as long as the funds are not attached to a political agenda (hence qualifying as interest activity), corporations can and do provide funds for institutes. Moreover, through bequests and large contributions, a number of institutes have endowments that produce revenue to support their activities. The amounts vary. The Brookings Institution, for instance, has an endowment of about $100 million, whereas CSIS has about $9 million in endowed funds.

A fourth source of operating funds is individual contributions. Among the major think tanks, the Heritage Foundation, which lists 43 percent of its income from this source, probably leads the way. Another source is sales of books and journals or magazines. Most research institutes publish their research, normally for a price, and this feeds into the budget. Finally, some institutes receive funding from government-sponsored research. The bellwether in this category is the RAND Corporation, which was created in 1948 largely to serve as a think tank for the newly independent U.S. Air Force and which still conducts much of its research for the Air Force and the Army.

*Ideological Leanings*    Another characteristic sometimes applied to research institutes is their general ideological or political persuasions. A number of institutes created in the 1970s were established out of the conservatives' belief that their lack of political success was the result of their lack of a formal, articulated agenda that could be used to appeal to the public or to provide a program for aspiring conservative candidates. The most prominent case in point of this phenomenon is the Heritage Foundation.

Think tanks run the political gamut. During the latter 1970s and early 1980s, for instance, the American Enterprise Institute became associated with the moderate wing of the Republican party. (A number of people associated with the Ford administration affiliated with it after Ford's loss to Jimmy Carter in 1976.) The Brookings Institution, on the other hand, has always been identified with more liberal positions and has sometimes been referred to as the "Democratic think tank," as has the Center for National Policy.

*Affiliations*  Think tanks may also be categorized in terms of three basic forms of association in the foreign and defense policy area.

The first and dominant pattern includes the private, freestanding research institutes which represent the original pattern that was established. When many people talk about the think tanks, they are talking about these. All the institutes identified in Table 6.1 belong to this type.

Some institutes are also associated with universities. The number is growing as universities, facing diminishing traditional federal sources of research funds, have adopted entrepreneurial strategies to attract funding by establishing centers, institutes, and the like. Among the most prestigious and best established entities are the Center for Science and International Affairs (a cooperative enterprise of the Massachusetts Institute of Technology and Harvard University), the Foreign Policy Research Institute (affiliated with the University of Pennsylvania), the Institute for Foreign Policy Analysis (associated with the Fletcher School of Tufts University), and the Hoover Institution (formally private but with a working relationship with Stanford University).

Yet another form of affiliation is with a governmental organization. Each of the military services, for instance, maintains its own in-house think tank to investigate and advise it on matters of concern to it. These are generally associated with the war colleges. Thus, the Army maintains its Strategic Studies Institute (SSI) at the U.S. Army War College in Carlisle Barracks, Pennsylvania, the Navy its Center for Naval Warfare Studies (CNWS) at the U.S. Naval War College in Newport, Rhode Island, and the Air Force its Aerospace Research Institute (ARI) at the Air University in Montgomery, Alabama. There are also instances of joint service activities, such as the Army-Air Force Center for Low-Intensity Conflict. The State Department also maintains the same kind of capability in its Center for the Study of Foreign Affairs.

As this discussion should indicate, the evolution of the think-tank phenomenon has been an eclectic affair. There are just about as many different kinds of think tanks as there are ways to categorize them. The pattern is continuing to evolve, particularly in the funding-tight 1990s, when the research institutes are being forced to compete with one another and with other institutions such as universities for dwindling resources.

## Patterns of Function and Activity

The research institutes and the policy intellectuals that staff them engage in a variety of different activities. Different organizations, of course, place greater emphasis on some functions than on others, and the pattern is evolving, as are the organizations themselves. Some of these activities are shared with interest groups; some are distinct.

The activities and functions can be divided into research, publications, expert advice, "talent bank," a focal point for like-minded individuals, and the media connection. The first and most fundamental category is *research*. Since the conduct of research was the reason why most of these organizations came into being in the first place, this should not be surprising. Moreover, much of the prestige and early influence of the original research institutes was the result of their adherence to objective, scholarly pursuit of knowledge based in social scientific methods of inquiry.

The research emphasis, which produces and disseminates knowledge applicable to dealing with societal problems, distinguishes the think tanks, giving them their character and identity. Moreover, the analyses they perform are the basic "product" they have to sell to the system; it is the way they can help set the political agenda and influence the public debate. In the absence of a research base, think tanks would be little more than interest groups representing the policy intellectual community.

The concern about the continuing purity of research efforts coming from the institutes arises from two bases. The first is the emergence of the activist, openly political think tank. The Heritage Foundation is the prototype. The organization openly admits that it engages in inquiry for the purpose of promoting the conservative agenda and that it publicizes only those research findings that support its point of view. The fear is that this emphasis will undercut the reputation for scientific integrity that has been important to think-tank influence in the past.

The second source of concern is financial. In the 1990s the sources of funds needed to support the research institutes contracted at the same time that other funding sources, such as government grants, also became more scarce. As a result, the think tanks must compete with one another. Often the things that most successfully "sell" contributors relate to overt political influence, once again with the potential consequence of compromising the organization's scientific purity.

The research institutes promote their research through *publications,* which may take several forms. One is the commissioning and publishing of books on topics of public interest. One fairly common pattern is for the think tank to employ a visiting scholar for a period of time (a year or two) with the express purpose of producing a book. Ideally, these books attract broad public readership, or at least the attention of policy-makers. The results can be added prestige for the think tank, influence on the policy process, and, not least importantly, revenue to support the institute. The Brookings Institution has always supported a vigorous book list, as has CSIS through its *Washington Papers* series, and the Council on Foreign Relations through its own press.

Another form of publication is technical reports. The RAND Corporation disseminates short, technical reports that are available to policy-makers and the general public. Staff members also write so-called op-ed articles for the opinion and editorial pages of leading national newspapers, such as the *New York Times, Washington Post*, and the *Christian Science Monitor*. In addition, a number of think tanks produce journals that are used as research sources by scholars and others conducting policy relevant research. A representative list with foreign and defense policy relevance includes the *Brookings Review* (Brookings Institution), *Cato Journal* (Cato Institute), *Foreign Policy* (Carnegie Endowment), *Defense Monitor* (Center for Defense Information), *Washington Quarterly* (CSIS), *Policy Review* (Heritage), *World Policy Journal* (World Policy Institute), and *World Watch* (Worldwatch Institute).

Many research institutes provide *expert advice* to government in a number of ways. Some organizations, for instance, contract with the government to provide specific expertise on technical matters. This activity is more often associated with consultants (sometimes known as Beltway Bandits because of their locations along the Washington Beltway and the alleged quality of their work) but is occasionally done by think tanks as well.

More commonly, however, the research institutes act in more subtle ways. A staff member who has just completed a major study may be asked to provide expert testimony to a congressional committee or to serve on a presidential commission investigating an area in which the organization has expertise. At the same time, that expertise can also be applied to watchdogging governmental activities. The Defense Budget Project, directed by Gordon Adams and sponsored by the Center on Budget and Policy Priorities before his OMB appointment, critically analyzes the defense budget proposal produced by the Defense Department and publishes and circulates that critique throughout the government.

In addition, think tanks provide a *"talent bank"* (the term used by the Nixon administration) for the government. This process works in two directions. On the one hand, when an administration leaves office and is replaced by another, some personnel dislocation always occurs among the several thousand officials who hold political appointments and find that their services are no longer required as a new president forms his own distinctive team. Many officials so removed do not want to leave the "Washington scene" altogether and even have aspirations of returning to senior government service in the future.

For such people, appointment to a position in one of the research institutes can provide an attractive option that serves both the individual and the organization. From the individual's viewpoint, a think-tank appointment can serve as a safe haven, a sanctuary between periods of government service wherein the person can remain abreast of what is happening in Washington. From the organizational vantage point, the association of important former governmental officials can enhance both the prestige and expertise of the organization.

In the other direction, the staffs of the research institutes provide a ready talent pool for filling governmental positions. It has been argued, for instance, that the Brookings Institution, as well as the John F. Kennedy School of Government at Harvard University, provides a kind of "government in waiting" for any new Democratic president, just as the Heritage Foundation provided a source of policy inspiration and personnel availability for the Reagan administration. As the Clinton administration made appointments to the midlevel positions within the Pentagon and State Department, for instance, the think tanks provided fertile recruiting ground.

The think tanks are a *focal point for like-minded individuals*. This function formed one of the major purposes of formalizing the conservative movement through Heritage and other organizations following Barry Goldwater's crushing defeat by Lyndon Johnson in the 1964 election. The feeling was that conservatives had failed to develop and articulate a politically attractive agenda because they had no mechanism around which those of like persuasion could rally. A research institute with an active research and publication program can fill this bill. Research leading to the articulation of policy positions can help clarify the policy agenda for any group. A publications program utilizing books, technical reports, talking papers, or articles in a house-sponsored journal can help to circulate ideas and to establish networks of like-minded scholar-policy analysts.

A newly emerging function of think tanks is the *media connection*, and more specifically, the role of the *electronic expert*. This phenomenon is the result of the media's burgeoning need for information and expertise, combined with the opportunities for organizational and self-promotion that the electronic expert's role provides for the think tanks.

The media's needs dated back to the Vietnam period. Events, and especially their analysis and understanding, often went beyond the expertise of the television networks and print media who, for instance, did not possess staff experts on Southeast Asian history and politics or the principles of mobile-guerrilla warfare (the style of war employed by the North Vietnamese and their Viet Cong allies). Those media, with headquarters and major bureaus in the same locales as the major think tanks (which *did* have staff with expertise in those very areas), created an obvious marriage of convenience. The media's need was for experts who exuded authority, whereas the think tanks sought the exposure that having members of their staffs appearing on the evening news could provide.

This role has been expanding as a result of trends in electronic mediation. Once again, CNN is the trend setter. CNN by necessity engages in a great deal of news analysis in addition to reporting. To analyze the news requires expert authorities, and the think tanks are a fertile ground. But that is not all. In addition, CNN has also changed the extent and depth by which breaking news events, and especially foreign events, are covered. Knowing that CNN will produce very detailed coverage of an international crisis forces the other news organizations (wire services, leading papers, television networks) to cover events in more detail than ever before. The alternative is to concede news coverage supremacy to CNN. Unwilling to do that, the need for experts proliferates.

This new phenomenon, of course, reached an apex during the Persian Gulf War and the preparations for it. Each television network recruited its own complement of experts to appear daily to explain what had happened, as well as periodic appearances by others. Members of the staffs of the more aggressive research institutes (CSIS being among the most prominent) were among the most often seen. Unless there is a trend reversing the expansion of news coverage (which hardly seems likely), this trend is likely to continue and expand in the future.

## Conclusions

Both think tanks and interest groups can be seen in the context of the system of informal checks and balances on which the political system operates. Nearly every interest has a group to represent it and make sure its voice is heard; the think tanks span the range of intellectual points of view. In the overall context of the U.S. government, interest groups are a more important phenomenon than the think tanks. They are larger, more numerous, more visible, richer, and hence more powerful. The think tanks, on the other hand, are probably more represented and effective in influencing foreign and defense policy than in other areas, because international relations is an important area of social science inquiry. Were our focus not on foreign affairs, there would have been less reason to examine the think tanks in any detail.

The two kinds of institutions share similarities and differences. Both, for instance, seek to influence rather than to govern (although some think-tank staffers move in and out of government), but they do so differently and for different reasons. Interest groups act self-interestedly: they attempt to move public policy so that it will favor those they represent. The early think tanks in particular sought to improve government not out of self-interest but out of an academically driven sense of improving the government.

The purposes are reflected in the means used. Although both institutions seek to educate the public and those who govern, their methods differ. The tools of interest groups are persuasion (lobbying), education, and pressure. The extreme form of their actions are found in PAC activities. This is the natural result of acting out of self-interest: specific outcomes are highly personalized. Because they presumably act disinterestedly, the think tanks have persuasion based in expertise and objective knowledge as their major tool.

Some of these distinctions may be vanishing as at least some think tanks begin to operate more and more like interest groups. The politically activist, and especially conservative, movement within the research institute community during the 1980s has produced a hybrid—the think tank with a specific political agenda. The tools may remain educational in the broad sense, but they result from directed research. This research is aimed not at increasing the general pool of knowledge, but at providing knowledge that reinforces political predilections. Once again, the Heritage Foundation stands at the forefront of this variant.

Finally, the two institutions form a bridge between government and the broader society that is the subject of the next chapter. In broad terms, interest groups aggregate, articulate, and seek to influence the public at large. At the same time, the media are the object of some educational elements by both groups, and the growing phenomenon of the electronic expert provides a new linkage between the media and the think tanks.

## SUGGESTED READINGS

Bayes, Jane H. *Ideologies and Interest Group Politics: The United States as a Special Interest State in the Global Economy*. Novato, Calif.: Chandler & Sharp Publishers, 1982.

Chittick, William O. *State Department, Press, and Pressure Groups: A Role Analysis*. New York: Wiley-Interscience, 1970.

Miller, Stephen. *Special Interest Groups in American Politics*. New Brunswick, N.J.: Transaction Books, 1983.

Ornstein, Norman J. *Interest Groups, Lobbying, and Policymaking.* Washington, D.C.: Congressional Quarterly Press, 1978.

Smith, James Allen. *The Idea Brokers: Think Tanks and the Rise of the New Policy Elite.* New York: Free Press, 1991.

Watson, Bruce W., and Peter M. Dunn, eds. *Military Intelligence and the Universities: A Study of an Ambivalent Relationship.* Boulder, Colo.: Westview Press, 1984.

Weiss, Carol H. *Organizations for Policy Analysis: Helping Government Think.* Newbury Park, Calif.: Sage, 1992.

Zeigler, L. Harmon. *Interest Groups in American Society.* Englewood Cliffs, N.J.: Prentice-Hall, 1964.

# CHAPTER 7

# The Influencers II:
# The Public and the Media

Within the philosophy underpinning the U.S. political system, sovereignty ultimately resides with individual citizens, who in turn delegate part of that sovereignty to government. Governmental authority to carry on the duties of the state, including the authority to conduct foreign and national security policy, flows from and is limited by the amount of sovereignty that has been ceded by the people.

Those who govern pay a price for being given the sovereign authority to govern in the form of the principle of *accountability*. According to this principle, the people reserve the right to inspect what their government does in carrying out the public trust and hence to decide whether or not it is doing the job correctly. On the basis of public assessment, those who govern can be deemed adequate and retained or removed from office.

The media, as provided for and protected by the First Amendment guarantee of a free and unrestrained press, assist the public in rendering its judgments by investigating and publicizing the performance of those who govern. Because a large part of the media's job is to act as a watchdog against incompetent or corrupt governmental action, there is a natural adversarial relationship between the "fourth estate" (a term for the press, first used in the nineteenth century to contrast it with the three classes of citizen of England) and those in government.

## Difficulties in Applying Accountability

The relationship between the media and government is, of course, neither as simple nor as straightforward as it sounds, especially in the areas of foreign and defense policy. In order to begin to see the complication of the notions of authority and accountability between the government and the people, we can look at three sources of difficulty: control of the foreign policy agenda, secrecy, and public ignorance of foreign policy.

## Control of the Agenda

In the realm of foreign policy, unlike many domestic policy areas, Americans in or out of government do not always determine what kinds of problems they will deal with. Instead, in a great deal of foreign policy the agenda setters are foreign governments or elements within foreign countries who create situations to which the United States has to respond. Thus, the U.S. government had no control over whether or not the former state of Yugoslavia would dissolve in 1992. In fact, Secretary of State James Baker publicly hoped it would stay together as it was falling apart. The extraordinarily explosive and violent circumstances that arose as a result of that dissolution created the need for a policy response that the government would have preferred not to have made and that was inherited by the Clinton administration.

The inability to control the agenda makes it more difficult to apply the principle of accountability. Foreign governments do at times act to make the U.S. government look better or worse, depending on whether a particular government likes or dislikes the administration in office. The former Soviet Union, for instance, regularly acted during presidential election years to put the incumbent in a better or worse light, depending on whether they felt reelection was in *their* best interest.

This problem of agenda control is likely to expand as the blurring between domestic and international politics continues. Decisions made in Tokyo or Berlin can have a real impact on the status and well-being of American citizens, from determining who will have jobs to what will be the cost of interest on automobile loans. Assessing whether or not government has performed admirably is very difficult under these circumstances.

## Secrecy

A reasonable proportion of foreign policy, and especially national security policy, is conducted with at least some adversarial content. The ability to conceal what one knows and how one knows it often provides some advantage. The problem is that the inability to know everything the policy-maker does comes at the expense of the full ability to account for action. There is some tradeoff between democratic accountability and security. The debate, especially in a post–Cold War world, is how much compromise of democratic ideals remains necessary.

The need to conceal has both legitimate and illegitimate bases. On the positive side, it is sometimes necessary to conceal information that provides the basis for making a decision because to reveal that basis would compromise the source from which it came. This is known as source sensitivity and provides much of the rationale for classifying (restricting access to) information within the intelligence community and the government more generally.

The conduct of diplomacy provides another legitimate example. When negotiating with another country, the negotiator is trying to obtain concessions that will move a situation as close to the national interest as possible. The nature of negotiation is give and take, in which each side is willing to compromise in order to get what it wants. One never, however, admits in advance how much one is willing to give away, because once that is revealed, there is nothing left to bargain about.

With even legitimate instances of secrecy, public assessment of performance begins with only a partial record of what happened. How can we know if a source has to be protected from exposure or recrimination? If we do not know the bargaining position our negotiators bargained from, how can we know if the deal they got was the best one possible? The answer, of course, is that accountability is left imperfect.

The negative side of secrecy, of course, is that it may be imposed for the wrong reasons, such as to obscure the government's incompetent or illegal actions. In the Iran-Contra scandal, for instance, the facts of selling arms to Iran in exchange for assistance in gaining the release of hostages held in Lebanon and the diversion of arms-derived funds to the Nicaraguan Contras were kept secret from the American people and Congress. At least part of the reason was that the people would not have approved of the actions, either on the grounds that it was ill-considered policy or that it violated policy and even law.

### General Public Ignorance of Foreign Policy

Most analyses of what the public can and should do to affect and judge foreign and defense policy have concluded that the role has been and continues to be very limited, mostly in the form of passive reaction to initiatives made by the political executive.

The reason traditionally cited for the public's historical ineffectiveness in influencing the foreign policy process is the public's legendary ignorance of international affairs. A very small percentage of the population keeps abreast of foreign events, has traveled abroad, speaks a foreign language, or has taken formal courses at any level dealing with foreign cultures, history, or international relations. This ignorance, combined with widespread perceptions that foreign affairs are so intricate and involved as to be beyond the comprehension of the average citizen, reinforces the people's general ineffectiveness in influencing how government conducts foreign and national security affairs.

One of the central roles of the media is to try to reduce citizen ignorance. As a foreign policy actor, the media's relationship to the process contains several aspects. One of these aspects is whether the media are agenda setters, impelling consideration of policy activity by virtue of those events they cover, or whether they reflect the agenda presented by events and other policy actors. This question will be of mounting importance because of global television's increasing proficiency at covering graphically the instability and violence that is sundering a number of newly noncommunist and Third World nations. In other words, would the international system have been forced to take any action in Bosnia and Herzegovina had the slaughter of civilians in Sarajevo not been an undeniable and unavoidable fixture of the nightly news? Television brought Somali starvation into our living rooms; similar privation in such places as neighboring Sudan go unreported and hence unnoticed by the public or policy-makers. Does television make a difference?

The relationship between the media and those in authority is also relevant. As part of the scheme of things, this relationship is and should be a partly adversarial one, because part of the press's role is to expose governmental misdeeds and the attempts of officials to gain excessive power (the real concern of the Constitution's framers). The problem has become greater in recent years. On the one hand, we now have more media coverage of everything, including foreign and national security policy. On the other hand, the Vietnam and Watergate episodes greatly worsened relations between government and the media. In Vietnam, for instance, the media believed they had been duped into falsely reporting progress by the military before the Tet offensive of 1968 (an attack by the North Vietnamese that, if reported casualty figures had been truthful, they would not have had adequate personnel to stage). The media have been suspicious of military pronouncements ever since. For its part, many members of the military believed that the media's negative reporting of the war after Tet contributed to the American loss of the war. The most recent instance of this ongoing distrust was seen in military restrictions on press access to the battlefield in Operation Desert Storm.

The media's place can be viewed as triangular (although not as an iron triangle) as depicted in Figure 7.1. On one side of the triangle is the relationship between the public and the media. The main points of contention in that relationship include the degree to which the media provide the public with adequate and accurate foreign and defense policy information, the degree to which the public takes advantage of the information provided, and whether the media serve to lead or reflect public opinion (or both). The key new variable in the public-media relationship is the emergence in the last decade of the global electronic media and how

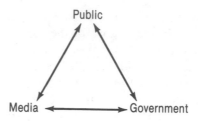

**FIGURE 7.1**   **Public–Media–Government Relationship**

this changes both the public's access to and awareness of foreign policy events and issues.

The second side of the triangle focuses on the relationship between the media and the government. The relationship is especially strained in the foreign and defense policy area because of the issue of secret (or classified) information. From the media's vantage point, very little information should be restricted and entirely too much information is classified. The media have the further suspicion that restriction is too often not based on legitimate need but to cover up misdeeds. Moreover, the only people legally bound to maintain the secrecy of classified information are those who have voluntarily done so as a term of employment with the government. Members of the media do not fall under that restriction, which is a source of discomfort to those charged with maintaining the confidentiality of information.

The third side of the triangle is the relationship between government and the people. The media serve as a conduit in this regard, since most of what people know about international affairs and the government's reaction to those events comes from the media. The major question is how well the media dispatch this role.

This brief introduction forms the basis of an inspection of both the public's and the media's role in the policy process. As stated at the outset, there is a conventional view of both, and especially of the public. Although we will reiterate the basic elements of the "conventional wisdom" about each, we will also attempt to explain how roles may be changing in the new international order.

## The Public

For most of U.S. history, and certainly before World War II, the public played a minor role in the nation's foreign policy. The major reason, of course, was that the public was only rarely affected by foreign policy occasions and hence had very little need or desire to be involved.

The permanent ascendance of the United States to a position of world leadership after World War II began the process of changing that attitude. As the leader of the Western coalition facing an apparently implacable Soviet enemy with whom war could come at any time, there was a need to convince the public that what the United States did in the world was morally right.

The question was the level and quality of public participation. At one extremity in the debate were the foreign policy professionals, who wanted the role to be as minimal as possible. Their most articulate spokesman was George F. Kennan, as detailed earlier. Kennan and others argued that the public role should be simply to accept and ratify the "wisdom" of the professionals. At the other extreme were more egalitarian voices who maintained that since it was the public that had to bear the burden of foreign policy decisions, they must be involved. The debate has never been resolved in a way that is acceptable to everyone.

One way to look at the traditional role of the public is as a parameter setter. Because the public does not possess great expertise in foreign affairs, it cannot set the agenda, nor is it likely to provide detailed guidance to policy-makers. What it can and does do, however, is to set broad outer boundaries (parameters) of policy that the public will accept. Within those boundaries, policy-makers have a reasonable discretion to act. When government exceeds those limits, its policy is in trouble. Government must therefore determine whether support will be forthcoming before it acts, especially if its actions will have a direct bearing on the citizenry. The U.S. government learned this lesson the hard way in the Vietnam War, where public opposition ultimately forced the United States to abandon the effort.

Interestingly enough, this relationship was stated in its most articulate form by a Prussian general staff officer over 150 years ago. In his seminal work *On War,* Carl von Clausewitz identified a "holy trinity" without whose support governmental effort (in his case the conduct of war) could not be sustained successfully. The elements of the trinity are the people, the army, and the government. Clausewitz maintained that the active support of each segment was critical to success.

In retrospect many observers, especially in the military, feel that the flaw in the Vietnam debacle was in ignoring the trinity. More specifically, the failure to activate public support (or opposition) before our intervention eventually led the public to turn on the war and the effort, as Clausewitz would have predicted, to collapse. That the military learned its lesson from Clausewitz and Vietnam was seen most forcefully in the Kuwaiti desert. That lesson was that the United States should never become involved in a major military effort again without an active show of support by the government and the people in the form either of a formal declaration of war or at least a mobilization of the body politic in the form of calling up the reserves.

This relationship between public and government was established in two ways. First, after Vietnam the armed forces were scaled down and restructured. The chief architect of this restructuring for the Army was General Creighton Abrams. He restructured roles and missions of the active and reserve components of the Army, so that critical roles were assigned mostly or entirely to the reserves. Thus, no major action could be undertaken without them. The effect was to ensure involvement at the grass-roots level of society. If the American people did not want to send their friends and neighbors to war, they could let the system know before action was taken by objecting to the mobilization.

Second, the Weinberger Doctrine, announced by Caspar Weinberger, President Reagan's secretary of defense, stated as Pentagon policy what Abrams had done operationally by laying out a set of criteria that had to be met before force should be employed. One of the major criteria was the assurance of broad and sustained public support.

Operation Desert Storm was the first application of this new understanding about the relationship between public and government. A first act in forming the force that would be dispatched to the Persian Gulf was a large-scale activation of reserve units. This was the first time the reserves had been called to overseas duty since the Korean War 40 years before. The reserves and the public acted favorably, thus giving the military the kind of assurance it sought.

Is the relationship between the government and the people on important foreign and defense policy concerns established in Desert Storm a precedent for the future or an aberration? To assess that question, we need first to look at the traditional view of the public's role and then to show how that role may be in the process of change.

### The Traditional Role: Multiple "Publics"

Much of the traditional literature on the public and foreign policy has stressed not what the public can and should do, but the limitations on that role. The source of that limitation is the historically high degree of general citizen disinterest and ignorance of the subject matter, which some argue makes their meaningful participation impossible.

Citizen limitation is normally depicted by dividing the electorate into a series of segments, often visualized as a set of concentric circles, as shown in Figure 7.2. The diagram divides the population in terms of its level of interest and expertise, with levels increasing as one moves inward toward the center of the circle.

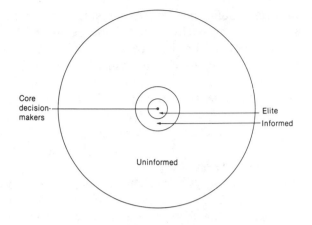

FIGURE 7.2     Foreign Policy "Publics"

*The Uninformed Public*   At the outer band of the circle is the uninformed (or inattentive) public. It is by far the largest portion of the population, encompassing 75 to 80 percent of the total. The uninformed public is defined as that portion of the population that does not regularly seek out information about international affairs. Operationally, this part of the public does not read stories about foreign affairs in newspapers or news magazines (if it reads these at all), does not read books on the subject, and avoids those parts of news broadcasts dealing with foreign policy.

Because of their lack of information, the uninformed public tends to become aware of or involved in foreign policy issues only under three circumstances. The first occurs when a foreign policy event has a direct bearing on them personally. Almost 30 years ago, conscription for the Vietnam War was of this nature, as was the boycott of the 1980 Moscow Olympics and, more recently, the mobilization of the reserves for Operation Desert Storm.

A second circumstance occurs when broad publicity is given to international events. Publicizing the plight of Kurdish refugees fleeing Saddam Hussein's forces in the wake of Desert Storm created a public awareness that would have otherwise been lost on all but the most dedicated student of foreign policy. The unrelenting, daily barrage of reportage about the American hostages held in Teheran at the beginning of the 1980s was similarly impossible to ignore. Suffering in the Balkans presents a similar situation.

In the third circumstance, conscious efforts are made to mobilize public opinion by the government or others. This ploy is used in particular by incumbent presidents: it is usually true that the public is less critical of foreign policy actions than domestic actions and will generally rally behind the president in foreign policy matters. As a result, the president can often build a consensus behind his position that would be more difficult to build around a domestic policy. Richard Nixon's trip to Egypt in 1974 to divert attention from the Watergate scandal which would shortly force his resignation from the presidency is a particularly strong example. (His approval ratings in the polls temporarily rose over 20 points during the visit.) An analogous effort from outside the government might be the campaign, spearheaded by Chrysler Corporation's Lee Iacocca, to convince Americans that much of the malaise of the U.S. automobile industry is the result of unfair trade practices by Japan.

These efforts do not always work. During the heat of the presidential campaign in late June 1992, a beleaguered President Bush complained to a group of reporters that his foreign policy accomplishments appeared unappreciated by the public. Specifically, he bemoaned, "We had [Russian President Boris] Yeltsin here in the Rose Garden, and we entered into a deal to eliminate the biggest and most threatening intercontinental ballistic missiles — the SS-18s of the Soviet Union — and it was almost 'Ho-hum, what have you done for me recently?'" (*New York Times*, July 1, 1992, p. A10). The point is that in a post–Cold War world, nuclear arms reductions probably do not qualify under any of the circumstances that activate the interest of the vast majority of the population.

The attention of the unattentive public is thus difficult to capture and tends to emerge only over large, highly visible events. For the most part, the attention provided by this group is sporadic, short term, and highly malleable. On the majority of foreign policy issues, members of this group simply have no coherent, elaborated opinions. Rather than being agenda setters in any sense of the term, they are much more likely to have their opinions shaped by others. Moreover, this group tends to be demographically distinct: lower educational and occupational attainment, geographic isolation from the major policy centers, and the like.

This grim depiction of the vast majority of the population's orientation toward foreign and defense policy forms the base for much of the elite critique of democratic participation in the foreign policy process. Indeed, as long as most of the population remains uninterested and unknowledgeable in this field, it is difficult to make a case for their inclusion as more than broad boundary setters. If one finds this situation both regrettable and unacceptable in a rapidly internationalizing community where foreign policy has direct and continuing relevance to all Americans, then we can raise the question — explored in the next section — of whether there are viable strategies for change.

*The Informed Public*  The second concentric circle in Figure 7.2 represents the informed (or attentive) public. As the diagram indicates, this is the second largest population segment, including 10 to 20 percent of the population. As the juxtaposition of titles suggests, the definition of the informed public is virtually the opposite of that of the inattentive public; members of the informed public *do* regularly seek out information on international affairs. They do so by such means as reading foreign policy stories in newspapers and magazines and watching television coverage of international events.

Several groups of people typically fall into the ranks of the informed public. Local civic leaders who influence the opinions of their communities are one group, as are local journalists, clergy, and others to whom the public at large turns to help them form opinions.

For most members of the informed public, their contact with foreign policy events is indirect rather than direct. Generally, they have relatively few, if any, direct contacts with the process, although that is changing as more and more localities come into direct relationships with foreign investors or because a defense installation or defense contractor does business in their area. With some exceptions, however, this means that informed public members achieve their understanding of foreign and defense policy issues at second hand and vicariously rather than through personal self-action or self-interest.

This relationship to foreign and defense policy affects the informed public's quality and depth of understanding on these issues. With the exception of a foreign or defense policy that directly affects their lives (e.g., a foreign automobile manufacturer building a plant in their vicinity or a military base closing), members of the attentive public are likely to have general rather than detailed knowledge. A clergyman, for instance, may be aware of black on black violence as an inhibitor to change in South Africa; he is unlikely to associate the tribal roots of the two leading black movements in the country (the Xhosa-dominated African National Congress and the Zulu-based Inkthata party).

The informed public does play a role in the foreign policy process. It does not set the agenda but is instead reactive: it learns generally of issues and expresses a general reaction that helps form the parameters within which policy can be crafted. At the same time, the status of members of the attentive public within their communities means that they inform other members of their community with less interest in issues and interpretations of those issues. As such, their role is to convey information and opinion.

*The Effective Public*    The third group is the effective (or elite) public. Defined as that part of the public that actively seeks to influence the foreign and defense policy process, this group consists of a relatively small number, generally considered as something less than 5 percent of the overall population.

Frequently associated with the elite public are policy-makers, national opinion leaders, and foreign policy experts. Policy-makers, actual members of government at the national and, to a somewhat lesser degree, state levels are active in foreign policy matters but are not primarily foreign and defense policy experts (see the discussion of core decision-makers below). Thus, for instance, a congressman from the upper Middle West will not necessarily be an expert on defense matters, but he or she does have a lively concern about European Community policies that effectively exclude American wheat from the European market. Similarly, the governor of a Sun Belt state has a multitude of domestic concerns that consume most of his or her energies, but textile imports and sales of citrus fruits to Japan also create a foreign policy interest.

The national opinion leaders are people whose positions and expertise make them molders of opinion and setters of agendas. Examples include members of the national media whose jobs bring them into direct contact with foreign and defense issues and personalities, or former government officials with recognized expertise — men such as Kissinger and Brzezinski.

Finally, the foreign policy expert community is made up of people who by training and experience have detailed knowledge but who do not happen to be in government. This group consists of scholars in relevant disciplines (international relations or economics, foreign or defense policy, contemporary diplomatic history), leaders of large interest groups with a direct foreign or defense interest, and experts in the research organizations or think tanks.

Distinguishing the effective public from the informed public is both their depth of knowledge and the centrality of foreign and defense matters to their personal and professional lives. Members of the elite public not only read national newspapers (e.g., the *New York Times*, the *Washington Post*, or the *Los Angeles Times*) and news magazines (*Newsweek*, *Time*, or *U.S. News and World Report*), but they also read (and write) articles in specialized journals (e.g., *Foreign Affairs, Survival*) and books on relevant subjects.

In addition, the professions in which the elite public involves itself leads to a certain level of activism and policy advocacy, for example, criticism of government policy and advocacy of alternative policies. This activity is often associated with being part of the "shadow government in waiting," those Democrats who are not in governmental positions during Republican administrations and vice versa. As such, individuals in this group can be the elite public part of the time and core decision-makers at other times.

Given the need for access to information and the policy process, members of the elite public have historically been physically concentrated as well, especially on the Eastern seaboard, notably Washington, D.C., and New York City, the nation's political and economic capitals, respectively. Journals like *Foreign Affairs* are regularly displayed on the news-stands of downtown Washington, for instance, and the Washington bureaus of the news networks provide excellent opportunities for exposure and influence for people such as the electronic experts discussed in Chapter 6.

*Core Decision-Makers*    The final group at the center of the series of concentric circles in Figure 7.2 are the core decision-makers. Although they may not be a part of the general population per se, this group encompasses individuals who are responsible for the actual formulation and execution of foreign and defense policy. This group is also the smallest, numbering several hundred people within the government, because of the requirement of formulating policy. While almost every professional in the Department of Defense or State could be said to be involved in implementing policy at some level, the role of most of them is quite restricted. They essentially apply (implement) policy made by others (although they may have some input into the decisions made) rather than decide on basic policy.

Those who actually make policy occupy key roles in both the executive and legislative branches. Within the executive, the most numerous are found at the levels of assistant secretary and above in the State and Defense departments, the international divisions of other cabinet-level agencies, and the National Security Council staff. Within the legislative branch, the most prominent examples are the chairs and ranking minority members of the most important congressional committees and their senior staffs. Thus, the chairs and ranking opposition members of the Foreign Relations, Armed Services, and Select committees on intelligence, and the chairs of the Appropriations subcommittees on defense and foreign policy matters are obvious examples.

The distinctions between core decision-makers and elite public are also imprecise. As noted, some individuals move back and forth between the two designations as their status changes. Moreover, some individuals are not clearly and unambiguously in one or the other. The assistant secretary of defense for policy, the assistant secretary of state for Far Eastern affairs, or the chairs of the Foreign Relations or Armed Services committees clearly are part of the core by virtue of their positions. On the other hand, individuals with an interest and some expertise in the area are more difficult to locate. Before he became president, Bill Clinton was probably on the boundary between the elite and the informed public on foreign and defense matters, and Vice President Albert Gore was somewhere around the boundary between the elite public and the core decision-makers.

This conventional analysis of the public's role is pessimistic and negative. It essentially argues that the vast majority of the population is uncaring and ignorant about foreign and defense policy issues to the point that their opinions can be largely ignored or easily molded to fit the policy-maker's agenda. In this view, only those in the two inner circles — the elite public and the core — have the experience and expertise to make intelligent decisions on these issues. The view thus supports the elitist school of thought about the public role.

This is an unsatisfying situation in a rapidly changing world in which international affairs increasingly influence the public agenda and individual lives. A question that may reasonably be asked is whether this situation is acceptable in the world of the future and what, if any, signs of change may be on the horizon.

### Sources of Change

The traditional absence of interest in foreign and national security policy among many Americans is grounded in their lack of knowledge of foreign affairs and their perception that this area of policy had no particular relevance for them. These two bases are, of course, linked: people do not learn about foreign affairs because of its seeming unimportance, and they do not know enough about foreign relations to realize its salience.

What can change these traditional attitudes? Is it possible for more uninformed Americans to become the informed public and for the informed public to move onto higher levels of involvement and understanding? While this matter is admittedly speculative, we can point to at least four forces that could make a dent in the ignorance/disinterest syndrome, a syndrome that has limited public effectiveness in the foreign policy arena: greater availability of information, educational reform, increased public awareness of the relevance of foreign policy, and attempts to mobilize public opinion.

**Greater Access to Information**   This factor is largely the product of the telecommunications revolution that is both intertwining the global economy and politics and is producing a cascade of greater information about foreign and defense policy problems. President Clinton, as "seminar leader," can easily be pictured expanding his televised economics seminar to foreign policy.

The key element here is global television, especially television operations such as CNN, which both collect and disseminate the news worldwide. Moreover, a variety of related technologies including the video camcorder, satellite linkages, and fiber optics give television the ability to provide instantaneous coverage and transmission of events happening, thereby adding to the drama of breaking events.

The impact of all these changes on how both Americans and citizens of other countries are affected in terms of their attitudes to foreign affairs remains speculative. Moreover, we do not yet have a perspective on this technological revolution. CNN, for instance, did not exist 12 years ago, and the ability to provide instantaneous coverage over thousands of miles is even newer than that. The early derision of CNN has quite been overturned. When dramatic events occur around the globe, people turn in large numbers to CNN, as they did during the Persian Gulf War. As a result, large numbers of citizens have become aware of things they heretofore had ignored.

Without Bernard Shaw's unrelenting coverage, for instance, would we have learned very much about the Chinese government's suppression of the "democracy movement" in Tiananmen Square in 1989? of the plight of the Kurds in the wake of the Persian Gulf War in 1991? of Serbian barbarity against the citizens of Bosnia and Herzegovina in 1992? At the same time, how much does selectivity of coverage (the slaughter in Mozambique, for instance, has been uncovered by the media and ignored by governments) affect the foreign policy agenda? Global television, of course, cannot give the citizenry a sophisticated understanding of problems and policy, but it can whet people's appetite and make ignorance less sustainable. To move greater numbers outside the ranks of the uninformed requires a second force: educational reform with an emphasis on international affairs.

*Educational Reform*  The need for educational reform has become a popular shibboleth of the 1990s, with President Clinton a leading standard-bearer. Spurred on by the dismal rankings of American children in science and mathematics compared to children in other countries, there is a clear mandate, if not funding base, to improve the educational system.

One area in which education has failed most emphatically is in giving the school-age population wide exposure to global problems. The litany is disturbingly familiar: less than 5 percent of American students study a foreign language (and far fewer become proficient), most students lack even basic geographical knowledge, and even among college students, less than 3 percent ever take a course in foreign affairs, international relations, or foreign culture.

That picture is changing, albeit slowly. At the collegiate level, increasing numbers of colleges and universities are adding an international education requirement to basic graduation requirements. At the precollegiate levels, organizations such as the American Geographical Society are spearheading efforts to increase the international content of curricula at the high school level and earlier. For these efforts to be maximized, increased funding for education will be needed; funding has proven a major barrier in most states in the past several years.

*Increased Relevance of Foreign Policy*   The changing nature of the national security problem caused and stimulated by the collapse of communism has more than an abstract importance to U.S. citizens. In the absence of a Soviet enemy to confront, the United States needs less military personnel and hence less military equipment and support services, all of which have provided many jobs for Americans in the past. At a more specific level, the announcement in July 1992 that the United States would no longer produce the enhanced, weapons-grade plutonium from which nuclear weapons are fabricated has direct implications for people in Rocky Flats, Colorado, and Oak Ridge, Tennessee, areas where those activities have traditionally been performed.

The internationalization of economic activity has created the need for a more sophisticated understanding of international dynamics. Indeed, those who learn to take advantage of the emerging system will prosper and those who do not will suffer. The very public nature of Clinton's commitment to the economy will almost certainly lead to greater appreciation of the dimensions of the problem.

For this kind of emphasis, the state of South Carolina may provide a model. Over two decades ago South Carolina accelerated its involvement in international affairs using the James F. Byrnes Center at the University of South Carolina as a catalyst. The state has been highly successful in arranging trading relationships with foreign countries and in attracting desirable foreign investment in the state. When the first BMW automobile rolls off the Spartanburg, South Carolina, assembly line in 1994, it will be a testimony to the power of international knowledge.

*Mobilizing Public Opinion*   In the past our national leaders appealed for overt mass public support only when the most dramatic and personal events occurred such as those involving peace and war. That situation will almost certainly change. Not only are international events more directly relevant and more visible to more Americans than before, but also the blurring of domestic and foreign policy means that more support will have to be generated to back those policies that could affect domestic priorities. The emergence of so-called humanitarian vital interests, with a heavy moral overtone that tugs at the public heart, represents an additional stimulus with which the Clinton administration will have to come to grips.

The case of assistance for Boris Yeltsin and the Russian Republic in the spring and summer of 1992 provides an example. Historically, a foreign nation's request for aid would have been a routine matter and would not have generated much controversy. In a period of fiscal stringency in which domestic policy priorities were being neglected, however, aid to Russia was juxtaposed with domestic needs. As some critics asked loudly and publicly, should the United States be underwriting change in the Russian economy when it cannot feed and house the homeless? Hardly anyone could argue that assisting Russia was a bad idea or not in the national interest, but enough were able to question the priority of the effort that Yeltsin was sent back to Russia largely empty-handed.

If public awareness and participation in foreign and defense policy-making is to increase, then obviously the cycle of ignorance and disinterest will have to be broken. And if that is to happen, greater publicity will have to be given to foreign events, and more effective explanation of the salience of those events to people's lives will have to be presented. The media will have to play a leading role in that process.

## The Media

The term *media* is a shorthand term used to describe those individuals and organizations who collect and disseminate information (news) about what is happening in the world. The media are divided into the so-called print media, consisting of newspapers and news magazines, and the electronic media, consisting of radio and television.

### The Print Media

Of course, the print media are older than the electronic. As stated earlier, their independence to observe and report on the operation of government is included in the First Amendment of the Constitution, and it was justified as a means of preventing the undue accumulation of power by individuals or governmental institutions. Their independence is assured because all the print media are independently owned by individuals outside government and are unregulated by governmental agencies. The operative principle to insure continued independence is the doctrine of "no prior constraint" on publication. This doctrine, first articulated in a 1931 Supreme Court case (*Near v. Minnesota*), states that there can be no prior censorship by government of reportage. (A practical exception is reportage of ongoing military campaigns that might provide information to the enemy.)

The print media cover foreign and defense policy through the flagship newspapers, news magazines, and the wire services. Probably the most influential are the flagship newspapers such as the *New York Times* and *Washington Post*, which have the time and resources to assign reporters and bureaus full time to coverage of foreign and international events, and the national newspapers, publications that do not have a specific geographical locale (*USA Today*, *The Wall Street Journal*, and *The Christian Science Monitor*). These are the newspapers read by people in the policy process, the elite public, and the better informed members of the attentive public. The function of the major news magazines is to provide depth and interpretation to events initially reported by the newspapers. Finally, the wire services, such as the Associated Press or Reuters, provide foreign and defense policy news to local newspapers that do not have the independent ability to collect and report on foreign affairs on their own.

### The Electronic Media

The electronic media, unlike the print media, are subject to at least cursory regulation through the licensing process by the Federal Communications Commission (FCC). FCC regulations basically ensure that radio and television stations do not use transmission bands that interfere with one another's signals; less formally, in their reportage they are expected to honor the principles of equal time to political candidates, the right of rebuttal, and the so-called fairness doctrine in reporting.

The electronic media cover foreign and defense policy issues through the major television and, to a lesser extent radio, networks and report the news to their affiliates. In addition, the emergence of CNN has created more or less the equivalent of the national newspapers in the form of a television station devoted solely to the news. Finally, local television and radio stations rely on sources such as the newspaper wire services and television feeds to report foreign and defense news.

### Role of the Media

The media's function in the area of defense and foreign policy, though still evolving, has been controversial. To understand how the media stand between the people and the government, we will first look at the traditional functions the media performs, noting how they are influenced by the nature of international affairs. We will then discuss how technological change, principally in the electronic media, is changing and expanding those functions.

### Traditional View of the Media

The media basically observe and report the activities of government and the actions and thoughts of individual political figures. In this role, they are sometimes in active sympathy and cooperation with those on whom they report, and sometimes they are not. The media also serve as watchdogs of the public interest, particularly in areas where they perceive the possibility of breaches of the public trust. In this role, the government and the media are almost always adversaries.

In reportage generally, but especially in the area of foreign and defense policy, the media do not, and really do not even attempt, to communicate evenly with the entire public. This is largely the result of the general public's lack of interest and the kinds of media that cover the area. Readership of the flagship newspapers, for instance, is demographically defined in terms of educational level, wealth, and means of livelihood, as is viewership of outlets such as CNN. In other words, the foreign and defense policy-reporting mechanism is directed at the relatively well educated and affluent, and it is transmitted through those channels that the educated and affluent read and watch.

Any attempt to harness the media to the task of broadening citizen awareness and participation in the foreign and defense policy process must begin with this awareness. Either broader segments of the public must be drawn to the national media, or foreign and defense reportage must be expanded in those channels from which the masses receive their information—local newspapers, local television, and local radio.

Media activity in the foreign and defense policy area can be thought of in terms of five different functions.

***Collection and Reportage of the News***    Through this function, the media observe what the government (and the broader world) are doing and inform the public of those actions. Collection and reportage of the news is also presumably the most objective and least controversial, but the nature of foreign and defense occurrences complicates the straightforward reportage in several ways.

Specifically, there are generally too many things happening worldwide for the media to cover simultaneously. Thus, the media are necessarily selective in what they cover and report, and some people will inevitably conclude that not all the worthiest items are being covered. People in the Third World, in particular, complain that they receive media attention only in times of wars, natural disasters, and other cataclysmic events. The wide range of events that occur worldwide does, however, stretch the resources of any news-gathering outlet to cover everything. Moreover, foreign events are often idiosyncratic and unpredictable, making orderly planning more difficult. Another difficulty in coverage occurs because governments often seek to hide or obscure events that are unfavorable to them. The telecommunications revolution is making obscuring unpleasantries more difficult, however.

*Investigation or Watchdogging*    At the simple level of reportage, print or electronic journalists may do little more than reiterate what public officials tell them. By self-appointment, however, reporters feel the need to determine the veracity of public pronouncements and to report instances in which they believe the public trust has not been well served. This function, which has increased dramatically in the last quarter-century, often places government officials and the media at loggerheads.

The event that more than any other triggered an adversarial and untrusting relationship between government and the media was the Vietnam War, as we mentioned earlier. In the early stages of the war (roughly 1965 through 1967), reportage of the war was largely favorable to the military; the press corps dutifully reported progress in the war based on briefings at Military Assistance Command Vietnam (MACV) in Saigon known as the "five o'clock follies." According to the progress reported to the media and dutifully transmitted to the American people, the enemy's forces were being rapidly depleted to the point that when U.S. commanding General William Westmoreland reported late in 1967 that he saw "the light at the end of the tunnel," the assertion was not widely disputed.

The Tet offensive of early 1968 broke the bond between the media and the government. When CBS anchorman Walter Cronkite saw the first film footage of Viet Cong in the American Embassy compound, he is reported to have said, "What the hell is going on here?" What was going on was the end of media trust in the government's conduct of defense and foreign policy. That relationship, and the media's consequent perceived need not to take the government at its word, was reinforced by events such as the Watergate scandal, the Iran-Contra scandal, and the exclusion of the press from the U.S. invasion of Grenada in 1983 (the first reports of which were received in the United States over Radio Havana).

*Interpretation*    Because of the general public's ignorance of international affairs, explaining the flow of events is a particularly important function. Many people simply do not have the knowledge base to put foreign and defense policy questions in focus and perspective. In the absence of media interpretation, they would have only government officials, whose explanations are often motivated by self-interest, to provide context.

This function, though valuable, is also controversial because of the media's alleged ignorance of the subtleties and nuances of many foreign and defense issues. Most print and electronic journalists are not trained in foreign affairs any more than the average citizen is. The problem is even more severe in the defense policy area. Since the draft was rescinded at the end of 1972, most young Americans—including the vast majority of reporters—have had no military experience on which to base expertise. The media at least partially understands this deficiency, which helps explain why so many of the electronic experts covering the Persian Gulf War were retired military officers.

The national press, both print and electronic, is also alleged to have a liberal bias. Part of the basis for this allegation is geographical: the national press is concentrated in New York and Washington, which are generally more liberal than much of the rest of the country. It is also partly the result of the fact that more liberal, reformist young men and women tend to be drawn to the media. Many members of the defense establishment believe this liberal bias is also antimilitary, thereby adding to the strained relationship between the media and the military.

Another consideration is that foreign and defense policy interpretation must occur largely in close proximity to events, when their full meaning cannot be known and when some or all of the parties involved may be directed to keep certain facts secret. The danger of the media's "instant analysis" is that when false interpretations of events are offered and accepted, they may continue to affect perceptions even after corrections have been made. When the government itself takes actions to withhold information from the media, thereby crippling its ability to interpret—as often occurs in military operations—the potential for friction between officials and the media is magnified.

*Influencing Public Opinion on Issues*    Like all the other functions, this, too, is tinged in controversy. Whether the media do in fact influence opinion or whether they simply reflect the opinions that they believe the public already holds is a matter for some debate. The overt expression of opinions occurs primarily on the editorial pages of newspapers, but how many people read or are influenced by editorial positions? Journalists claim that the influence is minimal or even nonexistent, but those in government believe that the editorial power of the national flagship newspapers or the television networks is very great.

Some of the media's critics also point out that the press has power to influence and does not have to bear responsibility for the consequences of advocacy. In this argument, political leaders' statements of opinion have personal consequences; if poor policies are advocated, the voters can demand retribution. However, when William Randolph Hearst created the bandwagon that forced President William McKinley to declare war on Spain, McKinley, not Hearst, would have been forced to bear the consequences had the action proven unsuccessful. Of course, the extent of this problem relates directly to the extent of power the media are believed to have.

In this connection, there is the question of how the media seek to influence opinion. In the traditional sense, the editorial page of the newspaper or clearly identified electronic media editorials have been considered legitimate, provided fairness and access by other opinions are available. The controversy emerges when editorial bias sneaks into the objective "news hole" in the form of biased selection of stories, biased reportage, and the like. The question that arises then is whether the media are serving the function of informing or whether they are propagandizing. This same criticism is also directed at television news analysis shows such as "60 Minutes" and "20/20."

*Agenda Setting*   The media try to influence what important issues become part of the public agenda, how the public should perceive these agenda items, and what policy outcomes are desirable. The problem enters in when media attempts to frame issues collide with government efforts to frame the agenda.

Instances of this collision in the foreign and defense arena are legend and are often most heartfelt. The modern prototype, of course, was Vietnam, especially after the Tet offensive of 1968. Beyond the simple disillusionment with the military's truthfulness on that occasion, many members of the media came to believe that the war was unwinnable and that U.S. withdrawal was the proper course. This conclusion was openly expressed and was reflected in the kind of stories chosen and in the way those stories were presented. The media can also change their minds quickly, altering their projected images of events. Despite coverage that bordered on cheerleading in support of intervention in Somalia, within days of its authorization leading columnists and the editorial page of the *New York Times* were already questioning the attainability of the political objective.

This problem, which often manifests itself in the media's alleged distortions of complex realities, is especially serious for television, particularly at the national level. Foreign and defense issues are normally complex and controversial, requiring considerable sharing of information with a public that is unequipped to make its own judgments. Television, on the other hand, is the medium of the short, pithy explanation; the 45-second "sound bite" with a vivid optical imprint, the specialty of television, is quite unlike the leisurely analysis provided by a *New York*

*Times* or *Newsweek* feature. Network news stories are rarely more than a minute and a half long, and that may not be long enough to form other than cursory impressions.

Though brief, the impressions created by the visual media can be very strong and influential, especially when violence and suffering are depicted. A 30-second film clip of Bosnians being attacked on the streets of Sarajevo can create an enormously strong anti-Serbian reaction that may or may not be justified. It can also impel governments into action and lead to strong public appeals to force government actions, as occurred when CNN showed pictures of the Kurds in southern Turkey as Saddam Hussein's forces reacted to their uprising following the end of the Persian Gulf War. U.N. Secretary Boutros-Ghali, in a 1993 interview, argued such reporting piqued the public conscience and forced leaders to react.

These examples of media activity and its impact are traditional, the stuff of journalism textbooks. A whole new area of possible activity is being created by the fruits of the high-technology revolution manifested in the telecommunications revolution.

## Impact of the Telecommunications Revolution

As noted earlier, a series of technologies associated with the enormous growth in knowledge generation, dissemination, and assorted derivative technologies are transforming the modern world of production, economics, and communications. This high-technology revolution is being aided by advances in telecommunications and is substantially enhancing the ability to acquire and disseminate information, which is the heart of the media's role.

The electronic media are the major beneficiaries of this process. In subtle ways that neither practitioners nor theoreticians yet understand, these advances are changing the international affairs that are the substance of foreign and defense policy, as well as the way policy is made.

Because we currently lack a theoretical understanding of this phenomenon during the 1980s and 1990s, we can only view the impact impressionistically, using examples. To that end, we will now explore how the telecommunications revolution is transforming foreign and defense policy by strengthening the role of the media or downgrading the importance of more traditional policy mechanisms.

*Increased Ability to Influence Events*    Global television represented by outlets such as CNN is a prime factor in this increased influence. Telecommunications advances have made the world increasingly transparent to media coverage and reportage. When we combine the ability to reach out almost everywhere with technologies such as the video cam-corder, there is very little that happens in the world that the media miss. That fact in and of itself affects what and how governments do their business.

Possibly the most dramatic instance of this transparency occurred in the summer of 1991 in Moscow, where a group of conspirators launched a temporarily successful coup against then Soviet President Mikhail S. Gorbachev. In earlier days, when the media could be and were excluded from the inner workings of the former Soviet government, this event might have proceeded quietly and countercoup activities such as Russian president Boris Yeltsin's very public resistance might have been brutally suppressed.

This time, however, worldwide television was there, and the coup leaders did not know what to do about them. Reporters covered and transmitted live visual images everywhere, and the coup leaders flinched. The day after the coup took place, the collective leadership felt obliged to hold a televised, live news conference explaining that there really had not been a coup and promising to restore Gorbachev after he became "well." (They said he was ill.) At that point the coup was doomed.

That is not the only example. Although we may not know for certain for a long time, the Eastern Europeans' complete rejection of communist leaderships in 1989 and 1990 must in part be attributed to their access to Western European television and the glaring disparities it revealed in the standard of living in the East. The only leader who lied and denied the disparities was Romania's Nicolai Ceausescu; he was also the only leader executed by his own people. One clear outcome of the telecommunications revolution is that it will be increasingly more difficult for governments to suppress information—to lie—which has always been a major tool of authoritarian governments.

*Impact on the Policy Process*    One way in which this impact occurs most strongly is through a phenomenon known as media diplomacy, whereby governments conduct some of their relationships with other governments through the media, sending information back and forth about positions and the like through interviews with CNN and other outlets. The media also intrude through the extensive coverage of diplomatic negotiations that until very recently we always held in heavily guarded secrecy.

Relations between the United States and the former Soviet Union illustrate the use of the media as a conduit for information between governments. For example, in 1991, on the eve of Gorbachev's visit to the United States to conclude negotiations on strategic arms reductions (START), the Soviet government apparently had a last-minute change of position on one of the important issues to be discussed. The problem the

Soviets now faced was to relay this change to the highest levels of the U.S. government in the most efficient way possible. The traditional method would have been to call in the U.S. ambassador and ask him to transmit the message back to Washington. Feeling this method would be too slow, the Soviets instead called the CNN bureau chief, who reported the story quickly on the network. The Soviets doubtless sought out CNN because they knew President Bush watched CNN. In a similar vein, President Bush used global television to voice his displeasure with the attempted coup against Gorbachev.

The extensive coverage of diplomatic events also represents change. It has always been a canon of diplomacy that it should be as quiet and confidential as possible, thereby creating an atmosphere of candor and flexibility in which compromises can be reached. (If positions are publicly known, compromise becomes more difficult because then it becomes necessary to back away from original positions, thus giving the appearance of losing ground.) Massive media coverage has changed that. It is not unusual for negotiators to end their negotiating session with a press conference to discuss what happened in the meeting, a heretofore unthinkable idea. Events such as the Earth Summit in the summer of 1992 were as much media events as anything else.

Public figures are still in the learning stages of being "television actors." When Saddam Hussein held the British children—his effective hostages—on his lap during the early stages of Desert Shield, he probably thought he was being reassuring, but it did not come off that way. By contrast, as President-elect, Clinton skillfully used his conduct of the Little Rock seminar to demonstrate to the public and to Wall Street, too, his seriousness, maturity, and grasp of complex economic issues.

*The Media as Part of the Process*    At one level, the way the media cover events influences public perceptions and thus help structure the responses that government can make. At the same time, media figures such as ABC's Ted Koppel, through the "Nightline" program, actually become active parts of the process. Koppel held teleconferences with participants to disputes on late-night television that earned him the nickname of "television's secretary of state."

The impact of such activity is not well established, but it is undoubtedly substantial. Certainly, media coverage of natural or man-made disasters creates a vividness of perception, as well as a common view of events, that would not be possible in the absence of those images. Our image of the Balkan disaster in Bosnia and Herzegovina, for instance, would have been much more clouded had it occurred 30 years ago, or especially nearly 80 years ago, when the result was World War I.

*The Media as Publicist, Interpreter, and Agenda Setter*    This role is likely to be true because, as a result of the global reach of the electronic media, the volume of material to which the public and policy-makers are potentially exposed will continue to expand exponentially.

Through their choices of what to publicize among a volume of events and issues beyond their ability to broadcast and the public's capacity to absorb, the media will help define the public agenda. This same increased volume and diversity of coverage will also mean that the public will be exposed to more and more unfamiliar situations for which they will require interpretation. The media are logical candidates for at least part of that role.

The emergence of 24-hour-a-day news broadcasting outlets such as CNN will create a much larger "news hole" for the media to fill. Thus, coverage will have to be expanded to areas that have not heretofore received very much coverage. On a global level, the ripe candidate will be the Third World (much of Asia, Africa, Latin America), which has been demanding greater exposure of its problems and will almost certainly get it. Once again, the problem lies in the shortage of expertise in the public that requires the media to explain what television is covering.

A beneficiary of this factor is almost certainly going to be the electronic experts, those academics from the universities and think tanks, former government officials, and retired military officers who possess knowledge of global issues that the media staffs frequently do not have. This factor is almost sure to become more prominent as the media expand their coverage to ever more exotic corners of the globe.

These are only a few suggestions of how the media will become more important in the future. How its role will evolve is difficult to predict: the pace of technological, economic, and political change is so rapid that establishing a sense of direction is almost impossible — and precise prediction is fool's work. For example, if someone had predicted five years ago that a coup against a democratizing government in the Soviet Union would be foiled at least in part because of the Western news media's live coverage of the event, who would have believed it?

## Conclusions

The roles of both the public and the media in the foreign and defense policy-making process are changing. In the past the traditional roles of both were relatively modest. The general public was basically compliant and reactive, allowing the elite to craft policy unless it went beyond public tolerance written in the most general terms. As for the media, it always focused more on the domestic agenda, because it lacked the physical and technological ability to report extensively and in a timely fashion on all but a thin slice of international reality.

Both circumstances have changed. As the boundary between domestic and foreign policy has blurred and the direct, personal impact of foreign policy has increased, so has the public interest. In the days of the Cold War, the content of what the public was exposed to was more heavily oriented toward national security. With the Cold War over, international economic foreign policy factors are more important, as are glaring abuses of the human condition. These are less abstract and more personal: they affect jobs and livelihoods and hence have greater salience than, say, the deterrent effect of a particular ballistic missile.

From this change may come greater public interest in foreign and defense policy, gradually widening the population that forms the attentive public. Academics and others have been calling for such interest in the past with little effect; direct personal self-interest may provide a more effective lever.

The telecommunications revolution has been more important in expanding the media's role in the foreign and defense policy area than in domestic politics. All its advances are enhancing the ability to cover the domestic scene, but that ability was already present in abundance. The ability to cover and interpret foreign policy events was always more circumspect, bounded by the speed with which oral descriptions and pictures could be transmitted from the far-flung corners of the globe. Technology has now made it as physically possible for news organizations based in New York or Washington to air news about events in Africa as it is to cover occurrences in Ohio.

The media's coverage of the 1992 election marked the beginning of a new relationship between politicians and the media. The extensive use of free guest appearances on shows like "Larry King Live" by Bill Clinton and H. Ross Perot showed that politicians had attained a new awareness of how to co-opt the media. In effect, they turned a campaign into entertainment. The success of the Perot "infomercial" suggests a format that Clinton and future presidents may want to use to educate and influence the public on complex foreign and defense issues.

The public and the media share more than an individually enhanced role in the foreign and defense policy-making process. Their roles are also intertwined. A basic limitation on the public's ability to receive and interpret information in the past was access to information in a timely way. Ten years ago, for instance, it was not technologically possible to buy today's *New York Times* in almost any community and CNN was a struggling infant considered primarily an oddity. Today, 75 cents will buy today's *Times* nearly everywhere, and over 50 million homes receive CNN. In other words the availability of timely information has exploded.

Neither the public nor the media will likely dominate the foreign and defense policy-making process anytime soon, if ever. Although the greater public knowledge of issues provided by the media is not a threat to the roles of formal governmental institutions and experts, the government must be more aware and sensitive than before—which is what democratic government is about.

## SUGGESTED READINGS

Almond, Gabriel. *The American People and Foreign Policy*. New York: Harcourt, Brace & World, 1950.

Bailey, Thomas A. *The Man in the Street: The Impact of Public Opinion on Foreign Policy*. New York: MacMillan, 1948.

Brody, Richard A. *Assessing the President: The Media, Elite Opinion, and Public Support*. Stanford, Calif.: Stanford University Press, 1991.

Cohen, Bernard C. *The Press and Foreign Policy*. Princeton, N.J.: Princeton University Press, 1963.

Cohen, Bernard C. *The Public's Impact on Foreign Policy*. Boston: Little, Brown & Co., 1973.

Graber, Doris A. *Public Opinion, the President and Foreign Policy*. New York: Holt, Rinehart & Winston, 1968.

Landecker, Manfred. *The President and Public Opinion: Leadership in Foreign Affairs*. Washington, D.C.: Public Affairs Press, 1968.

Rosenau, James N. *National Leadership and Foreign Policy: A Case Study in the Mobilization of Public Support*. Princeton, N.J.: Princeton University Press, 1963.

Rosenau, James N. *Public Opinion and Foreign Policy: An Operational Formulation*. New York: Random House, 1961.

Smith, Perry M. *How CNN Fought the War: A View from the Inside*. New York: Carol Publishing Group, 1991.

Spragens, William C. *The Presidency and the Mass Media in the Age of Television*. Washington, D.C.: University Press of America, 1979.

Wittkopf, Eugene R. *Faces of Internationalism: Public Opinion and American Foreign Policy*. Durham, N.C.: Duke University Press, 1990.

# CHAPTER 8

# Case Studies: FSX and Desert Storm

The dynamics of the policy process are best revealed by the way it deals with concrete foreign and defense problems. To this end, we have selected two recent cases that show both the complexity and idiosyncrasy of the policy process at work. One case deals with the controversy generated when the Japanese sought to develop a new jet fighter aircraft during the 1980s and a debate arose as to whether or to what extent the United States should provide that aircraft. The other case involves the decision process leading to Operation Desert Storm, the military campaign launched to force Iraq to withdraw its forces from conquered Kuwait, and subsequent developments. Because it is so recent, many of the specific details of the Desert Storm decision process are not yet publicly available and must be inferred from public decisions and materials.

The two cases are different in a many respects, including content and focus. The FSX controversy, as it evolved, had both strong economic and national security content; the kind of jet fighter the Japanese ultimately developed would have an impact both in the areas of defense and economics. Desert Storm, while having some economic overtones—the United States and the West's continued access to reasonably priced Persian Gulf petroleum—was almost exclusively framed and viewed as a traditional national security problem with a military solution.

The two cases also differed in terms of the urgency of the situations. When Iraq's armed forces smashed across the Kuwaiti frontier and rapidly occupied the entire country, there was an apparent need to respond with alacrity. This need for quick reaction was made all the more important because Iraq apparently had the ability to continue to march further south and occupy the rich Saudi oil fields along the Persian Gulf coast as well. This action would have greatly endangered Western oil access. FSX, on the other hand, was a developmental program that would be years in the making. Begun in the middle 1980s, the first FSX aircraft (if there ever are any) is not scheduled to be completed until 1997.

Another difference lay in the visibility of the two situations. Desert Storm, of course, was a highly visible event, occupying center stage in the American consciousness and policy process from the August 2, 1990, invasion of Kuwait until the end of the 100-hour ground offensive that broke the Iraqi occupation and ended ground hostilities at midnight, February 27, 1991. By contrast, the FSX negotiations proceeded almost entirely outside the public eye. They were not launched by any dramatic event that captured public attention; in fact, most of the negotiations were conducted quietly and privately in the traditional manner of diplomacy. The attentive public became aware of the issue only when it became an interbranch battle between the new Bush White House and Congress in January 1989.

Yet another difference was the complexity of the issues involved. Of the two situations, the FSX proved to be by far the more complex and thus the more difficult to resolve. Its intricacy arose from two basic sources. On the one hand, both governments, but especially the U.S., experienced some difficulty in deciding whether to treat the problem as a national security or an international economic concern at a time when the lines between the two were becoming increasingly hazy. On the other hand, contentiousness emerged because of infighting within the executive branch itself as well as between the executive and legislative branches.

The decision process in Desert Storm, as we know to date, was far less complex. This campaign was a classic military response to a geopolitical problem, the kind of situation for which the traditional National Security Council system had been designed, even if the problem lacked the communist–anticommunist context in which the system was devised. As the crisis evolved, the branches of government fought not over whether to respond, but only over how and when. The only complicating factor, which actually served to reinforce the administration's desired course of action, was the participation of a United Nations revitalized by the event.

A difference flowing from the others centered on the actors who were most prominently involved in the two occasions. Both began in the executive branch within the context of the traditional NSC system with the Departments of Defense and State predominating. Desert Storm largely remained within that context, as the president and his closest advisers, Vice President Quayle, Secretary of State Baker, Secretary of Defense Cheney, National Security Adviser Scowcroft and his deputy (and later DCI) Gates, and CJCS Powell — all core members of the system — were tightly in control of the evolving situation. Even congressional input was rarely sought — to the annoyance of many members of Congress.

A wider net of participants was necessarily brought into the decision process surrounding the FSX. Because the deal had potential economic consequences at a time when the U.S.-Japanese economic relationship was coming under scrutiny, the executive agencies that had primary responsibility for international economic policy (e.g., the Commerce Department and the Office of the Trade Representative) were ultimately drawn into an adversarial relationship with the State and Defense departments.

As we will see, one lesson of this bruising experience may be the need, on matters where jurisdictions overlap, to include coequal agencies with economic responsibilities on the NSC, as first suggested in Chapter 1. In the Clinton administration, those elements of the Economic Council with direct responsibility for industrial policy would quickly have been engaged in, or even dominated, the process.

A final dissimilarity between the two cases involves agenda setting. In Operation Desert Storm, the primary agenda setter was Saddam Hussein, whose initial invasion created the policy problem and whose continued intransigence dominated the agenda. Desert Storm is a textbook case in which a foreign policy issue is defined by external forces beyond the control of U.S. policy-makers, whose role becomes reactive: how does the United States respond to a situation thrust on it?

The agenda setting is less clear-cut in the FSX case. Certainly, the Japanese decision that it needed a new fighter aircraft precipitated the situation, but the Japanese did not wholly control either the agenda or its outcome throughout. Because of the historic relationship between Japan and the United States, Japan's reluctance to appear militaristic, and Japan's traditional deference, the Americans were allowed largely to frame the options. Much of what makes FSX noteworthy is the internal U.S. struggle over which of the options it had framed would ultimately be the option chosen.

There are also points of similarity between the two cases. First, a portion of each involved the adversarial relationship between Congress and the executive that has been a recurring theme in this book. Part of the reason, of course, is that both occurred within the context of Republican control of the presidency and Democratic control of the legislative branch. Partisanship was clearly more evident in Desert Storm: almost all the senators and representatives who opposed early authorization of combat operations were Democrats. In both cases, the two branches' lack of mutual trust was evident; politics did not end at the water's edge.

Second, both cases, especially FSX, suggest the need to consider reform of the system. As we will see, FSX was a picture of bureaucratic confusion and rivalry within the executive branch that arose out of its failure to involve all interested parties early on and thus to produce a unified and acceptable administration position. In the case of Desert Storm, the administration's apparent inability to stick by an articulated long-term political objective to be served by the operation continues to raise the question of whether a relatively small, insulated set of actors can adequately deal with the large, complex issues of national security. Moreover, this instance of U.S.-U.N. military interaction offers some premonition for present (Somalia) and future operations.

We will view these two crises in ascending order of complexity, if in opposite chronological order. Both are long-term situations in that neither has achieved resolution: as yet there are no FSX jet fighters and there will not be for some years, and the continuing controversy with Iraq's Saddam Hussein that dominated the period before, during, and after Desert Storm continues.

## Case Study: The United States, Iraq, and Desert Storm

The U.S.-led response to Iraq's invasion, conquest, and annexation of its tiny neighbor, Kuwait, between August 1990 and the end of February 1991 riveted public attention in the United States and, thanks to global television, most of the rest of the world as well. The Persian Gulf War as it is generically known was highlighted by the brilliantly conceived and executed U.S. military plan, Desert Shield (the activity before offensive action began) and Desert Storm (the offensive air and ground campaigns). Television galvanized our attention; where one was when the bombing of Baghdad began on January 16, 1991, may be as defining a moment for some Americans as where they were when the first reports of John Kennedy's assassination was to an earlier generation.

Our purpose here is not to rehash the military side of Desert Storm. Rather, we will view the episode from the vantage point of Desert Storm as a foreign policy and policy-making problem. In this larger sense of the event, we will examine (1) the period before the Iraqi invasion, when the United States was actively engaging the Iraqi leader through a generally low-key campaign within the executive branch that sought to bring him into the international mainstream; (2) the invasion of Kuwait on August 2, 1990, the raising of forces to oppose the invasion and, most importantly from our vantage point, the executive branch's appeal to the Congress, as well as the United Nations, to authorize the use of force; and (3) the period since the end of military hostilities, with some attention to whether the Americans achieved the goals they set out to achieve in the war and how controversy over the postwar situation became a partisan issue in the 1992 presidential campaign.

### The Pre-Invasion Period: The Courtship of Saddam

The tangled events leading to Desert Storm can be seen adequately only in light of the complex international politics of the Persian Gulf region and U.S. efforts to stabilize those politics in order to reasonably insure a steady flow of Persian Gulf petroleum to the West. It is a history of changing sides and changing fortunes.

Iran and Iraq are geopolitically the most important states of the region in terms of size, population, and military potential. They are also historic enemies whose enmity dates back at least to the days of Persia and Mesopotamia in biblical times. From the early 1950s until the end of the 1970s, the United States aligned itself closely with Iran and especially Shah Reza Pahlevi, whom we supplied with military equipment in return for his guarantee that the oil would flow. During this period (when Saddam Hussein rose to power in Iraq), the United States and Iraq were adversaries who did not even recognize one another diplomatically.

That changed when the fundamentalist Iranian Revolution overthrew the shah in 1979. To the Ayatollah Ruhollah Khomeini and his supporters, the United States was the "great Satan" to be universally opposed. To that end, the U.S. embassy in Teheran was seized and its personnel made captive in late 1979. Iranians with connections to the Americans were arrested and often executed. The United States had dramatically lost its principal ally in the region.

In September 1980 Iraq declared war on and attacked Iran in a war that would last eight years. Iraq's Saddam Hussein believed he could gain an easy victory over an Iranian military whose leadership ranks had been decimated because of connections with the Americans and endear himself to other Arabs by defeating the hated non-Arab Persians and extinguishing the appeal of the militant Shiite fundamentalism of the Iranian leadership.

In this situation, the United States began to shift toward support of Iraq, first assisting in arming the Iraqis and by 1984 suggesting normalization of relations between the two countries. (U.S. diplomats had been expelled from Iraq in 1958.) Prior to the fall of the shah of Iran, it might be noted, Iraq's Saddam Hussein had been viewed as the major destabilizing force in the region; this perception faded as he was compared with the Iranians. Saddam, however, did not change; it was our perceptions that changed.

When the Iran-Iraq War ended in 1988, Iraq was in trouble. It had won modestly on the battlefield, particularly when it resorted to terrorist missile attacks against Iranian cities and chemical weapons attacks against Iranian forces as well as against its own Kurdish minority in 1988 (facts overlooked by the Bush administration). It had, however, suffered considerable damage that needed repairing, and it had run up huge debts—upwards of $40 billion—mostly with Saudi Arabia and Kuwait.

To assist recovery from the war, as well as to bolster Saddam Hussein's political position within Iraq, whose citizens had wearied of wartime deprivations, Saddam Hussein proposed that Kuwait and Saudi Arabia show their gratitude for Iraqi opposition to Iran by forgiving the loans and by providing massive new credits to help finance Iraqi recovery. Both the Saudis and Kuwaitis refused to cancel the loans and were circumspect about new loans.

This left Saddam Hussein with a problem, which was how to raise the money for recovery. He proposed to do so by gaining the support of the Organization of Petroleum Exporting Countries (OPEC) to limit production and thus drive up the price of all oil, including Iraqi, as a source of needed revenues. The Saudis and Kuwaitis refused to cooperate. To make matters worse, the Kuwaitis were in effect "poaching" Iraqi oil reserves at the Rumalia oil fields by "angle drilling"—that is, starting oil wells on the Kuwaiti side of the border, then angling the pipes under the border and syphoning off oil from its Iraqi sources.

The United States was not sitting idly by through all these activities. Instead, it was engaging in a low-profile program of cooperation with the Iraqis, the origins of which have yet to be publicly shared. The United States was providing credits to Iraq (through the Commodity Credit Corporation of the Agriculture Department), ostensibly to allow the Iraqis to buy grain and other foodstuffs. The problem was that the Iraqis found ways to exchange those credits for cash that could be spent on other products, including weapons. Hearings in Congress in July 1990 showed that Iraq owed the U.S. government over $2 billion in loans. Most prominently, Senator William Cohen (R-Me.), ranking member of the Senate Intelligence Oversight Committee, revealed that some of these monies were spent on triggers for nuclear devices that were nearly delivered illegally to Iraq in the spring before their invasion of Kuwait.

Although middle-level officials of the Agriculture and Commerce departments apparently suspected and reported these diversions (which have come to be known as "Iraqgate"), it is not clear how widely senior officials in the White House knew about them. Intent on courting Saddam, at a minimum there was less than vigilant pursuit of any wrongdoing. There have been accusations of wrongdoing and coverup that constitute an inevitable agenda item for President Clinton; whether he will pursue the accusations is not known at this point.

These actions were first revealed in early 1990 by members of Congress demanding sanctions against Iraq; the sanctions were opposed by the Bush administration. The administration's spokesman, John Kelly, assistant secretary of state for Near Eastern and South Asian affairs, explained that sanctions would dilute the United States' "ability to exercise a restraining influence on Iraqi actions."

The invasion of Kuwait temporarily diverted attention from this growing scandal. When the war was over, however, it became a major source of foreign policy contention in the 1992 presidential election that has yet to be resolved.

The administration was also systematically misreading and underestimating Saddam Hussein's intentions as the crisis in the Persian Gulf deepened. When Kuwait refused to accede to Iraqi demands to suspend loan payments, then to support a price hike in petroleum, and finally to cease angle drilling at Rumalia, Saddam issued increasingly bellicose threats. The Kuwaiti royal al-Sabah family, the Saudis, and the Americans at the highest levels ignored the threats. Even as CIA intelligence estimates detailed the massing of Iraqi troops in southern Iraq near the Kuwaiti frontier, U.S. Ambassador April Glaspie met on July 25, 1990, with the Iraqi leader, where, according to Iraqi transcripts of the meeting, she stated that "We have no opinion on the Arab-Arab conflicts, like your border disagreement with Kuwait."

The major recurring theme of U.S. relations with Iraq prior to the invasion of Kuwait was one of misperception and underestimation of what Saddam would and would not do. The United States possibly acted solipsistically, assuming that given a situation, Saddam would act the way we would. If that was the case, we were wrong; Saddam is not, of course, motivated by the same drives as Americans, nor does he view different options in the same way.

The question we must raise, even if we cannot answer it satisfactorily, is why were these mistakes made? One possible answer was the nature of decision-making in the Bush White House. As we have already seen, foreign and national security policy-making was concentrated among those very close to the president. None of these men was a Middle Eastern or Iraqi expert, and their primary focus was on the geopolitical balance in the region, which they saw the courtship of Saddam as serving.

In the absence of wider consultation, that group may have seen the situation as they wanted to and may have assumed of Saddam Hussein what they wanted to. Certainly, the expertise at the lower levels of the State and Defense departments was available to warn of the pitfalls of policy that could have been activated at, say, the Policy Coordinating Committee level. But were these experts consulted? If they were, why were they not heeded? If not, was it fear of being the executed messenger that inhibited responsible opposition? The full value of the episode requires an answer to these questions. At any rate, those who had nurtured Saddam Hussein were proven terribly wrong on August 2, 1990, as Iraq overran Kuwait.

### Post-Invasion Politics: Organizing and Authorizing the Military Response

The administration's response to the invasion was swift and decisive, showing the Bush national security apparatus at its very best. Neither then nor subsequently did the Bush team dwell on why it had been wrong earlier, beyond Ambassador Glaspie's subsequent testimony to the Senate Foreign Relations Committee that "We didn't think he [Saddam Hussein] was that stupid."

U.S. and world reactions to the invasion were swift. On August 2, President Bush condemned the invasion and announced the imposition of economic sanctions against Iraq. A three-pronged process against the invasion began in hopes of rolling it back. It included gaining international backing through the United Nations; forming a military coalition to carry out such authorizations as the United Nations provided; and convincing the U.S. Congress to authorize the use of U.S. forces to expel Iraq from Kuwait.

*Gaining International Backing*   Turning to the United Nations represented an important precedent as to how to legitimize international action and gain international consensus to oppose the aggression. The United Nations could only condemn the action because of the precedent involved: Saddam's action against Kuwait was the first time in the history of the world organization that one member nation-state had invaded and conquered another member. If the United Nations had failed to act on that occasion, its continuing international relevance would have been highly suspect. By virtue of its own Charter, the United Nations could only legitimately authorize an expulsion of Iraq from Kuwait and restoration of Kuwaiti sovereignty. That was all it was asked to do at the time, and that was the extent of the coalition's mandate as long as it retained U.N. auspices. Whether or not the Bush administration used this limit to minimize the debate on American purposes, it certainly accepted them.

It was the second time that the United Nations had ever been able to invoke the principles of collective security found in its Charter (although the action did not exactly conform to Charter provisions). The end of the Cold War and the emerging international cooperation between the United States and the Soviet Union, which had not yet dissolved itself, made action possible. Whether intentional or not, it set in motion the widening use of the United Nations to legitimate international responses to military emergencies, setting up yet another foreign policy issue for the future Clinton administration.

U.N. actions took the form of four Security Council resolutions of gradually increasing severity. They are important because a similar process has been invoked more recently in both Bosnia and Herzegovina and in Somalia. If the United Nations is to be an important tool to President Clinton (as he has indicated by elevating the ambassadorship to cabinet rank), the utility of this tool requires some examination.

The first resolution, Security Council Resolution 660, passed on the day of the invasion; it simply condemned the invasion, demanded Iraqi withdrawal, and vowed to take subsequent actions if compliance did not occur. The vote was 14 to 0, with one abstention (Yemen). On August 6, with no withdrawal forthcoming, Security Council Resolution 661 was passed, imposing mandatory economic sanctions against Iraq, by a vote of 13 to 2. (Cuba and Yemen voted against it.) Up to this point, the actions were not truly precedent-setting; economic sanctions had been imposed before—against South Africa and former Rhodesia (now Zimbabwe).

Precedent began to be set on August 25, when the Council passed Resolution 665 by a vote of 13 to 0, with Yemen and Cuba abstaining. This resolution authorized the use of naval forces to enforce the economic embargo against Iraq, including halting "all inward and outward maritime shipping in order to inspect and verify their cargoes and destinations." A similar resolution was passed against Serbia in December 1992.

This partial authorization of the use of force set the stage for the final authorizing action on November 29, 1990. Resolution 678 authorized member states to "use all necessary means" to remove Iraq from Kuwait if the Iraqis did not withdraw by January 15, 1991. This resolution passed by a vote of 12 to 2 (Yemen and Cuba again in opposition), with one abstention (the People's Republic of China). This was only the second time in its history that the United Nations had authorized the use of force (the other being in Korea in 1950) and the first time the Security Council had been able to take such action. (The General Assembly passed the "Uniting for Peace" resolution in 1950.) The power was used again in December 1992 to authorize the use of force in Somalia.

*Forming a Multilateral Military Coalition*   Although the vast bulk of the forces mobilized to oppose Saddam were American, Secretary of State James Baker assembled a coalition eventually numbering over 25 different nations. The roster of states was assembled after no more than a summary consultation with the congressional leadership. The first state to volunteer forces was Egypt, which was joined by a number of European states (Great

Britain, France, and Czechoslovakia), Arab states (Saudi Arabia, Syria, Oman, the United Arab Emirates, Morocco, and others), and other states ranging from Australia, Canada, and Argentina to Sierra Leone, Bangladesh, and Pakistan. These coalition members augmented the eventual U.S. force of 425,000, bringing coalition strength to 695,000.

The nations came for numerous reasons. Britain and France sent significant contingents largely because of their continuing interest in the region; both had been mandatory powers in the region between the world wars. The Egyptians came because Baker arm-twisted them into joining: owing the United States a significant debt and desirous of additional military credits, they could be convinced by promises to fulfill their needs. As for Syria's President Hafez al-Assad, he saw an opportunity to humiliate a hated rival, Saddam Hussein.

The degree of Arab participation surprised many observers at the time, but it probably should not have. Just as Saddam's action had violated a basic principle of the United Nations that virtually demanded a U.N. response, so, too, did he transgress against a basic, if unwritten, rule of the Arab world when he conquered and on August 8 formally annexed Kuwait. That basic principle was that the 1919 boundaries by which the Arab states gained their independence are not to be altered by force. The Arab states had no choice but to respond and restore the status quo.

***Convincing the U.S. Congress***   The most difficult prong of the strategy involved persuading the U.S. Congress to authorize the use of force against Iraq. When the president initially responded to the invasion by condemning it and sending troops to Saudi Arabia to deter further aggression, no dissent emanated from Congress. Congressional support extended to the resolutions invoking U.N. economic sanctions, the callup of the reserves announced on August 22, and even to Bush's statement before Congress on September 11 that force might be necessary. Broad bipartisan support continued into November, as Operation Desert Shield grew to a U.S. force of over 200,000.

The event that shattered the consensus and evoked an interbranch, partisan disagreement occurred on November 8 and 9. The first action, announced by President Bush, was his intention to increase troop strength by 200,000, to a total force of about 430,000. The second, announced by Secretary of Defense Cheney, was to cancel troop rotations back from the Gulf; those deployed would be there for the duration.

The two announcements had the effect of throwing down the gauntlet to Congress by making early military action likely or even inevitable. On November 11, Senate Armed Service Committee (SASC) Chairman Sam

Nunn condemned the action as precluding the probability that the sanctions would be allowed to work. The troops, he argued, could not be expected to sit in the desert without rotation for as long as it took the sanctions to compel the Iraqis into compliance. Senator Nunn called hearings of the committee on November 27-29, at which he presented a number of expert witnesses, including two former chairmen of the Joint Chiefs of Staff (retired Air Force General David Jones and retired Admiral William Crowe, Jr.) and former Secretary of Defense James Schlesinger, all of whom counseled caution.

The president's actions brought the issue to a head by forcing Congress and the public seriously to confront an actual shooting war, a possibility that had generally been avoided in the hopes that sanctions would work.

The president and some members of Congress had simply come to believe either that the sanctions would never compel an Iraqi withdrawal or at least would not do so rapidly enough to sustain public support in the United States and elsewhere behind the effort. The other side, led by Nunn, suggested that the sanctions be given more time to see if they would work and asserted that the president's actions on November 8 and 9 precluded the successful application of the sanctions, virtually creating their failure as a self-fulfilling prophecy. It is not coincidental that the second view was being expressed before SASC on the very day that the United Nations passed Resolution 678 authorizing force. The fact that the second prong of policy-making (the United Nations) was proceeding at the same time as the third was engaged only inflamed executive-legislative animosities.

Another schism between the White House and Congress regarded the physical toll the war would take. There was widespread disagreement over likely outcomes. In the debate over authorizing the president to use force, for instance, Senator Edward Kennedy (D-Mass.) stated one side, suggesting that the war would be "brutal and costly" and could end with "thousands, even tens of thousands, of American casualties." The chairman of the House Armed Services Committee (HASC), Representative Les Aspin, countered with the belief that the war would be over in weeks, certainly not more than a month, and that casualties would be light. In retrospect, the correct assessment is obvious, but it was not so obvious at the time. (Aspin's "correct" view helped raise his prospects for appointment at Defense by Clinton.)

The debate became dormant as the congressional Christmas recess came and diplomatic efforts continued. When Congress returned in January, however, the January 15, 1991, deadline specified in Resolution 678 was impending, but without U.S. force it was a hollow threat. As a result, the president formally requested a resolution from Congress authorizing his use of force (the resolution being a lesser alternative to a formal declaration of war).

The Congress debated the request until January 12, when both houses voted. The results were highly partisan. In the Senate the vote was 52 to 47 in favor of the resolution, with 42 Republicans and 10 Democrats voting in favor and 2 Republicans and 45 Democrats voting against. In the House, the resolution passed more easily, by a vote of 250 to 183. Still, the results were partisan: 164 Republicans and 86 Democrats supported the resolution, while 3 Republicans, 179 Democrats, and 1 independent opposed it.

### Post-Desert Storm Politics: Snatching Defeat from the Jaws of Victory?

The smashing military victory, both the precision air war and the "100-hour ground war," seemed to vindicate the president's policy, despite some misgivings about stopping the ground action before the ground action had destroyed Saddam's armed forces. The president's approval rating reached 90 percent in the polls, the highest ratings for any chief executive since such polls have been taken.

Political controversy, however, became especially intense as the 1992 political campaign took shape. The president sought to portray Desert Storm as his finest foreign and national security hour, justifying his reelection to a second term. Democratic nominee Clinton and his running mate, Albert Gore, however, found significant fault in the aftermath of Desert Storm.

The controversy continues, particularly because of the continuing presence of an obviously combative, unrepentant, and assertive Saddam Hussein as president of Iraq. Whether his removal from office was a U.S. goal when the decision to resist the invasion of Kuwait was made or whether his death or removal was ever a policy objective is not known. At a minimum, either objective would have exceeded the U.N. mandate. At times, however, it appeared that this was the case; to those who believed that total success required a change of leadership in Baghdad, the job was not completed.

Controversy over Saddam's eventual disposition has arisen because of the expectation periodically stated by President Bush that his overthrow was desirable. As Operation Desert Shield built in the Saudi desert during the fall of 1990, the president adopted the rhetorical device of demonizing Saddam, calling him another Hitler. The clear implication was that this Hitler must be removed as the other Hitler had been. When he was not, those unsure of the objective could only wonder if it had been achieved. On February 15, 1991, in the midst of the aerial bombardment campaign, the president went a step further, imploring "the Iraqi military and the Iraqi people to take matters into their own hands and force Saddam, the dictator, to step aside."

This statement, presumably aimed at so-called moderate Sunni elements within Baghdad (most believe that any moderates had either fled the country or been executed) and possibly intended tactically to make the coming ground campaign easier, underscores another source of controversy: the administration's apparent vacillation on removing Saddam. On the one hand, the Arab members of the coalition could not accept this objective. Hence, its formal adoption as an objective would have splintered the coalition. On the other hand, the fact that the president kept repeating the desire made it look like an objective. If it was, then the U.S. "victory" was less complete than advertised. As far as we know, this broader desire was never part of policy and would have been widely opposed for broadening the war. Presumably, the president got carried away in his rhetoric. It suggests, if possible, that presidential pronouncements should strive for greater restraint in the future.

Another lingering controversy surrounds the destruction of Iraq's nuclear, biological, and chemical (NBC) weapons capabilities and its stock of ballistic missiles (Scuds). This was an overt purpose of the bombing campaign that began Desert Storm, but inadequate coalition intelligence capability within Iraq could not identify the location of all Saddam's weapons. The destruction of remaining capabilities was an explicit term of the ceasefire negotiated to end the war, as was the United Nations' monitoring and inspection of sites within Iraq suspected of hiding either the weapons or the missiles.

Saddam Hussein's very public reluctance to cooperate fully with U.N. inspection teams reached a crescendo in July 1992, when Iraq refused the U.N. inspection team access to the Agriculture Ministry, where the inspectors believed records on chemical weapons production were hidden. The impasse dragged on for over two weeks, and the Bush administration even vaguely threatened military action in the form of air strikes if Saddam did not comply. Finally, Saddam relented—having had plenty of time to remove any tell-tale files—and allowed U.N. inspectors access to the building.

Once again, Saddam appeared to triumph, much to the consternation of the Bush administration. Saddam had complied, but the United Nations came away empty-handed. He defied the United States by not letting U.S. members of the inspection team into the building. Finally, he came away as a hero to his own people, as thousands of cheering Iraqis took to the street hailing his defiance of the United States and the United Nations, all before the television cameras.

Yet another source of contention occurred directly at the end of the war. Although apparently not directed at them, President Bush's call to rebellion on February 15, 1991, was taken by the Kurds of the north of Iraq and the Shiites of the south as an invitation for *them*, as opposed to the Sunnis, to rise and overthrow the dictator. Fearing that the success of such rebellions would cut Iraq into three separate states none of which would provide a postwar counterweight to Iran, the president actively opposed their success. That opposition, however, was not shared with either group; at the time, a delegation of Kurdish nationalists in Washington was even denied a meeting with the State Department, where the administration's position might have been stated.

The result was a massive, ruthless attack by the remnants of the Iraqi military against both groups. Critics pointed out that had the ground war not stopped when it did, Iraq would not have had the wherewithal to engage in massive atrocities, especially against the Kurds. Large numbers of Kurds, fearing retributory slaughter, fled across the border into neighboring Turkey and Iran. Because CNN cameras happened to cover the resulting orgy of death and despair in roughly improvised refugee camps on Turkish mountain sides, the administration responded with a massive assistance program called Operation Provide Comfort. It could be argued that the operation would have been unnecessary had not President Bush appeared to incite the Kurds to rebellion, which triggered the retribution. Moreover, Provide Comfort (widened to include air cover for the Shiites of the south in 1992, as Operation Southern Watch) has major precedential potential as we explore in the concluding chapter.

Once again, Saddam Hussein benefited. Because the coalition allowed his forces to retreat intact to Iraq, he had the muscle to smash the rebellions. In the process, he reinforced his own internal political position by suppressing political opponents among the Kurds and Shiites.

The most lingering controversy is the diversion of agricultural credits to weapons purchases by Iraq, apparently with the knowledge of administration officials. It is not clear how high up the administrative hierarchy knowledge of the diversion went. The fact that the U.S. government nearly, if unwittingly, contributed to Iraq's nuclear weapons capability on the eve of the invasion of Kuwait cast an ominous tone over the 1992 election campaign.

The scandal illustrates what can happen when geopolitical ends are allowed to overwhelm other considerations and when those ends dictate a policy that is largely hidden from the American people and Congress, which authorized the credits but had to find out about the diversions on their own. This fact helped explain congressional zeal and the partisan content of the investigation as to what happened. How vigorously these allegations should be pursued—especially given the partisan potential—was an early problem for the Clinton administration.

The net effect of these lingering controversies has taken much of the glow off the triumph in the desert. It does nothing to detract from the skillful, professional manner in which the military conducted its part of the operation. Within its orders, it succeeded admirably. What these problems do reveal, however, was the apparent failure to sift carefully through all the options and their ramifications, something for which the interagency process is supposedly designed.

## Case Study: The FSX Wrangle

The FSX controversy marked a sea change in the worldview of U.S. policy-makers. At first glance it seemed to be a routine disagreement among friends regarding Japan's next-generation jet fighter, the FSX (an acronym for Fighter Support/Experimental). But the dispute became a lightning rod for pent-up policy disputes between the United States and Japan and—perhaps more importantly—within the United States' policy-making community. By the time it was finally resolved in the spring of 1989, the tangled episode had placed new strains on an already inflamed U.S.-Japan relationship, had tarnished reputations in both Washington and Tokyo, and, most importantly, had demolished the intellectual and policy wall that had previously separated security and economic issues in the thinking of the United States' policy elites. Before dissecting this complex tale, we need to establish its context amid the strategic U.S.-Japanese relationship.

### Context

After defeating Japan in World War II, the United States quickly transformed it into a Cold War ally. The logic behind the policy shift was simple and compelling: Japan's disciplined and well-educated population gave it an industrial potential that might tilt the global balance of power if Japan ever slipped into the communist orbit. At the same time, the shift of the Cold War's focus to Asia signaled by the 1949 communist triumph in China and the 1950 outbreak of the Korean War gave Japan a new strategic significance as a forward base for U.S. armed forces in Northeast Asia. With the codification of the security relationship in 1960 and the evolution of bilateral defense cooperation since the late 1970s, the U.S.-

Japanese partnership became a bulwark of regional stability in Asia and the Pacific.

With the United States providing Japan's strategic security shield and a postwar constitution that limited its own military efforts to modest conventional defense of its home islands, Japan was free to channel its prodigious energies into a single-minded drive for economic growth. Japan's sensational postwar economic renaissance both helped and hindered the critical relationship with the United States. On the one hand, Japanese prosperity made it a dramatic Cold War showcase of the superior performance of democratic, market-oriented systems. On the other hand, Japan's aggressive pursuit of export markets increasingly made it an economic rival of its strategic patron.

By the 1980s the competitive aspects of the relationship were receiving new emphasis in U.S. circles, particularly as Tokyo began racking up large and growing trade surpluses with the United States. Among the United States' policy elites and opinion leaders, a darker view of Japan began to take hold. Japan, it was argued, owed much of its success to its obsessive, predatory exploitation of the wide-open U.S. market while systematically denying outsiders fair and equal access to its own market. Exaggerated though it was, this image of a Japan that does not play fair gained broad currency in the United States.

Despite the growing economic frictions between the two nations, policy-makers in both Washington and Tokyo clung to the informal doctrine that a policy wall should separate the security and economic agendas. From Tokyo's point of view, this doctrine was an exceedingly good deal, since it meant that no matter how frustrated the Americans became by Japanese economic behavior, the United States was unlikely to end its commitment to defend Japan or diminish its considerable military presence in the region. For Washington's part, the doctrine of separating economics and security reflected the pervasive Cold War conviction, shared for 45 years by Democrats and Republicans alike, that the global struggle against communism and Soviet expansionism was the overriding foreign policy issue to which all other policy agendas would have to be subordinated. Should the Cold War turn against the West, the reasoning went, it would make little difference who was guilty of trade protectionism or other economic sins.

The agreed primacy of the security agenda meant that the executive agency created to deal with that agenda—the Department of Defense— would automatically become a bureaucratic heavyweight in directing the overall U.S.-Japanese relationship. Other agencies, such as the Commerce Department or the Office of the U.S. Trade Representative, would, of course, play some role too, but their policy domains were regarded as second-echelon, and even a bit drab when compared to the high-stakes drama of deterrence, espionage, and crisis management. It followed that the policy-making role of these economic agencies would be decidedly inferior to that enjoyed by the Pentagon and the State Department.

Unsurprisingly, when the Defense Department looks at the world, it typically does so with little regard for international economic consider-ations. Nor do Pentagon policy-makers typically proceed from a sophis-ticated grasp of international economic issues. Instead, their career paths require a diligent focus on practical military matters and geostrategic concerns. Hence, the de facto bureaucratic alliance between the Defense Department and the State Department on the crucial U.S.-Japanese relationship meant that security issues would be kept separate from—and superior to—the mundane world of economics.

America's security–economics dichotomy reflected the deep strain of laissez faire in the thinking of U.S. policy-makers and the mass public. According to this belief, economic outcomes are best left to the unfettered play of the free market system, both at home and abroad. The United States' easy dominance of the global economy after World War II was widely taken as proof of the superiority of its system of minimal government intrusion in the marketplace and maximum economic freedom for producers and consumers to determine economic outcomes. It was an article of faith that the same free market principles that had produced the United States' economic primacy would, if expanded internationally in the form of liberalized global trade and capital flows, ignite a comparable economic boom abroad. The Japanese and, for that matter, all other countries would surely see the light and become ardent converts to U.S.-style free market capitalism.

The confluence of these geopolitical, intellectual, and bureaucratic factors defined the policy-making environment in which the FSX contro-versy evolved. As it mushroomed into a major conflict between the United States and its most important Asian ally, it challenged, as few other issues have before or since, the traditional U.S. practice of separating security policy and economic policy.

### The Dispute, Part I: Washington versus Tokyo

In the early 1980s bureaucrats in the Japan Defense Agency began weighing alternatives for replacing their Air Self Defense Force's aging inventory of F-1 fighters, Japan's first-ever domestically developed and produced fighter. (Commonly referred to as JDA, the agency is ordinarily regarded as Tokyo's version of the Pentagon, but it enjoys a much less influential position in Japan's policy-making process than the Pentagon plays in the U.S. process.) The range of options was quickly narrowed to two: purchase of existing foreign aircraft (which, given the alliance relationship, would certainly mean *U.S.* aircraft) or development of a new indigenous Japanese fighter.

These early discussions among Japanese policy planners showed solid support for the so-called all-Japan option — that is, an ambitious high-technology aircraft program that would be designed, developed, and produced in Japan. This sentiment was especially strong in JDA's Technical Research and Development Institute and its Bureau of Equipment, as well as within the Air Self Defense Force, defense-oriented industrial circles, and the powerful Ministry of International Trade and Industry (MITI).

Their reasoning was that an all-Japan FSX would be a logical step in the evolution of Japan's technological know-how and manufacturing capability. In addition, doing so would merely repeat the established practice of the United States' major European allies who had their own national military aircraft programs. Between 1982 and 1985, the all-Japan faction worked diligently to overcome objections to its proposed option within Japan's policy community and among opinion elites. Hence, by 1985 Tokyo was at the brink of proceeding with the indigenous development option and expected little objection from Washington should it do so.

Meanwhile, as U.S. diplomatic and military officials in Tokyo and Washington became aware of evolving Japanese thinking, they began a quiet campaign to try to persuade Japanese policy-makers to overrule the indigenous development plan. Chief among them were three working-level figures, all of whom were well versed in Japanese politics: Gregg Rubinstein, a career Foreign Service officer who in the mid-1980s was serving in the Mutual Defense Assistance Office in Tokyo; Navy Commander James Auer, then the Pentagon's principal officer on Japan policy; and Kevin Kearns, another Foreign Service officer, who replaced Rubinstein at the U.S. Embassy in Tokyo in 1986.

One of the arguments presented to the Japanese was that the development and production of a small number of fighters (less than 150 were planned) would make the plane's per-unit cost extremely high. Given the growing closeness of defense cooperation between the two nations, the Americans argued, Japan's limited defense expenditures could better serve mutual objectives by simply buying U.S-built F-16s.

The F-16 would be available immediately and, at $15 million per plane, at a fraction of the cost of an indigenously developed FSX. Not only would it be cheaper, but the F-16 Fighting Falcon was a proven world-class fighter. Less than two minutes after engine start, the F-16 can be traveling at the speed of sound at 30,000 feet. For speed, manueverability, and cost, the F-16 was far and away the best value available to Japan.

U.S. officials also feared that, in order to pay for the FSX, the Japanese would be tempted to seek overseas customers for it, thus ending that nation's long-standing policy against selling arms abroad. Given the immense cost of domestic development, the Americans reasoned, Japan's policy of refusing to sell arms abroad would be harder to sustain. By the 1980s Japan's inherent right to self-defense was generally conceded, even among its Asian neighbors with bitter memories of Japanese aggression in World War II, but the prospect of an arms-exporting Japan would surely undermine the fragile trust and goodwill that Tokyo had gradually rebuilt since 1945. Finally, the Americans argued, an all-Japan FSX would lack what defense planners call "interoperability," or the smooth fit with U.S. military tactics, forces, and equipment.

Quiet pressure from Rubinstein, Auer, and Kearns was having little impact on JDA bureaucrats determined to proceed with indigenous development. At the same time, the overall U.S.-Japanese relationship was steadily deteriorating. Despite a series of sector-specific trade talks and a deeply devalued dollar, the bilateral trade deficit ballooned in the mid-1980s. In 1987 it reached an eye-popping $56 billion out of a worldwide U.S. trade deficit of $160 billion. Moreover, in March 1987 it was revealed that the Toshiba Machine Corporation had illegally exported machine tools to the Soviet Union which would permit the Soviets to make quieter submarine propeller blades, thus making their submarines harder to detect.

Growing numbers in Congress were venting their constituents' anger at Japan's perceived intransigence on trade and outrage at the cynicism of a prominent Japanese corporation. Why, they wondered, would the Japanese now refuse to buy the cheaper and superior F-16, a move that would help reduce the trade deficit, improve defense cooperation, and soothe a badly strained relationship? In the wake of the Toshiba Machine scandal, the U.S. Senate passed, by a vote of 96 to 0, a sense of the Senate resolution calling on Japan to buy its new fighter from the United States.

Despite the mounting economic and political strains, the Pentagon continued to try to compartmentalize the security and economic agendas. In April 1987, for example, it dispatched the so-called Sullivan mission to Tokyo to make a definitive U.S. assessment of the JDA's case on behalf of an all-Japan FSX. Headed by Assistant Deputy Undersecretary of Defense Gerald Sullivan, the mission consisted of military experts drawn from the Pentagon, but it contained no representatives from other agencies. Notably absent was any representation from the Department of Commerce, which was increasingly the hub of those in the executive branch who viewed Japan as an economic threat to the United States and who believed the United States should take a tougher stand on bilateral issues involving trade, technology, and competitiveness.

To be sure, the Sullivan mission's final report would indeed prove to be instrumental in turning Japan's Ministry of Foreign Affairs and Ministry of Finance against JDA's plan for indigenous development. But the report's arguments were grounded in narrow security policy calculations of cost-effectiveness and defense interoperability. Indeed, given the makeup of the Sullivan mission, its worldview is scarcely surprising.

Hence, the Pentagon's efforts, though competent from a solely security-oriented perspective, suffered from that very narrowness of outlook. And Pentagon dominance of the U.S. stance toward the FSX meant that non-Pentagon perspectives received scant attention. By treating the FSX largely as a matter of defense policy, the Defense Department left unaddressed a whole host of nonmilitary policy matters raised by the project. Chief among these was the question of Japan's broader intentions regarding the commercial jet aircraft market, an area still dominated by U.S. producers. By viewing the immediate matter in isolation from the emerging agenda of international economic competitiveness, U.S. policy-makers were acting without an overall strategic concept of the larger U.S. interests in the issue at hand or the broader objectives which the United States should pursue.

Sensing the political fallout of a Japanese decision for the all-Japan option, Secretary of Defense Caspar Weinberger traveled to Tokyo in June 1987 for talks with his counterpart, Defense Minister Kurihara. Insisting that the controversy over the FSX "went to the heart of the U.S.-Japan relationship," Weinberger pressed Kurihara to embrace a third option: *codevelopment*. Under this scheme, the two nations would jointly develop the FSX, using an existing U.S. fighter as the technological base.

By this point, Pentagon and State Department officials believed (1) that Tokyo would never agree to an outright purchase of U.S. aircraft and (2) that the momentum building in Japan for indigenous development threatened the overall bilateral relationship. Hence, codevelopment was seen as a sensible "third way" through which the United States could claim victory for its goal of strengthening deterrence through enhanced bilateral defense cooperation and interoperability. In addition, the Pentagon and State Department saw codevelopment as a way of shoring up the overall U.S.-Japanese relationship. It promised an economic benefit for the United States through the prospective sale of U.S. equipment and technology to Japan.

In Tokyo, the Foreign Ministry agreed with Weinberger that the FSX threatened the overall partnership with the United States and adroitly muscled aside the Defense Agency to win Prime Minister Nakasone's support for the U.S. codevelopment proposal. On October 12, 1987, Nakasone announced his government's decision to work with the United States in the joint development of the FSX. Later that month, General Dynamics' F-16 was selected as the base on which codevelopment research and production would build.

Before work on the project could proceed, however, the two governments would need to negotiate a Memorandum of Understanding (MOU) that would formally codify the terms of the project. Among the issues requiring precise specification in the MOU were the amount of U.S. technology to be transferred to Japan, the division of work between the two nations in both the development and production phases, and U.S. access to new technologies developed by the Japanese in the course of FSX development.

The Pentagon and the State Department paid remarkably little attention to these "details," leaving their resolution to low-level delegations. Their focus had been on getting Japan to agree to codevelopment based on an existing American aircraft in order to counter the mounting anti-Japanese sentiment brewing in Congress. In this way the security partnership could be protected from the intrusion of economic considerations.

Kevin Kearns, a participant in the talks, began to sense that the United States and the Japanese were pursuing very different agendas in their new undertaking. The United States continued to stress such aspects as cost effectiveness, rapid introduction of an advanced fighter into Japan's Air Self Defense Force, and maximum interoperability, all of which would clearly call for minimal modifications of the F-16. Japanese negotiators, however, were insisting on extensive modifications of the F-16, a move that would entail, among other things, a massive transfer of U.S. technology to Japan, a great deal of work for Japanese firms, and the assistance of the U.S. contractor, General Dynamics, in any problems it might encounter.

To Kearns, this showed that the Japanese were simply up to their old tricks, taking advantage of the United States' preoccupation with security issues to reap maximum economic benefits. In 1988, Kearns was able to secure a State Department internship on the staff of the Senate Foreign Relations Committee. Knowing that the MOU would ultimately require congressional approval, Kearns had strategically positioned himself for what he increasingly viewed as a campaign to save U.S. foreign policy from its economic naïveté.

In November 1988 the MOU was completed. Under its terms, U.S. firms would get 40 percent of the projected cost of developing four FSX prototypes. When the project moved to the production phase (120 airplanes would be built, beginning in 1997), a second MOU would be negotiated, but the United States assumed that it would get a comparable work share as in the development phase. It was also agreed that so-called derivative technology, that is, new technology derived by the Japanese from U.S. F-16 technology, would be transferred to the United States without charge. The companion licensing agreement between General Dynamics and its Japanese collaborator, Mitsubishi Heavy Industries, was completed in January 1989.

The matter was now ready to go before the Congress, which would have 30 days in which to block it. Unless it did so, the MOU would then be in effect. But note the timing: January 1989 meant that the FSX agreement would be passed into the hands of the newly formed Bush administration and would be subject to the scrutiny of a newly installed Congress. What had until now been a rather technical issue of secondary importance was about to become the first foreign policy crisis of the Bush administration.

### The Dispute, Part II: Washington versus Washington

In the early months of 1989 the FSX agreement became a political lightning rod for critics who believed that the United States needed to take a more aggressive stance toward Japan on trade, technology, and competitiveness issues. They had concluded that the Pentagon, with its traditional security policy worldview, had left those issues largely unaddressed in the MOU. The Commerce Department emerged as an unexpectedly feisty player of bureaucratic politics because of (1) the naming of Robert Mosbacher, a close personal friend of President Bush, as the new secretary of commerce, (2) a desire within the Department of Commerce to settle old scores with the Pentagon for the shabby way it had been treated during the FSX negotiations — at one point Karl Jackson, then deputy assistant secretary of defense for East Asia, simply refused to provide his Commerce counterpart, Maureen Smith, with a copy of the MOU; as a Pentagon official put it, "We just told Commerce to buzz off"; and (3) new language in the 1989 Defense Authorization bill which now required the Pentagon to include the Commerce Department in negotiating MOUs. Taken together, these three factors made the Commerce Department a suddenly self-confident challenger of Pentagon and State Department primacy on U.S.-Japanese relations.

The Defense Department was left leaderless at this critical juncture as the nomination of former Senator John Tower to be the new secretary of defense ran aground on charges that Tower was a hard-drinking womanizer. By the time Dick Cheney was picked in place of the doomed Tower, critics of the FSX deal had rallied important bureaucratic allies and had seized the momentum.

Finally, Congress began to mobilize against the FSX MOU. The opposition was bipartisan, with Senator John Danforth, a Missouri Republican, seeing Japan's refusal to purchase U.S. fighters as yet another instance of Japanese protectionism, while to Senator Jeff Bingaman, a Democrat from New Mexico, the issue was one of preserving the United States' lead in commercial aircraft technology. To him and others, the FSX would transfer vital U.S. technology to an ally who would simply use it to make its own firms more competitive against the Americans.

The arrival of the State Department's Kevin Kearns on Capitol Hill was important, too, for the Senate Foreign Relations Committee now had on staff a determined opponent of the FSX deal who was intimately familiar with its terms and who had developed an alarming analysis of its implications. Working principally through North Carolina Republican Senator Jesse Helms, Kearns orchestrated a masterful setback for FSX supporters (and, in the process, thoroughly alienated himself from his colleagues at State). On January 18, 1989, using notes prepared by Kearns, Senator Helms seized the confirmation hearings of Secretary of State-designate James Baker to force the perplexed Baker to agree to a review of the FSX MOU.

FSX supporters in the State Department tried to fudge the issue by hastily conducting their own cursory "review," which they forwarded to Baker. But the Kearns-led insurgency would have none of it; they insisted on nothing less than a full-dress interagency review. An interagency review was the one thing that supporters of FSX had feared the most, for it meant that the long-muted skeptics at Commerce, Labor, the U.S. Trade Representative's office, and the White House Office of Science and Technology would now have their say.

Bowing to pressure from Congress and the Commerce Department, President Bush—at the urging of Baker and National Security Adviser Brent Scowcroft—directed the NSC to conduct the review and to make certain that all interested agencies were heard from. The inevitable interagency shootout took place at the February 10, 1989, meeting of the NSC's Policy Coordinating Committee. State and Pentagon representatives repeated the now-familiar security policy case for the MOU as it stood, but the meeting was dominated by opponents of the deal from Commerce, the Labor Department, the Office of the U.S. Trade Representative, and the White House Office of Science and Technology.

Startled by the breadth of opposition, Bush ordered that a definitive review be undertaken and that a unified interagency report on the FSX be submitted to the NSC by March 10. Significantly, NSC chief Scowcroft yielded to Robert Mosbacher's insistence that the Commerce Department share supervision of the review with the Pentagon. Both as symbol and as substance, this meant that the economic agenda had now taken its seat at the foreign policy head table right alongside security policy.

The Pentagon-Commerce study was ready in time for the NSC's March 15 meeting, which Washington insiders knew would be the showdown event on U.S. policy toward the FSX. The 16-page paper included a balanced summation of three areas of disagreement between the security policy community at the Pentagon and State Department, on the one hand, and the trade–technology–competitiveness faction centered in the Commerce Department. The disputes involved work share, computer source codes, and derivative technology flowback to the United States.

As to work share, Commerce insisted that the United States get a formal agreement from Japan that 40 percent of the work in the production phase would go to U.S. firms. The Pentagon argued that this agreement was unnecessary at this stage and could be taken up when the second, production-phase MOU was ready for negotiation. With regard to source codes, Commerce argued against allowing Japan access to the sophisticated computer software that controlled the F-16's flight and weapons systems. The Pentagon countered that much of the weapons-control software could safely be transferred but agreed that the flight-control codes should be withheld. Finally, Commerce urged further clarification of the derivative technology flowback provision, while the Pentagon argued that the MOU was clear enough as it stood.

The March 15 meeting of the NSC gave the FSX opponents one more chance to weigh in with their objections. The Pentagon-State alliance was nearly swamped in a sea of vigorous objections voiced by Trade Representative Carla Hills, White House Chief of Staff John Sununu, Secretary of Commerce Mosbacher, and Energy Secretary James Watkins. When the meeting was over, President Bush decided that before proceeding further with the deal, "clarifications" with the Japanese would have to be secured.

Thus, on March 20 Japan's Ambassador Matsunaga was summoned to the State Department. There he was presented with the new U.S. demands. Perhaps the most significant aspect of the meeting was the composition of the U.S. delegation: Secretary of State Baker was there, of course, as was the new secretary of defense, Dick Cheney. But joining them was none other than Secretary of Commerce Mosbacher. The meeting merits a footnote in the history of U.S. foreign policy-making because it marked the first time that a Commerce secretary took part in defense cooperation talks with a foreign government.

### The Dispute, Part III: Washington versus Tokyo (Again)

Japan's policy community watched with dismay as Washington's policy factions and bureaucratic rivals turned the FSX into a political Kabuki-by-the-Potomac. Despite the Americans' insistence that they were merely seeking "clarifications," to the Japanese it appeared that Washington was forcing renegotiation of what Tokyo regarded as a completed agreement. Although their public reactions were couched in typical Japanese politeness, in private Japanese policy-makers were fuming. From where they sat, it was the United States who had barged uninvited into what was initially an all-Japanese development project and demanded that the United States participate in a joint effort based on an existing U.S. airplane. Now, to add insult to injury, the United States was in effect calling Japan a technology thief who could not be trusted.

Others in Japan were not at all reluctant to lash out at what they regarded as the United States' new habit of blaming Japan for its own economic ills and its heavy-handed treatment of its most important ally. The conservative nationalist Shintaro Ishihara, for example, wrote that "development by Japan of a fighter craft Japan built itself with its own advanced technology would give it absolute authority over its own airspace, and this would alter both the meaning and the value of the Japan-U.S. defense alliance. The United States then would be unable to continue patronizing Japan in the area of defense."

Tokyo's policy-makers, however, concealed their bitterness and decided to grant the United States the policy "clarifications" it was demanding. Japan's decision to do so was based on its belief that it was too late to pull out of FSX codevelopment or to begin a new all-Japan fighter development program owing to the looming need to replace the aging F-1s. Japan believed, too, that failure of the FSX development would be a grave setback for defense cooperation between the United States and Japan. Through the FSX project, not only would Japan receive sophisticated aircraft technology from the United States, but also the United States would acquire cutting-edge know-how from Japan. To Tokyo, the strategic benefits of strengthening the intricate web of defense and technological interdependence between Japan and the United States outweighed its immediate anger at Washington's high-handed treatment. Thus, on April 28 the two sides announced that they had successfully "clarified" the MOU by agreeing to most of the Commerce Department's objections.

### The Dispute Resolved and Its Lessons

With the ball back in Washington's court, a now-unified executive branch submitted the "clarified" MOU to Congress for its approval. Kevin Kearns and his allies on Capitol Hill believed that the new deal was better than the original but still not a good one for U.S. interests. However, the united front presented by Defense, State, and Commerce was enough to overcome congressional skepticism, though just barely so. On May 16,

1989, the Senate approved the MOU on a close vote of 52 to 47. Had three votes gone the other way, FSX would have died in Congress.

That it did not means that the new fighter plane will indeed be codeveloped. It remains to be seen if the dark fears of FSX critics that the deal will boost Japan's commercial aircraft industry will in fact materialize. It is possible that the United States will gain significant benefits through the derivative technology flowback provision. Under its terms, the United States will acquire the fruits of Japan's research and development on the aircraft, including the commercially important field of composite materials fabrication. Japan is determined to devise new manufacturing processes for building the FSX wing using co-cured carbon fiber, a sophisticated way of making stronger and lighter aircraft components. Should the Japanese succeed in doing so, the United States will indeed have obtained a handsome economic dividend for its early investment in the F-16.

If the jury remains out on the long-term fruits of the FSX, the verdict is entirely clear on the U.S. policy-making process that produced it. What the FSX saga tells us is that U.S. policy-makers can no longer compartmentalize trade and defense issues. Nor can the United States continue to elevate the traditional geostrategic agenda of security and defense above the emerging agenda of trade, technology, and global competitiveness. The United States can no longer function as a kind of technology 7-Eleven where allied nations can drop in for a quick order of U.S. defense know-how, which can then be used commercially in the competition for global markets.

It follows that the numerous strands of U.S. policy must now be coordinated in ways that were not necessary before. That, in turn, means that the proliferating roster of policy players must be coordinated more than ever before. Developing a coherent strategy of assuring the nation's physical *and* economic well-being will place greater burdens on the NSC's interagency machinery. It may even be necessary to replace the NSC structure with a new interagency apparatus that is less grounded in the security imperatives of the Cold War and more attuned to the nontraditional issues of global interdependence coming to the fore in the post–Cold War world.

President Clinton's National Economic Council may be the vehicle for this coordination. The new Council, chaired by the investment banker Robert Rubin, has as its mandate the overall coordination of the many strands that together make up domestic *and* international economic policy. Its charge is to help the president attain a measure of coherence in policy domains as diverse as health care, taxes, monetary policy, investment, and trade issues. But the creation of the new Council does not assure that economic issues will necessarily be better integrated into the nation's overall international strategy than has been the case in the past. What the FSX case shows is the pressing need to develop policy-making procedures that routinize consideration of the economic component of national security decisions and the security and diplomatic implications of economic decisions. Thus, Clinton's new National Economic Council, while a step in the right direction of rationalizing the nation's economic policies, does not assure the coordination of these policies with the political and military components of U.S. foreign policy.

## Conclusions

Both cases discussed in this chapter are probably representative of the kinds of problems that the policy-making process will confront in the future. In addition, in both cases the existing policy process did not perform as well as it might, thus suggesting the desirability of reforming that process.

With regard to the representativeness of the cases for the post–Cold War world, the FSX case, of course, had its gestation in the Cold War context, and the agreement apparently resolving it preceded by a matter of months the revolutions of 1989 that signaled the end of the Cold War. At the same time, Cold War security obligations played a part in Japan's professed need for a new fighter aircraft.

What makes the case representative is its economic content and the convergence of sometimes contradictory economic and geopolitical interests in foreign policy. The net result of the FSX process was, of course, codevelopment of an aircraft by the United States and Japan. Such arrangements are becoming increasingly frequent in associated industries, such as the automotive and electronic industries, where joint ventures and joint ownership are becoming more and more frequently the norm. Not all of these joint activities become foreign policy issues as the FSX did, but the impact of economic considerations on foreign policy is a major part of the post–Cold War world.

So, too, is the convergence of economic and national security criteria and the need to reconcile the two sets of interests. With the Cold War competition ended and in the absence of a compelling and powerful enemy, the traditional case for national security predominance defined militarily will almost certainly decrease. As a result, the actors representing the Defense and State departments will have to share the process more with other agencies such as Commerce, as they were grudgingly forced to do in FSX. Moreover, FSX is both an example of an intermestic problem

(American aerospace jobs, Japanese defense) and the kind of competitiveness issue that energizes many within the Clinton Economic Council. It is a classic Bill Clinton issue.

The challenge posed by Iraq's invasion and conquest of Kuwait is instructive of the kinds of traditional national security concerns the system will have to deal with in the future. The conflict occurred in the Third World, where much of the remaining instability and potential for violence resides. Moreover, ethnic and geopolitical concerns — the Kurdish question in Iraq, Saddam Hussein's assertion that Kuwait was rightly the nineteenth province of Iraq — are the kinds of problems being faced today in the disintegrated communist world in places such as Yugoslavia and parts of the former Soviet Union. Iraq may be a worst case of sorts: there are relatively few other leaders with the combined resources and ambitions that Saddam Hussein has displayed. Nonetheless, these are the kinds of situations that the United States may find itself tempted to engage in in the future. The issue also served to stimulate interest in the United Nations as the legitimating agent of choice for authorizing the use of force in the post–Cold War world.

Another common point between the two cases returns us to a theme that has recurred throughout the book. In both instances studied here, the decision mechanisms for making and executing policy — principally the interagency process — were of dubious adequacy to deal with the problems presented to it.

In the case of FSX, the obvious shortcoming was the failure to involve the Commerce Department and other economic interests early on in the process of developing a U.S. position on the Japanese fighter. The Clinton "cluster" approach to policy areas may remedy this problem. The Economic Council's composition suggests (as do the president's own policy preferences) that the Council will have equal clout in similar situations to the NSC "cluster" in the future. When we look back at how the FSX controversy evolved, we see that it almost certainly would have been handled differently within such an institutional arrangement.

The shortcomings of Desert Storm may be more personal than institutional. Here, the failure to anticipate and deal in advance with largely predictable consequences of different actions may well have been the result not of inadequate resources so much as the failure to utilize all available resources. Although the record of how policy was made is not yet public, the glimpses we have through sources such as Bob Woodward's *The Commanders* suggests that the decisions were made by a very small group: mostly the president, vice president, chairman of the JCS, secretaries of state and defense, national security adviser, director of central intelligence, and a few other key assistants such as Paul Wolfowitz at Defense and some members of Vice President Quayle's staff. Little available evidence exists that the extensive network of bodies described as the interagency process in Chapter 5 played an extensive part.

Just how much the context in which foreign and defense policy-making has changed and will change is a matter of looking at the future. It is necessarily a speculative venture, since the future has the disadvantage (from the analyst's point of view) of not having yet happened. Such speculation, and the impact of projected change on the policy process, is the subject of Chapter 9.

## SUGGESTED READINGS

Aspin, Les. *The Aspin Papers: Sanctions, Diplomacy, and War in the Persian Gulf Crisis*. Washington, D.C.: Center for Strategic and International Studies, 1991.

Bulloch, John, and Harvey Morris. *Saddam's War: The Origins of the Kuwait Conflict and the International Response*. Boston: Faber & Faber, 1991.

Carpenter, Ted Galen, ed. *America Entangled: The Persian Gulf Crisis and Its Consequences*. Washington, D.C.: Cato Institute, 1991.

Congressional Quarterly. *The Middle East*. 7th ed. revised. Washington, D.C.: Congressional Quarterly Press, 1991.

Ennis, Peter. "Inside the Pentagon-Commerce Turf War." *Tokyo Business Today*, October 1989, pp. 22–26.

Otsuki, Shinji. "The FSX Controversy Revived." *Japan Quarterly*, October-December 1989, pp. 433–443.

Otsuki, Shinji. "The FSX Problem Resolved?" *Japan Quarterly*, January-March 1990, pp. 70–83.

Prestowitz, Clyde. *Trading Places: How We Are Giving Our Future to Japan and How to Reclaim It*. New York: Basic Books, 1989.

Sifry, Michael L., and Christoph Cerf, eds. *The Gulf War: History, Documents, Opinions*. New York: Random House, 1991.

Spar, Debora. "Co-developing the FSX Fighter: The Domestic Calculus of International Co-operation," *International Journal*, Spring 1992, pp. 265–292.

# CHAPTER 9

# The Policy Process
# and the Future

To comment on the volatility of the international system at this point is to restate the obvious. Nonetheless, change continues to be the norm in the world, and the ability of U.S. policy mechanisms, as well as the foreign policy mechanisms of other leading countries, to adapt to that change will be determinative of how the world looks at the end of the millennium.

The Clinton administration is faced with responding to substantive challenges and to the need for structural adaptation in a changing environment. The international challenges consist of (1) ethnically based violence in a series of states on the margins of the developing world and (2) a series of economic and political dynamics associated with democratization and the spread of market economies. Both are inherently important as precedent-setting events for the international order and as problems that will influence structural adaptation.

## Ethnic Violence

A number of serious problem situations confront policy-makers today, and how they are disposed of will largely define the international and national security problems for some time to come. These situations are the ethnonationalist violence between the Christian Serbs and Muslim Bosnians in Bosnia and Herzegovina; the ongoing confrontation between Iraq and the United Nations and the United States over Iraqi armament in violation of terms of the ceasefire ending the Persian Gulf War in 1991 and the United States' protection of Kurdish and Shiite rebels in Iraq; and the international response to Somali violence and suffering.

These crises share several characteristics that will likely provide glimpses of the kinds of foreign and defense policy problems we are likely to face in the future. The first of these characteristics is that they all occur at the *margins of the Cold War international system.*

Calling the Persian Gulf marginal may at first glance seem dubious given the centrality of the region's oil reserves to Western economic vitality. As a central player in international politics, however, the region's importance is relatively recent. Conflict in the area is endemic, but until the end of the Cold War removed the controls that the superpowers exercised over client states (notably Soviet influence in Iraq), its instability was moderated by mutual U.S.-Soviet interest in avoiding escalation of conflicts to the point they might be dragged in on opposite sides. Only in the fluidity of the transition from the Cold War system to what will replace it would Saddam Hussein have unleashed the forces he did.

The marginality in what is left of Yugoslavia is easier to document. The Balkans have been and remain an extremely volatile area that have provided, among other things, the tinderbox that ignited World War I. The period between the declaration of the Republic of Yugoslavia in 1929 and the death of Marshal Josip Tito in 1980 was one in which authoritarian rule dampened the nationalistic and religious hatreds that resurfaced in 1992. The marginality of Bosnia and Herzegovina is reinforced by its lack of petroleum.

Despite its obvious tragedy, Somalia is even lower in priority within the hierarchy of interests. One of the key reasons for Somalia's bleak long-term prospects, even if starvation is halted, is the crushing lack of Somali human or natural resources on which to build a stable system. The only way that Somalia can become important enough to justify employing force is to assert humanitarian vital interests. Given the number of potential Somali-type situations, setting criteria for involvement is a crucial task for the Clinton administration.

Another shared characteristic is the existence of *multinationalism* (multiple nationalities within countries) as an important precipitating problem. The continuing Iraqi problem has two facets. Its international facet combines Iraq's attempts to possess and maintain stores of nuclear, biological, and chemical (NBC) weapons and ballistic missiles and the continuing military menace that an Iraq so armed poses to its neighbors.

The internal facet of the Iraqi problem displays the multiple nationalities dimension. Three major groups dominate the Iraqi scene: the Arab Shiites, who form a majority of the physical population but who do not rule; the Arab Sunnis, who are the second largest population segment and Saddam Hussein's support group; and the Kurds. Geographically, the Kurds inhabit the north of Iraq, the Shiites the south, and the Sunnis the center area surrounding Baghdad.

Saddam Hussein has sought to suppress—even exterminate—the other groups; such action also clearly violates U.N. ceasefire agreements. In 1991 the campaign against the Kurds sent large numbers fleeing to well-publicized refugee camps in Turkey and Iran that led to Operations Provide Comfort and Southern Watch by the United States. This constitutes an indirect form of support for the idea of humanitarian vital interests (indirect because unstated).

The three national groups that dominate in Bosnia and Herzegovina are Bosnian Muslims, Greek Orthodox Serbs, and Roman Catholic Croats. The focus in this crisis has been on Serbian actions against the Bosnian Muslims. In retaliation for Bosnia and Herzegovina's declaration of independence from Yugoslavia, the Serbs (Serbia, along with Montenegro, constitute what is left of Yugoslavia) attacked in areas in Bosnia and Herzegovina where Christian Serbs lived in large numbers. The purpose was "ethnic cleansing," forcing the Muslim population to leave so that the areas could be reclaimed by Yugoslavia. The most visible symbols of Serbian action were the war zone in Sarajevo (site of the 1988 Winter Olympics) and the "detainment" camps where large numbers of Muslims were being physically held under conditions of abject privation. In Somalia, "turf" battles between warring clans gave violence and starvation its political dimension.

A third shared characteristic is the *role of global television* in publicizing each crisis to the point that none could be ignored. When the Kurds fled under wretched, deadly circumstances to the Turkish mountainsides, it was CNN that made the world (including President Bush) aware of their plight and prompted Operation Provide Comfort, as noted. As part of the operation, the United States also established U.S.-occupied exclusion zones in northern Iraq that would be exempt from Iraqi sovereignty to allow the Kurds to return to Iraq without fear of renewed assaults by Iraqi forces.

Television played a similar role in Bosnia and Herzegovina, forcing the major international players to focus on a situation they would rather have ignored. The pictorial account of the siege of Sarajevo was unrelenting: the footage of a Serbian mortar attack against a cemetery in Sarajevo interrupting the funeral of a three-year-old girl and wounding her grandmother was particularly riveting. The discovery and photographing of the gaunt prisoners in the Serbian camps by the British Independent Television Network (ITN) forced world attention to remain on the situation. And in the case of Somalia, television images of starving Somali children were too vivid to require elaboration here.

The three crises also represent a likely *new focus for U.S. national security*. Since the end of the Cold War, the U.S. national security establishment has been adrift, searching for a new focus to supplant the Soviet military menace. Operation Desert Storm provided a respite in that refocusing and, because of the way it was fought, allowed the U.S. military to implement strategies and tactics that had been devised for European warfare. The future, however, is dimmer.

The internal struggle in Iraq and the horrors in Bosnia and Herzegovina and Somalia are of a different, and more perplexing, order than either the Cold War confrontation or the Iraqi invasion. All are in essence highly complex, intractable internal struggles, and it is not clear whether the U.S. military is organized for such problems, or even if any outside intervention could improve the situation. Most of the U.S. military hierarchy oppose the commitment of U.S. forces, and especially ground forces, in Bosnia and Herzegovina, either unilaterally or as part of a U.N.-sponsored peace enforcement force. The small U.N. peacekeeping force failed in 1992 because neither side (or at least the Serbs) wanted peace on the current terms. With no peace to enforce, what could the national security establishment do? It clearly preferred to do nothing militarily. The comparison of the detention camps to Nazi concentration camps made inaction a decreasingly viable option for the new Clinton administration. Similarly, Somali suffering, and the realization that only the United States could possibly alleviate it, made response in that area seem inevitable.

These crises represent important precedents for future policy-makers. With the confrontation between East and West ended, the locus of international instability and violence will certainly shift to the margins: the remnants of the old Second (communist) World and the Third World. Multinationalism and its resultant nationalist furies and passions will be a major part of the causes of violence.

Historically, such situations have simply been ignored or only verbally decried by the major powers because vital interests were absent there. Global television's role in maintaining a focus on Bosnia and Herzegovina and Somalia may be a harbinger for the future. The horror of these situations has inflamed public opinion, despite the lack of traditionally defined vital interests, and it will do so again in the future. Finally, all this occurs within the context of a debate about the future of U.S. foreign and national security policy to face the "new world order."

How the United States responds to these problems in the future will have enormous precedential significance. If the United States responds in Bosnia as it has done in both Iraq (Provide Comfort/Southern Watch) and Somalia, the principle of intervention in the ethnic chaos that marks so much of the Second and Third Worlds will clearly be established. In that case, what criteria will be used to decide when and where to act that do not seem hopelessly cynical?

Because the United States cannot assume the role of global policeman (and the American public will not endorse such a role), intervening in every case of grotesque violence, the question of selection criteria is important. Although any concrete set of criteria may exclude some situations and thus in effect encourage violence among those excluded, some guidelines must exist.

One criterion that has been suggested is so-called doability: engagement where success seems likely, and avoidance where it does not. This criterion has been cited to explain the reluctance to become engaged on the ground in Bosnia: intervention would be too difficult both militarily and politically. In contrast, Somalia posed few military problems. The result, as the saying goes, is, "The Army does deserts, it doesn't do mountains." The problem is that it also says we avoid the hard jobs, the macho stuff that energizes the military.

The intractable political problems that underlie these three situations make the call on intervention even more difficult. The Saddam–Kurd–Shiite dispute is really about political power in Iraq; the ethnic violence in Bosnia is over political control of Bosnian soil; and the Somali killing is about who, if anyone, can form a viable government to succeed the Siad Barré government which was toppled in 1991. The problem is that neither the U.S. nor army military force for that matter can solve these problems. We may be able to stop the shooting or starving for as long as we remain, but eventually we will leave, and unless the parties themselves make peace among them, the situations may well revert and end up in frustration for us.

The other policy issue is the relationship between the United States and the United Nations in these situations, which boils down to a matter of jurisdiction and control. The question of jurisdiction revolves around who authorizes the use of force. In Bosnia and Somalia, the U.N. Security Council has authorized all actions; Provide Comfort/Southern Watch was a unilateral U.S. action.

The Somali situation illustrates this question of jurisdiction. By Security Council resolution, the United States was in essence "deputized" to enter Somalia and restore enough order to permit relief supplies to reach the starving masses. The United States accepted, but insisted that U.S. forces remain strictly under American command, a position it felt was politically necessary. For the United Nations' part, Secretary General Boutros Boutros-Ghali insisted that he have control since this was a U.N. operation. The issue peaked early in the operation over whether or not the mandate included disarming the Somali gang "technicals": Boutros-Ghali insisted that disarmament was essential if order was truly to be reestablished (an undoubtedly valid assessment); the Americans countered that the mission was not within the mandate and was probably impossible (also undoubtedly correct). The result was a compromise: the Americans remained under their own control, did not admit disarmament as part of their mandate, but nonetheless disarmed any armed Somalis with whom they made contact. The question of principle remained and will have to be resolved by President Clinton.

## Economic and Political Change

The international system is in the process of change in other ways as well. As argued here and elsewhere, this system will have to confront the economic problem of how to compete in a truly global, rapidly changing economy. It will also have to deal with the disintegration of the Second (communist) World, both in the current context of change in Eastern Europe and the former Soviet Union, but elsewhere over time. Finally, the emphasis in the future will likely be on problems in the Third World, with both national security and economic implications.

Domestic and foreign concerns have become most blurred in the international economic system. National economies as distinct, nationally controlled entities are rapidly disappearing, and in their place, a genuinely global economic structure is emerging.

Economic change is manifested in internationalization both of the capitalist production system and the enlargement of economic areas. The internationalization of the productive system has been seen most dramatically in the emergence of the so-called stateless corporations. The global electronics and communications firms fall into this category, and the automotive industry is not far behind.

This phenomenon, fueled by the high-technology revolution, is creating a tier system, wherein the economies of the most dynamic countries are becoming so intertwined as to be nearly inextricable. The clearest example, despite periodic difficulties, is the relationship between Japan and the United States in areas such as automobile manufacture.

The other part of internationalization involves the rise of new, large trading zones. For the United States, the North American Free Trade Area agreement between the United States, Canada, and Mexico is at the top of the agenda. By removing all tariff and other barriers, the idea is to promote trade and hence stimulate sluggish economies. Because some jobs and industries will also move within the zone, some American jobs will therefore be lost, principally to Mexico and the lower wage demands of Mexican workers. Because creation of the free trade area will mean that some jobs now performed in, for example, North Carolina will be lost to the Yucatan, foreign and domestic policy lines are once again blurred. How to blend U.S. economic growth and NAFTA implementation will be the major intermestic problem for the Clinton administration early in its term.

The creation of a tiered economic system in which the most advanced reinforce one another's prosperity also places great emphasis on national economic competitiveness. The litany in this area has become familiar: if the United States is to compete in the future, it must invest in research and development, education, roads and bridges, and a host of other things, all matters high on the Clinton agenda.

All the items that are normally associated with competitiveness have traditionally been viewed as part of the domestic, not foreign, policy agenda. Those issues have been propelled to the forefront by the international environment and the United States' continuing place in it. Education is no longer simply a national, or state, or local concern; rather, it has become an important part of the foreign policy agenda, with important national security implications. The ability to produce the most advanced and sophisticated weapons, such as those that were so much in evidence in Desert Storm, requires a population sufficiently well educated to conceptualize, design, and manufacture them. Thinking in these broad terms is said to be one of President Clinton's specialties.

Another economic concern is the ability of national governments to control and regulate the activities of their corporations and firms in an internationalized environment. In traditional national security terms, we talk about the *instruments of national power*, of which economic power is one (along with political and military power). The idea that a nation's economy can somehow be harnessed to national governmental ends implies the government's ability to order and control economic activity. When a firm, such as a stateless corporation, has headquarters and manufacturing facilities in several countries, as well as facilities owned by citizens of several nation-states, it is not entirely clear how one state can harness the resources of that corporation to its national ends.

The tragedy of dissolving Yugoslavia shows the problems of the Second World in their most dramatic current sense. The bloody Yugoslav experience may provide a glimpse into the future; most notably, there are areas of the former Soviet Union where the same kinds of multinational mix could ignite. The prospect is all the more chilling because when Tito reformed the Yugoslav state after World War II, he consciously modeled it on the Stalinist state. This model had several common elements. First, it was based on a series of so-called republics federated together: 15 in the former Soviet Union, 6 in Yugoslavia. In both cases, the borders between the republics were more or less arbitrarily drawn, especially the boundaries established by Stalin. Second, all the republics were multinational to begin with, and the government encouraged greater intermixture through migration. Third, the populations that were intermixed were separated by deep and lingering ethnic, religious, or nationalistic rivalries. The result was supposed to be a melting pot that would produce a Yugoslav or a Soviet man, not a Croatian or a Ukrainian man. Obviously, at least from current perspectives, this transformation did not take place.

The simmering hatreds were not apparent because the strong, coercive communist governments were able to suppress the older animosities. In the process, the seeming intergroup tranquility was mistaken for a real transformation, an illusion supported by what now appears to have been very bad social science theory.

The democratization that accompanied the revolutions of 1989 and the voluntary breakup of the Soviet Union had the unintended and unanticipated consequence of releasing the pent-up hatreds and frustrations that had festered, not disappeared. As the old states dissolved, the only sources of association left for people were the old ones: nationalism and religion. The result was resurgent nationalism, often at its worst. In the less destructive manifestation of nationalism, some states have voluntarily dissolved themselves: former East Germany merged into the Federal Republic, Czechoslovakia became separate Czech and Slovak states, and the former Soviet Union divided into 15 states, 11 of which are loosely aggregated as the Commonwealth of Independent States.

The problem is that such disaggregation is often only the first step to a more dangerous manifestation: intercommunal violence of the sort raging in the remnants of Yugoslavia. The basis of this violence goes back to the communist policies that created states with artificial boundaries, including population segments of historical animosity. Policies that encouraged migration simply exacerbated this problem.

The violence that is taking place in Bosnia and Herzegovina, as Orthodox Christian Serbs "cleanse" large parts of Bosnian territory of Muslims (who are actually ethnic Serbs, although they identify themselves nationally as Muslims when asked), is intended as the preface to creating a "Greater Serbia" that will be incorporated back into Yugoslavia. With less fanfare, Croatia for a time did much the same thing in Bosnian areas adjacent to Croatia.

Unfortunately, this is not an isolated situation. Because Yugoslavia models itself on the Soviet pattern, many former Soviets have always regarded Yugoslavia as a kind of laboratory for the old Soviet Union. Similar conditions of ethnic mixture exist in places as disparate as Moldova bordering on Romania and the southern areas of the old Soviet Union where religious differences are layered on national differences. The result is a tinderbox waiting to ignite.

The question is what, if anything, can be done to avoid the spread of the horror and atrocity that has accompanied the fighting in Bosnia. As the reluctance of the international system to intervene in that situation demonstrated, the problems are basic and may be capable of solution only through bloodletting. It is a gruesome prospect and one that global television will not allow us to ignore or forget.

As the international system demonstrates its impotence in the Balkans, people in the former Soviet Union with similar problems receive ambivalent, even contradictory messages. On one hand, the message is that since you are on your own if violence erupts, it must be avoided at nearly any cost. On the other hand, those who would "ethnically cleanse" parts of the Soviet Union have to conclude that violence may succeed. The prospect is especially appalling to Russia, since the largest number of former Soviet nationalities living outside their nations are Russians. They have had a foretaste already in Moldova. What would the Russians do if a movement arose akin to the Serbian campaign against Bosnia in one of the remote former Soviet republics against Russians, and the system reacted impotently?

This problem is not unique to the Second World; the same kinds of problems may well extend to large parts of the Third World. As the forces of democratization begin to permeate the Afro-Asian world, the Yugoslav model could be the model for much of the developing world as well.

Some of the same ingredients found in the Second World are present in large measure in much of the Third World, excluding most of Latin America where conflict is class-based with some racial overtones (Indians versus those of European background). Because independence from colonial rule was granted to the colonial unit, the need for federation occurred, especially in the larger states such as Nigeria and India. Owing to previous habitation patterns and loyalties that predated colonialism, the areas are very multinational. In large parts of Africa, for instance, nationalism equates with tribalism, and there may be literally hundreds of tribes, with distinct languages, histories, and loyalties enclosed within state boundaries. Religious differentiation based in the penetration of Christian and Islamic missionaries in Africa add to these differences. Population migration has also been a factor and is accentuated where there are differentiations in skill levels among tribal groups. Finally, most have existed within the confines of authoritarian governments—in Africa, mostly militarily based—that have managed to keep at least minimal order.

Democratization will come to these areas as surely as it has to the old Second World. In the long run, Americans can only applaud such a development, for it represents the triumph of their political philosophy, the universalization of American values. What the reality of Bosnia and Herzegovina and the prospect in the former Soviet Union suggests is that the transition may occur in a crucible of blood. Beyond the human tragedy of the Muslim Serbs and others in Bosnia and Herzegovina, that is the symbolic significance of the international community's coming to grips with this situation.

The heart of this problem is how to balance out these dynamics. In the short run, democratization will often lead to outpourings of animosity manifested in bloodshed into which we will be tempted to become engaged. In the long run, the process can lead to economic prosperity and political stability. The question for the Clinton administration is to determine how to fashion a policy and strategy for minimizing the pain of getting from the short-run costs to the long-run benefits.

These are all extremely complex, relatively new problems. The internationalization of economic activity has occurred so quickly that our understanding of it lags behind; the debate over NAFTA has brought forth absolutely contradictory predictions that underscore the conceptual disarray. Everyone expected problems in Yugoslavia, but hardly anyone guessed their depth and trauma or the possibility that they could be precedent-setting for other areas. The recognition that this is a harbinger for the Third World is only slowly seeping in.

## Structural Adaptation

The international environment is posing a new agenda to which U.S. foreign policy-makers, as well as their counterparts elsewhere in the Western world, will have to adjust. As the outline of these problems suggest, they are both relatively new and likely difficult, even intractable. They are also agenda items with which the current foreign and defense policy-making machinery has had comparatively little experience. What structural adaptations, if any, will the new agenda require?

The first and most obvious adaptation is in the area of response to challenges in the international economic system. During the Bush years, governmental efforts to understand and influence the dynamics of the evolving global system appeared to be piecemeal, reflecting the administration's reluctance to involve the government in the private sector. The U.S. trade representative, Carla S. Hill, stood at the pinnacle, because she had had cabinet status since 1989, but her office lacked the extensive bureaucracy that provides expertise for other actors such as the secretaries of state or defense. International economic concerns are represented in a number of cabinet-level agencies that do business overseas, but normally at the level of the assistant secretary or lower. Within the interagency process, an economic representative (an assistant secretary of the Treasury) was found only at the fourth level (the Policy Coordinating Committee).

The Clinton administration has responded by creating an economic "cluster" of agencies coequal collectively to the NSC: the Economic Council. The appointment of the economic team as the first act of the transition, followed by the December 1992 economic seminar in Little Rock and punctuated by the appointment of a close personal friend and adviser, Mickey Kantor, to be U.S. trade representative, symbolizes this reorganization.

The major objections to the Council are both philosophical and bureaucratic. Philosophically, the conservative Republican administrations that were in power for the past 12 years had difficulty with any agency that might have appeared to be directed toward industry, especially if such an agency's advocacies amounted to propounding an industrial policy (the idea that the government should help direct and coordinate the direction of industrial development). The United States is the only major country in the world that does not have such a policy. Bureaucratically, agency heads from which personnel would be drawn oppose the idea because it effectively erodes their mission and power.

A second area ripe for redirection and possible revision is the definition and structure of national security. The current system, developed and shaped to deal with the Cold War, does not necessarily respond as well to the changing world environment. The definition of national security is rapidly being broadened to include nontraditional areas such as economics, environmental protection, counternarcotics, counterterrorism, and a host of other conditions that affect the well-being of Americans. Secretary Aspin's proposed reorganization of DOD reflects a sensitivity to these changes.

Most of these concerns have had no official place in the formal national security system represented by the interagency process (see Chapter 5). Areas such as counternarcotics and counterterror are represented indirectly since these tasks are assigned — at relatively low priority — to the Defense Department. Others, such as the environment, lacked a prominent place; the promotion of environmental technology as a central part of industrial policy and competitiveness creates a higher priority.

A reworking of the NSC system, probably from the level of the Deputies Committee and below, could address this problem by creating permanent institutional positions for agencies and interests from the expanded list of national security concerns. This change would, in effect, move those areas from the status of peripheral or occasional actors to the core. The result could well be better coordinated policy.

A third area that is changing is the enhanced role of the United Nations in U.S. policy. During the Cold War, the United Nations was not central to the implementation of U.S. policy, simply because on most major issues, the United States and the USSR were on opposite sides. Since each possessed a veto in the Security Council, that body was effectively paralyzed from acting on important matters.

The end of the Cold War, as we have already stated, has revived the United Nations. Growing U.S.-Russian cooperation (the Russian Republic occupies the Security Council seat formerly held by the Soviet Union) has meant that a veto is not automatic. China remains the sole communist state with the veto but has chosen to abstain rather than vetoing important resolutions.

The first two instances in which the U.N. Security Council authorized the use of force were in 1990 (the Persian Gulf War) and 1992 (to end Serbian aggression against Bosnia and Herzegovina). Clearly, the Security Council is becoming the central legitimizing mechanism for collective military action, which itself is a trend for dealing with Second and Third World violence. This being the case, the United Nations is and will continue to become a central element in formulating and executing national security policy.

The Bush administration's organization of the government did not directly reflect this enhanced importance. The chief U.S. policy-maker regarding the United Nations is the U.S. ambassador to the United Nations. This position reported to the State Department through the deputy secretary (the number two person in the department) and had generally been held by career diplomats with little political clout.

If the United Nations is to be more prominent, the representation of those who know and deal with it should expand as well. The Clinton administration made such an adjustment during the transition by elevating the U.N. ambassadorship to cabinet rank. A precedent for this decision exists: President Dwight D. Eisenhower gave Henry Cabot Lodge, Jr., this status, and the same was true of Ambassador Adlai Stevenson under John F. Kennedy and Lyndon B. Johnson.

A final area of concern has to do with the Second and Third Worlds. The Cold War system was clearly directed at the Second World but not in the current manner of assessing its disintegration. Similarly, the Third World has always been viewed as less important than other parts of the world. As a result, fewer resources, including the development and nurturing of expertise, have been devoted to Third World countries.

Changing that situation may not involve structural change so much as a reallocation of resources and attention within the present structure. Enhancing attention within the national security arena to nontraditional problems will have the effect of doing some of this, since a number of those problems, notably the environment and narcotics, have strong Third World connotations. The failure to strengthen these assets will likely doom the United States to repeat mistaken policies toward a Third World inadequately understood.

## Conclusions

The world environment that is simultaneously the stimulant for and the forum in which U.S. foreign and defense policy occurs is changing rapidly. Numerous analysts have attempted to sort out the dynamics of change and the directions and emphases the new environment will take. Our emphasis has been slightly different. Our central theme and thesis has been that not only is the environment changing, but so, too, must the mechanisms by which the United States interacts with the world change. The Cold War mechanisms worked admirably to keep that competition from going hot (war). The disappearance of that threat suggests the need to adapt and fine-tune those mechanisms for a "new world order."

### SUGGESTED READINGS

Allison, Graham, and Gregory F. Treverton, eds. *Rethinking America's Security: Beyond Cold War to New World Order*. New York: W. W. Norton, 1992 (A Council on Foreign Relations Book).

Art, Robert J., and Seyom Brown, eds. *U.S. Foreign Policy: The Search for a New Role*. New York: Macmillan, 1993.

Kennedy, Paul. *The Rise and Fall of the Great Powers: Economic Change and Military Conflict from 1500–2000*. New York: Random House, 1987.

Klare, Michael T., and Daniel C. Thomas. *World Security: Trends and Challenges at Century's End*. New York: St. Martin's Press, 1991.

Lafeber, Walter. *The American Age: United States Foreign Policy in the 1980s*. New York: W. W. Norton, 1989.

Nye, Joseph S., Jr. *Born to Lead: The Changing Nature of American Power*. New York: Basic Books, 1990.

Snow, Donald M. *Distant Thunder: Third World Conflict and the New International Order*. New York: St. Martin's Press, 1992.

Starr, Martin K., ed. *Global Competitiveness: Getting the U.S. Back on Track*. New York: W. W. Norton, 1988 (An American Assembly Book).

# INDEX

*Wall Street Journal*, 222
War colleges, 199
War of 1812, 160
War Powers Resolution, 34, 123, 149,
    157–168
Warsaw Pact, 1, 7, 14
*Washington Post*, 201, 222
Watergate scandal, 50, 53, 109, 156,
    209, 214, 224
Watkins, James, 256
Weinberger, Caspar, 60, 121, 122, 172,
    176, 197, 212, 252
  Weinberger Doctrine, 212
Westmoreland, William, 224

Wilson, Woodrow, 35, 129
Wirth, Tim, 96
Wolfowitz, Paul, 260
Woodward, Bob, 153, 260
Woolsey, James, 150
World Bank, 115
World War I, 160
World War II, 95, 108, 160
Wright, Jim, 140


Yeltsin, Boris, 63, 220, 228
Yugoslavia, 4, 15–18, 23, 25, 62, 152,
    153, 207, 260, 263, 268, 269